Kaplan Schweser's Path to Success

Level II CFA® Exam

CFA®

Welcome

As the head of Advanced Designations at Kaplan Schweser, I am pleased to have the opportunity to help you prepare for the CFA® exam. Kaplan Schweser has decades of experience in delivering the most effective CFA exam prep products in the market and I know you will find them to be invaluable in your studies.

Our products are designed to be an integrated study solution across print and digital media to provide you the best learning experience, whether you are studying with a physical book, online, or on your mobile device.

Our core product, the SchweserNotes™, addresses all of the Topics, Study Sessions, Readings, and LOS in the CFA curriculum. Each reading in the SchweserNotes has been broken into smaller, bite-sized modules with Module Quizzes interspersed throughout to help you continually assess your comprehension. After you complete each Topic, take our online Topic Quiz to help you assess your knowledge of the material before you move on to the next section.

All purchasers of the SchweserNotes receive online access to the Kaplan Schweser online platform (our learning management system or LMS) at www.Schweser.com. In the LMS, you will see a dashboard that tracks your overall progress and performance and also includes an Activity Feed, which provides structure and organization to the tasks required to prepare for the CFA exam. You also have access to the SchweserNotes, Module Quizzes, and Topic Quizzes content as well as the SchweserNotes Videos (if purchased), which contain a short video that complements each module in the SchweserNotes. Look for the icons indicating where video content, Module Quizzes, and Topic Quizzes are available online. I strongly encourage you to enter your Module Quiz and Topic Quiz answers online and use the dashboard to track your progress and stay motivated.

Again, thank you for trusting Kaplan Schweser with your CFA exam preparation. We're here to help you throughout your journey to become a CFA charterholder.

Regards,

Derek Burkett

Derek Burkett, CFA, FRM, CAIA
Vice President (Advanced Designations)

Contact us for questions about your study package, upgrading your package, purchasing additional study materials, or for additional information:

888.325.5072 (U.S.) | +1 608.779.8327 (Int'l.)
staff@schweser.com | www.schweser.com/cfa

Book 1: Quantitative Methods and Economics

SchweserNotes™ 2022

Level II CFA®

SCHWESERNOTES™ 2022 LEVEL II CFA® BOOK 1: QUANTITATIVE METHODS AND ECONOMICS

©2021 Kaplan, Inc. All rights reserved.

Published in 2021 by Kaplan, Inc.

Printed in the United States of America.

ISBN: 978-1-0788-1690-8

CONTENTS

STUDY SESSION 1—QUANTITATIVE METHODS (1)

STUDY SESSION 2—QUANTITATIVE METHODS (2)

STUDY SESSION 3—ECONOMICS

LEARNING OUTCOME STATEMENTS (LOS)

STUDY SESSION 1

The topical coverage corresponds with the following CFA Institute assigned reading:

1. Introduction to Linear Regression

The candidate should be able to:

a. describe a simple linear regression model and the roles of the dependent and independent variables in the model. (page 1)

b. describe the least squares criterion, how it is used to estimate regression coefficients, and their interpretation. (page 3)

c. explain the assumptions underlying the simple linear regression model, and describe how residuals and residual plots indicate if these assumptions may have been violated. (page 6)

d. calculate and interpret the coefficient of determination and the F-statistic in a simple linear regression. (page 9)

e. describe the use of analysis of variance (ANOVA) in regression analysis, interpret ANOVA results, and calculate and interpret the standard error of estimate in a simple linear regression. (page 9)

f. formulate a null and an alternative hypothesis about a population value of a regression coefficient, and determine whether the null hypothesis is rejected at a given level of significance. (page 13)

g. calculate and interpret the predicted value for the dependent variable, and a prediction interval for it, given an estimated linear regression model and a value for the independent variable. (page 16)

h. describe different functional forms of simple linear regressions. (page 17)

The topical coverage corresponds with the following CFA Institute assigned reading:

2. Multiple Regression

The candidate should be able to:

a. formulate a multiple regression equation to describe the relation between a dependent variable and several independent variables, and determine the statistical significance of each independent variable. (page 28)

b. interpret estimated regression coefficients and their p-values. (page 29)

c. formulate a null and an alternative hypothesis about the population value of a regression coefficient, calculate the value of the test statistic, and determine whether to reject the null hypothesis at a given level of significance. (page 30)

d. interpret the results of hypothesis tests of regression coefficients. (page 30)

e. calculate and interpret a predicted value for the dependent variable, given an estimated regression model and assumed values for the independent variables. (page 34)

f. explain the assumptions of a multiple regression model. (page 49)

g. calculate and interpret the F-statistic, and describe how it is used in regression analysis. (page 35)

h. contrast and interpret the R^2 and adjusted R^2 in multiple regression. (page 42)

i. evaluate how well a regression model explains the dependent variable by analyzing the output of the regression equation and an ANOVA table. (page 37)

j. formulate and interpret a multiple regression, including qualitative independent variables. (page 44)

k. explain the types of heteroskedasticity and how heteroskedasticity and serial correlation affect statistical inference. (page 49)

l. describe multicollinearity, and explain its causes and effects in regression analysis. (page 56)

m. describe how model misspecification affects the results of a regression analysis, and describe how to avoid common forms of misspecification. (page 58)

n. interpret an estimated logistic regression. (page 62)

o. evaluate and interpret a multiple regression model and its results. (page 63)

The topical coverage corresponds with the following CFA Institute assigned reading:

3. Time-Series Analysis

The candidate should be able to:

a. calculate and evaluate the predicted trend value for a time series, modeled as either a linear trend or a log-linear trend, given the estimated trend coefficients. (page 73)

b. describe factors that determine whether a linear or a log-linear trend should be used with a particular time series and evaluate limitations of trend models. (page 78)

c. explain the requirement for a time series to be covariance stationary and describe the significance of a series that is not stationary. (page 81)

d. describe the structure of an autoregressive (AR) model of order p and calculate one- and two-period-ahead forecasts given the estimated coefficients. (page 82)

e. explain how autocorrelations of the residuals can be used to test whether the autoregressive model fits the time series. (page 83)

f. explain mean reversion and calculate a mean-reverting level. (page 84)

g. contrast in-sample and out-of-sample forecasts and compare the forecasting accuracy of different time-series models based on the root mean squared error criterion. (page 85)

h. explain the instability of coefficients of time-series models. (page 86)

i. describe characteristics of random walk processes and contrast them to covariance stationary processes. (page 87)

j. describe implications of unit roots for time-series analysis, explain when unit roots are likely to occur and how to test for them, and demonstrate how a time series with a unit root can be transformed so it can be analyzed with an AR model. (page 88)

k. describe the steps of the unit root test for nonstationarity and explain the relation of the test to autoregressive time-series models. (page 88)

l. explain how to test and correct for seasonality in a time-series model and calculate and interpret a forecasted value using an AR model with a seasonal lag. (page 93)

m. explain autoregressive conditional heteroskedasticity (ARCH) and describe how ARCH models can be applied to predict the variance of a time series. (page 97)

n. explain how time-series variables should be analyzed for nonstationarity and/or cointegration before use in a linear regression. (page 99)

o. determine an appropriate time-series model to analyze a given investment problem and justify that choice. (page 100)

STUDY SESSION 2

The topical coverage corresponds with the following CFA Institute assigned reading:

4. Machine Learning

The candidate should be able to:

a. describe supervised machine learning, unsupervised machine learning, and deep learning. (page 110)

b. describe overfitting and identify methods of addressing it. (page 112)

c. describe supervised machine learning algorithms—including penalized regression, support vector machine, k-nearest neighbor, classification and regression tree, ensemble learning, and random forest—and determine the problems for which they are best suited. (page 114)

d. describe unsupervised machine learning algorithms—including principal components analysis, k-means clustering, and hierarchical clustering—and determine the problems for which they are best suited. (page 118)

e. describe neural networks, deep learning nets, and reinforcement learning. (page 119)

The topical coverage corresponds with the following CFA Institute assigned reading:

5. Big Data Projects

The candidate should be able to:

a. identify and explain steps in a data analysis project. (page 128)

b. describe objectives, steps, and examples of preparing and wrangling data. (page 129)

c. describe objectives, methods, and examples of data exploration. (page 132)

d. describe objectives, steps, and techniques in model training. (page 136)

e. describe preparing, wrangling, and exploring text-based data for financial forecasting. (page 130)

f. describe methods for extracting, selecting and engineering features from textual data. (page 134)

g. evaluate the fit of a machine learning algorithm. (page 138)

STUDY SESSION 3

The topical coverage corresponds with the following CFA Institute assigned reading:

6. Currency Exchange Rates: Understanding Equilibrium Value

The candidate should be able to:

a. calculate and interpret the bid–offer spread on a spot or forward currency quotation and describe the factors that affect the bid–offer spread. (page 149)

b. identify a triangular arbitrage opportunity and calculate its profit, given the bid–offer quotations for three currencies. (page 151)

c. explain spot and forward rates and calculate the forward premium/discount for a given currency. (page 154)

d. calculate the mark-to-market value of a forward contract. (page 156)

e. explain international parity conditions (covered and uncovered interest rate parity, forward rate parity, purchasing power parity, and the international Fisher effect). (page 157)

f. describe relations among the international parity conditions. (page 163)

g. evaluate the use of the current spot rate, the forward rate, purchasing power parity, and uncovered interest parity to forecast future spot exchange rates. (page 164)

h. explain approaches to assessing the long-run fair value of an exchange rate. (page 164)

i. describe the carry trade and its relation to uncovered interest rate parity and calculate the profit from a carry trade. (page 166)

j. explain how flows in the balance of payment accounts affect currency exchange rates. (page 168)

k. explain the potential effects of monetary and fiscal policy on exchange rates. (page 169)

l. describe objectives of central bank or government intervention and capital controls and describe the effectiveness of intervention and capital controls. (page 172)

m. describe warning signs of a currency crisis. (page 173)

The topical coverage corresponds with the following CFA Institute assigned reading:

7. Economic Growth and the Investment Decision

The candidate should be able to:

a. compare factors favoring and limiting economic growth in developed and developing economies. (page 187)

b. describe the relation between the long-run rate of stock market appreciation and the sustainable growth rate of the economy. (page 189)

c. explain why potential GDP and its growth rate matter for equity and fixed income investors. (page 189)

d. contrast capital deepening investment and technological progress and explain how each affects economic growth and labor productivity. (page 190)

e. demonstrate forecasting potential GDP based on growth accounting relations. (page 192)

f. explain how natural resources affect economic growth and evaluate the argument that limited availability of natural resources constrains economic growth. (page 193)

g. explain how demographics, immigration, and labor force participation affect the rate and sustainability of economic growth. (page 194)

h. explain how investment in physical capital, human capital, and technological development affects economic growth. (page 195)

i. compare classical growth theory, neoclassical growth theory, and endogenous growth theory. (page 198)

j. explain and evaluate convergence hypotheses. (page 201)

k. describe the economic rationale for governments to provide incentives to private investment in technology and knowledge. (page 202)

l. describe the expected impact of removing trade barriers on capital investment and profits, employment and wages, and growth in the economies involved. (page 202)

The topical coverage corresponds with the following CFA Institute assigned reading:

8. Economics of Regulation

The candidate should be able to:

a. describe the economic rationale for regulatory intervention. (page 211)

b. explain the purposes of regulating commerce and financial markets. (page 212)

c. describe anticompetitive behaviors targeted by antitrust laws globally and evaluate the antitrust risk associated with a given business strategy. (page 213)

d. describe classifications of regulations and regulators. (page 213)

e. describe uses of self-regulation in financial markets. (page 214)

f. describe regulatory interdependencies and their effects. (page 215)

g. describe tools of regulatory intervention in markets. (page 215)

h. describe benefits and costs of regulation. (page 216)

i. describe the considerations when evaluating the effects of regulation on an industry. (page 217)

WELCOME TO THE 2022 LEVEL II SCHWESERNOTES™

Thank you for trusting Kaplan Schweser to help you reach your goals. We are pleased that you have chosen us to assist you in preparing for the Level II CFA Exam. In this introduction, I want to explain the resources included with these SchweserNotes, suggest how you can best use Schweser materials to prepare, and direct you towards other educational resources you will find helpful as you study for the exam.

Besides the SchweserNotes themselves, there are many educational resources available at Schweser.com. Log in using the individual username and password that you received when you purchased your SchweserNotes.

SchweserNotes™

These notes consist of five volumes that include complete coverage of all 17 Study Sessions and all 441 Learning Outcome Statements (LOS). Examples and Module Quizzes (multiple-choice questions) are provided along the way to help you master the material and check your progress. At the end of each major topic area, you can take an online Topic Quiz for that subject. Topic Quiz questions are created to be exam-like in format and difficulty, to help you evaluate how well your study of each topic has prepared you for the actual exam.

Practice Questions

Studies have shown that to retain what you learn, it is essential that you quiz yourself often. For this purpose we offer SchweserPro™ QBank, which contains thousands of Level II practice questions and explanations. Questions are available for each module, Study Session, and topic. Build your own quizzes by specifying the topics and the number of questions. SchweserPro™ QBank is an important learning aid for achieving the depth of proficiency needed at Level II. It should not, however, be considered a replacement for rehearsing with "exam-type" questions as found in our Schweser Mock Exams.

Mock Exams

Schweser offers six full-length mock exams: Schweser Mock Exams 1 through 6 each contain complete 88-question tests, with answer explanations. These are important tools for gaining the speed and skills you will need to pass the exam. You can use our Performance Tracker to monitor how you are performing compared to other Schweser Level II candidates.

How to Succeed

The Level II CFA exam is a formidable challenge (47 readings and 441 Learning Outcome Statements), so you must devote considerable time and effort to be adequately prepared. There is no shortcut! You must learn the material, know the terminology and techniques, understand the concepts, and be able to answer

88 questions quickly and mostly-correctly. Fifteen hours per week for 25 weeks is a useful estimate of the study time required on average, but different candidates will need more or less time, depending on their individual backgrounds and experience.

There is no way around it; CFA Institute will test you in a way that will reveal how well you know the Level II curriculum. You should begin early and stick to your study plan. Read the SchweserNotes and complete the Module Quizzes. Prepare for and attend a live class, an online class, or a study group each week. Take quizzes often using SchweserPro QBank, and go back to review previous topics regularly. At the end of each topic area, take the online Topic Quiz to check your progress. You should try to finish reading the curriculum at least four weeks before the Level II exam so that you have sufficient time for Mock Exams and for further review of those topics that you have not yet mastered.

I would like to thank Kent Westlund, CFA Content Specialist, for his contributions to the 2022 Level II SchweserNotes for the CFA Exam.

Best regards,

Dr. Bijesh Tolia, CFA, CA

VP of CFA Education and Level II Manager

Kaplan Schweser

The following is a review of the Quantitative Methods (1) principles designed to address the learning outcome statements set forth by CFA Institute. Cross-Reference to CFA Institute Assigned Reading #1.

READING
1

Introduction to Linear Regression

EXAM FOCUS

This introduction covers simple linear regression, which involves two variables: an independent and a dependent variable. Candidates should be able to construct a simple regression model and state the assumptions under which a linear model is valid. Given the estimated model parameters (coefficients), you should be able to use the model to predict the dependent variable. Finally, you may be required to interpret an ANOVA table and test the significance of estimated regression coefficients. Note that an *F*-test, in the context of a simple regression, is equivalent to a *t*-test of the significance of the estimated slope coefficient.

MODULE 1.1: LINEAR REGRESSION: INTRODUCTION

Video covering this content is available online.

LOS 1.a: Describe a simple linear regression model and the roles of the dependent and independent variables in the model.

CFA® Program Curriculum, Volume 1, page 5

The purpose of **simple linear regression** is to explain the variation in a dependent variable in terms of the variation in a single independent variable. Here, the term "variation" is interpreted as the degree to which a variable differs from its mean value. Don't confuse variation with variance—they are related but are not the same.

$$\text{variation in } Y = \sum_{i=1}^{n}(Y_i - \overline{Y})^2$$

- The **dependent variable** is the variable whose variation is explained by the independent variable. We are interested in answering the question, "What explains fluctuations in the dependent variable?" The dependent variable is also referred to as the *explained variable*.

■ The **independent variable** is the variable used to explain variations in the dependent variable. The independent variable is also referred to as the *explanatory variable*.

> **EXAMPLE: Dependent vs. independent variables**
>
> Suppose that we want to predict stock returns based on GDP growth. Which variable is the independent variable?
>
> **Answer:**
>
> Because GDP is going to be used as a *predictor* of stock returns, stock returns are being *explained* by GDP. Hence, stock returns are the dependent (explained) variable, and GDP is the independent (explanatory) variable.

Now, suppose that we want to use excess returns on the S&P 500 (the independent variable) to explain the variation in excess returns on ABC, Inc., (ABC) common stock (the dependent variable). For this model, we define excess return as the difference between the actual return and the return on 1-month Treasury bills.

We start by creating a scatter plot with ABC excess returns on the vertical axis and S&P 500 excess returns on the horizontal axis. Monthly excess returns for both variables from June 20x2 to May 20x5 are plotted in Figure 1.1. For example, consider the point labeled "May 20x4." In that month, the excess return on the S&P 500 was –7.8% and the excess return on ABC was 1.1%.

Figure 1.1:   Scatter Plot of ABC Excess Returns vs. S&P 500 Index Excess Returns

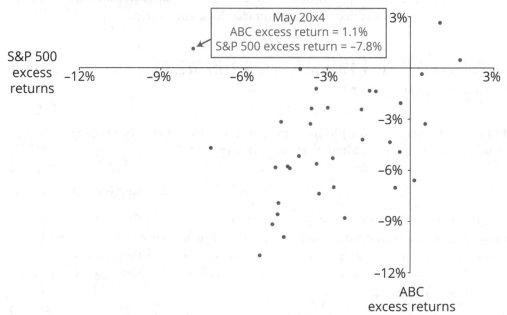

Sample Correlation Coefficient

The correlation coefficient, r, is a measure of the strength of the linear relationship (correlation) between two variables. The correlation coefficient has no unit of measurement; it is a "pure" measure of the tendency of two variables to move together.

The sample correlation coefficient for two variables, X and Y, is calculated as:

$$r_{XY} = \frac{\text{covariance of X and Y}}{(\text{sample standard deviation of X})(\text{sample standard deviation of Y})}$$

$$= \frac{\text{cov}_{XY}}{(S_X)(S_Y)}$$

The correlation coefficient is bounded by positive and negative 1 (i.e., $-1 \le r \le +1$), where a correlation coefficient of +1 indicates that changes in the variables are perfectly positively correlated (i.e., they go up and down together, in lockstep). In contrast, if the correlation coefficient is –1, the changes in the variables are perfectly negatively correlated.

The two variables in Figure 1.1 appear to be positively correlated: excess ABC returns tended to be positive (negative) in the same month that S&P 500 excess returns were positive (negative). This is not the case for all the observations, however (for example, May 20x4). In fact, the correlation between these two variables is approximately +0.40.

LOS 1.b: Describe the least squares criterion, how it is used to estimate regression coefficients, and their interpretation.

CFA® Program Curriculum, Volume 1, page 8

Simple Linear Regression Model

The following linear regression model is used to describe the relationship between two variables, X and Y:

$Y_i = b_0 + b_1 X_i + \varepsilon_i$, i = 1, ..., n

where:

Y_i = ith observation of the dependent variable, Y

X_i = ith observation of the independent variable, X

b_0 = regression intercept term

b_1 = regression slope coefficient

ε_i = residual for the ith observation (also referred to as the disturbance term or error term)

Based on the regression model stated previously, the regression process estimates an equation for a line through a scatter plot of the data that "best" explains the observed values for Y in terms of the observed values for X.

The linear equation, often called the line of best fit, or regression line, takes the following form:

$$\hat{Y}_i = \hat{b}_0 + \hat{b}_1 X_i, \ i = 1, 2, 3 \dots, n$$

where:

$\hat{Y}_i$ = estimated value of Y_i given X_i

$\hat{b}_0$ = estimated intercept term

$\hat{b}_1$ = estimated slope coefficient

 PROFESSOR'S NOTE

The hat "^" above a variable or parameter indicates a predicted value.

The regression line is just one of the many possible lines that can be drawn through the scatter plot of X and Y. The criteria used to estimate this line is the essence of linear regression. The regression line is the line for which the sum of the squared differences (vertical distances) between the Y-values predicted by the regression equation $\left(\hat{Y}_i = \hat{b}_0 + \hat{b}_1 X_i \right)$ and *actual Y*-values, Y_i, is minimized. The sum of the squared vertical distances between the estimated and actual Y-values is referred to as the **sum of squared errors (SSE)**.

Thus, the regression line is the line that minimizes the SSE. This explains why simple linear regression is frequently referred to as *ordinary least squares* (OLS) regression, and the values determined by the estimated regression equation, $\hat{Y}_i$, are called least squares estimates.

The estimated **slope coefficient** $(\hat{b}_1)$ for the regression line describes the change in Y for a one-unit change in X. It can be positive, negative, or zero, depending on the relationship between the regression variables. The slope term is calculated as:

$$\hat{b}_1 = \frac{\text{cov}_{XY}}{\sigma_X^2}$$

The **intercept** term $(\hat{b}_0)$ is the line's intersection with the Y-axis at $X = 0$. It can be positive, negative, or zero. A property of the least squares method is that the intercept term may be expressed as:

$$\hat{b}_0 = \overline{Y} - \hat{b}_1 \overline{X}$$

where:

$\overline{Y}$ = mean of Y
$\overline{X}$ = mean of X

The intercept equation highlights the fact that the regression line passes through a point with coordinates equal to the mean of the independent and dependent variables (i.e., the point $\overline{X}, \overline{Y}$).

EXAMPLE: Computing the slope coefficient and intercept term

Compute the slope coefficient and intercept term for the ABC regression example using the following information:

cov(S&P 500, ABC) = 0.000336 $\overline{\text{S\&P 500}}$ = –2.70%

var(S&P 500)   = 0.000522 $\overline{\text{ABC}}$ = –4.05%

Answer:

The slope coefficient is calculated as $\hat{b}_1$ = 0.000336 / 0.000522 = 0.64.

The intercept term is:

$$\hat{b}_0 = \overline{\text{ABC}} - \hat{b}_1 \, \overline{\text{S\&P 500}} = -4.05\% - 0.64(-2.70\%) = -2.3\%$$

The estimated regression line that minimizes the SSE in our ABC stock return example is shown in Figure 1.2.

This regression line has an intercept of –2.3% and a slope of 0.64. The model predicts that if the S&P 500 excess return is –7.8% (May 20x4 value), then the ABC excess return would be –2.3% + (0.64)(–7.8%) = –7.3%. The residual (error) for the May 20x4 ABC prediction is 8.4%, the difference between the actual ABC excess return of 1.1% and the predicted return of –7.3%.

Figure 1.2:   Estimated Regression Equation for ABC vs. S&P 500 Excess Returns

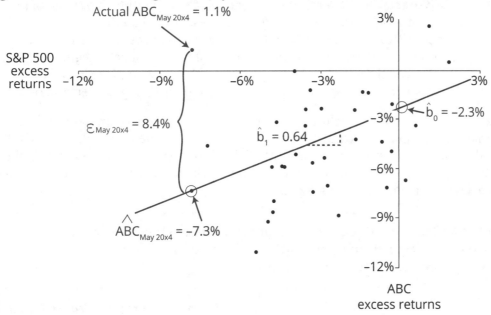

Interpreting a Regression Coefficient

The estimated intercept represents the value of the dependent variable at the point of intersection of the regression line and the axis of the dependent variable (usually the vertical axis). In other words, the intercept is an estimate of the dependent variable when the independent variable is zero.

We also mentioned earlier that the estimated slope coefficient is interpreted as the expected change in the dependent variable for a one-unit change in the independent variable. For example, an estimated slope coefficient of 2 would indicate that the dependent variable is expected to change by two units for every one-unit change in the independent variable.

EXAMPLE: Interpreting regression coefficients

In the ABC regression example, the estimated slope coefficient was 0.64 and the estimated intercept term was −2.3%. How would we interpret each coefficient estimate?

Answer:

The slope coefficient of 0.64 can be interpreted to mean that when excess S&P 500 returns increase (decrease) by 1%, ABC excess returns are expected to increase (decrease) by 0.64%.

The intercept term of −2.3% can be interpreted to mean that when the excess return on the S&P 500 is zero, the expected return on ABC stock is −2.3%.

PROFESSOR'S NOTE

The slope coefficient in a regression of the excess returns of an individual security (the *Y*-variable) on the return on the market (the *X*-variable) is called the stock's beta, which is an estimate of systematic risk of ABC stock. Notice that ABC is less risky than the average stock, because its returns tend to increase or decrease by less than the overall change in the market returns. A stock with a beta (regression slope coefficient) of 1 has an average level of systematic risk, and a stock with a beta greater than 1 has more-than-average systematic risk.

Keep in mind that any conclusions regarding the importance of an independent variable in explaining a dependent variable are based on the *statistical significance* of the slope coefficient. The magnitude of the slope coefficient does not (by itself) indicate the importance of the variable. Rather, a hypothesis test must be conducted to assess the importance of the variable.

LOS 1.c: Explain the assumptions underlying the simple linear regression model, and describe how residuals and residual plots indicate if these assumptions may have been violated.

CFA® Program Curriculum, Volume 1, page 17

Linear regression is based on a number of assumptions. Most of the assumptions pertain to the regression model's residual term (ε). The assumptions are as follows:

1. A linear relationship exists between the dependent and the independent variables.

2. The variance of the residual term is constant for all observations (homoskedasticity).

3. The residual term is independently distributed; that is, the residual for one observation is not correlated with that of another observation (meaning that the paired X and Y observations are independent of each other).

4. The residual term is normally distributed.

Linear Relationship

A linear regression model is not appropriate when the relationship between X and Y is nonlinear. Later, we will demonstrate that, in some cases, taking natural log of either X or Y may result in a linear relationship between the transformed variables. Figure 1.3 illustrates how a linear model is a poor fit when the relationship between X and Y is nonlinear.

Figure 1.3: Nonlinear Relationship

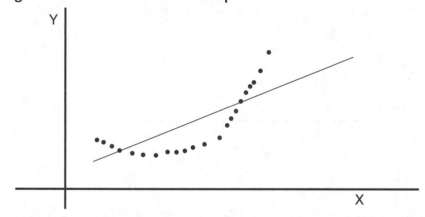

Homoskedasticity

Heteroskedasticity (i.e., absence of homoskedasticity) occurs when the variance of the residuals differs across observations. Figure 1.4 shows a scatter plot of observations around a fitted regression line. We can see that the model residuals are more widely dispersed around higher values of X than around lower values of X. If these observations were chronological, then it appears that the model accuracy has declined over time.

Figure 1.4: Heteroskedasticity

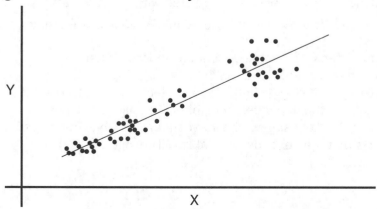

Independence

If the observations (*X* and *Y* pairs) are not independent, then the residuals from the model will exhibit **serial correlation**. Suppose we collect a company's monthly sales and plot them against monthly GDP. There may be a seasonality in sales such that December sales (unfilled dots in Figure 1.5) are noticeably farther from their predicted values (straight line) as compared to the other months (solid dots in Figure 1.5). If the observations are not independent, the seasonal observations will unduly influence the regression parameters.

Figure 1.5: Independence

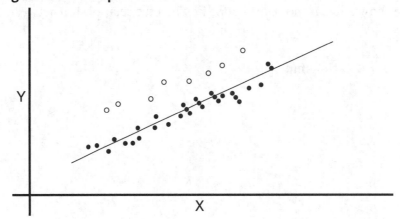

Normality

When the residuals (prediction errors) are normally distributed, we can conduct hypothesis testing for evaluating the goodness of fit of the model (discussed later). For a large sample size, using the central limit theorem, we can drop the normality assumption requirement.

MODULE QUIZ 1.1

To best evaluate your performance, enter your quiz answers online.

1. Which of the following is not a necessary assumption of simple linear regression analysis?
   A. The residuals are normally distributed.
   B. There is a constant variance of the error term.
   C. The dependent variable is uncorrelated with the residuals.

2. What is the *most appropriate* interpretation of a slope coefficient of 10.0?
   A. The predicted value of the dependent variable when the independent variable is zero is 10.0.
   B. For every 1-unit change in the independent variable, the model predicts that the dependent variable will change by 10 units.
   C. For every 1-unit change in the independent variable, the model predicts that the dependent variable will change by 0.1 units.

MODULE 1.2: GOODNESS OF FIT AND HYPOTHESIS TESTS

Video covering this content is available online.

Reading 1

LOS 1.d: Calculate and interpret the coefficient of determination and the *F*-statistic in a simple linear regression.

LOS 1.e: Describe the use of analysis of variance (ANOVA) in regression analysis, interpret ANOVA results, and calculate and interpret the standard error of estimate in a simple linear regression.

CFA® Program Curriculum, Volume 1, page 24

Analysis of variance (ANOVA) is a statistical procedure for analyzing the total variability of the dependent variable. Let's define some terms before we move on to ANOVA tables:

■ **Total sum of squares (SST)** measures the total variation in the dependent variable. SST is equal to the sum of the squared differences between the actual *Y*-values and the mean of *Y*.

$$SST = \sum_{i=1}^{n}\left(Y_i - \overline{Y}\right)^2$$

■ **Regression sum of squares (RSS)** measures the variation in the dependent variable that is explained by the independent variable. RSS is the sum of the squared distances between the predicted *Y*-values and the mean of *Y*.

$$RSS = \sum_{i=1}^{n}\left(\widehat{Y}_i - \overline{Y}\right)^2$$

■ **Sum of squared errors (SSE)** measures the unexplained variation in the dependent variable. It's also known as the sum of squared residuals or the residual sum of squares. SSE is the sum of the squared vertical distances between the actual *Y*-values and the predicted *Y*-values on the regression line.

$$SSE = \sum_{i=1}^{n}\left(Y_i - \widehat{Y}\right)^2$$

You probably will not be surprised to learn that:

total variation = explained variation + unexplained variation

or:

SST = RSS + SSE

Figure 1.6 illustrates how the total variation in the dependent variable (SST) is composed of RSS and SSE.

Figure 1.6: Components of Total Variation

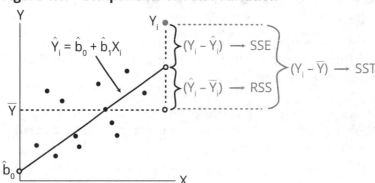

The output of the ANOVA procedure is an ANOVA table, which is a summary of the variation in the dependent variable. ANOVA tables are included in the regression output of many statistical software packages. You can think of the ANOVA table as the source of the data for the computation of many of the regression concepts discussed in this topic review. A generic ANOVA table for a simple linear regression (one independent variable) is presented in Figure 1.7.

Figure 1.7: ANOVA Table

Source of Variation	Degrees of Freedom	Sum of Squares	Mean Sum of Squares
Regression (explained)	1	RSS	$MSR = \dfrac{RSS}{k} = \dfrac{RSS}{1} = RSS$
Error (unexplained)	n – 2	SSE	$MSE = \dfrac{SSE}{n-2}$
Total	n – 1	SST	

PROFESSOR'S NOTE

k is the number of slope parameters estimated and *n* is the number of observations. In general, the regression df = k and the error df = (n − k − 1). Because we are limited to simple linear regressions in this topic review (one independent variable), we use k = 1 for the regression *df* and n − 1 − 1 = n − 2 for the error *df*.

Standard Error of Estimate (SEE)

SEE for a regression is the standard deviation of its residuals. The lower the SEE, the better the model fit.

$$SEE = \sqrt{MSE}$$

Coefficient of Determination (R^2)

The **coefficient of determination** (R^2) is defined as the percentage of the total variation in the dependent variable explained by the independent variable. For example, an R^2 of 0.63 indicates that the variation of the independent variable explains 63% of the variation in the dependent variable.

$$R^2 = RSS / SST$$

PROFESSOR'S NOTE

For simple linear regression (i.e., with one independent variable), the coefficient of determination, R^2, may be computed by simply squaring the correlation coefficient, r. In other words, $R^2 = r^2$ for a regression with one independent variable.

EXAMPLE: Using the ANOVA table

Complete the ANOVA table for the ABC regression example and calculate the R^2 and the standard error of estimate (SEE).

Partial ANOVA Table for ABC Regression Example

Source of Variation	Degrees of Freedom	Sum of Squares	Mean Sum of Squares
Regression (explained)	?	0.00756	?
Error (unexplained)	?	0.04064	?
Total	?	?	

Answer:

Recall that the data included three years of monthly return observations, so the total number of observations (n) is 36.

Completed ANOVA Table for ABC Regression Example

Source of Variation	Degrees of Freedom	Sum of Squares	Mean Sum of Squares
Regression (explained)	1	0.0076	0.0076
Error (unexplained)	34	0.0406	0.0012
Total	35	0.0482	

$$R^2 = \frac{\text{explained variation (RSS)}}{\text{total variation (SST)}} = \frac{0.0076}{0.0482} = 0.158 \text{ or } 15.8\%$$

$$SEE = \sqrt{MSE} = \sqrt{0.0012} = 0.035$$

The *F*-Statistic

An *F*-test assesses how well a set of independent variables, as a group, explains the variation in the dependent variable. In multiple regression, the *F*-statistic is used to test whether *at least one* independent variable in a set of independent variables explains a significant portion of the variation of the dependent variable. We will discuss the use of the *F*-test in multiple regression with more than one independent variable in the next topic review.

The *F*-statistic is calculated as:

$$F = \frac{MSR}{MSE} = \frac{RSS/k}{SSE/n - k - 1}$$

where:
MSR = mean regression sum of squares
MSE = mean squared error

Important: This is always a one-tailed test!

In multiple regression, the *F*-statistic tests *all* independent variables as a group.

The F-Statistic With One Independent Variable

For simple linear regression, there is only one independent variable, so the *F*-test is the *t*-test for statistical significance of the slope coefficient:

$$H_0: b_1 = 0 \text{ versus } H_a: b_1 \neq 0$$

To determine whether *b*1 is statistically significant using the *F*-test, the calculated *F*-statistic is compared with the critical *F*-value, F_c, at the appropriate level of significance. The degrees of freedom for the numerator and denominator with one independent variable are:

$$df_{numerator} = k = 1$$
$$df_{denominator} = n - k - 1 = n - 2$$

where:
n = number of observations

The decision rule for the *F*-test is: reject H_0 if $F > F_c$.

Rejection of the null hypothesis at a stated level of significance indicates that the independent variable is significantly different than zero, which is interpreted to mean that it makes a significant contribution to the explanation of the dependent variable. In simple linear regression, it tells us the same thing as the *t*-test of the slope coefficient. In fact, in simple linear regression with one independent variable, $F = t^2$.

> **EXAMPLE: Calculating and interpreting the *F*-statistic**
>
> Use the completed ANOVA table from the previous example to calculate and interpret the *F*-statistic. Test the null hypothesis at the 5% significance level that the slope coefficient is equal to 0.
>
> **Answer:**
>
> $$F = \frac{MSR}{MSE} = \frac{0.0076}{0.0012} = 6.33$$
>
> $$df_{numerator} = k = 1$$
> $$df_{denominator} = n - k - 1 = 36 - 1 - 1 = 34$$

The null and alternative hypotheses are: H_0: $b_1 = 0$ versus H_a: $b_1 \neq 0$. The critical F-value for 1 and 34 degrees of freedom at a 5% significance level is approximately 4.1. (Remember, it's a one-tail test, so we use the 5% F-table!) Therefore, we can reject the null hypothesis and conclude that the slope coefficient is significantly different than zero.

LOS 1.f: Formulate a null and an alternative hypothesis about a population value of a regression coefficient, and determine whether the null hypothesis is rejected at a given level of significance.

CFA® Program Curriculum, Volume 1, page 29

A *t-test* may also be used to test the hypothesis that the true slope coefficient, b_1, is equal to some hypothesized value. Letting $\hat{b}_1$ be the point estimate for b_1, the appropriate test statistic with n − 2 degrees of freedom is:

$$t_{b_1} = \frac{\hat{b}_1 - b_1}{s_{\hat{b}_1}}$$

The decision rule for tests of significance for regression coefficients is: Reject H_0 if $t > + t_{critical}$ or $t < -t_{critical}$

Rejection of the null means that the slope coefficient is *different* from the hypothesized value of b_1.

To test whether an independent variable explains the variation in the dependent variable (i.e., it is statistically significant), the hypothesis that is tested is whether the true slope is zero ($b_1 = 0$). The appropriate test structure for the null and alternative hypotheses is:

H_0: $b_1 = 0$ versus H_a: $b_1 \neq 0$

EXAMPLE: Hypothesis test for significance of regression coefficients

The estimated slope coefficient from the ABC example is 0.64 with a standard error equal to 0.26. Assuming that the sample has 36 observations, determine if the estimated slope coefficient is significantly different than zero at a 5% level of significance.

Answer:

The calculated test statistic is:

$$t = \frac{\hat{b}_1 - b_1}{s_{\hat{b}_1}} = \frac{0.64 - 0}{0.26} = 2.46$$

The critical two-tailed *t*-values are ±2.03 (from the *t*-table with df = 36 − 2 = 34). Because $t > t_{critical}$ (i.e., 2.46 > 2.03), we reject the null hypothesis and conclude that the slope is different from zero.

The *t*-test for a simple linear regression is the same as a *t*-test for the correlation coefficient between X and Y. The value of the *t*-statistic will be identical and the critical *t*-value (and hence the decision rule) will also be identical.

$$t = \frac{r\sqrt{n-2}}{\sqrt{1-r^2}}$$

Interpreting *p*-Values

The *p*-value is the smallest level of significance for which the null hypothesis can be rejected. When testing for the hypothesis that the coefficient is equal to zero versus not equal to zero, an alternative method is to compare the *p*-value to the significance level:

■ If the *p*-value is less than the significance level, the null hypothesis can be rejected.

■ If the *p*-value is greater than the significance level, the null hypothesis cannot be rejected.

MODULE QUIZ 1.2

To best evaluate your performance, enter your quiz answers online.

Use the following data to answer Questions 1 and 2.

An analyst is interested in predicting annual sales for XYZ Company, a maker of paper products. The following table reports a regression of the annual sales for XYZ against paper product industry sales.

Regression Output

Parameters	Coefficient	Standard Error of the Coefficient
Intercept	–94.88	32.97
Slope (industry sales)	0.2796	0.0363

The correlation between company and industry sales is 0.9757. The regression was based on five observations.

1. Which of the following is *closest* to the value and reports the *most likely* interpretation of the R^2 for this regression?
   A. The R^2 is 0.048, indicating that the variability of industry sales explains about 4.8% of the variability of company sales.
   B. The R^2 is 0.952, indicating that the variability of industry sales explains about 95.2% of the variability of company sales.
   C. The R^2 is 0.952, indicating that the variability of company sales explains about 95.2% of the variability of industry sales.

2. Based on the regression results, XYZ Company's market share of any increase in industry sales is expected to be *closest* to:
   A. 4%.
   B. 28%.
   C. 45%.

Use the following information to answer Questions 3 and 4.

A study was conducted by the British Department of Transportation to estimate urban travel time between locations in London, England. Data was collected for motorcycles and passenger cars. Simple linear regression was conducted using data sets for both types of vehicles, where Y = urban travel time in minutes and X = distance between locations in kilometers. The following results were obtained:

Regression Results for Travel Times Between Distances in London		
Passenger cars:	$\hat{Y} = 1.85 + 3.86X$	$R^2 = 0.758$
Motorcycles:	$\hat{Y} = 2.50 + 1.93X$	$R^2 = 0.676$

3. The estimated increase in travel time for a motorcycle commuter planning to move 8 km farther from his workplace in London is *closest* to:
   A. 31 minutes.
   B. 15 minutes.
   C. 0.154 hours.

4. Based on the regression results, which model is more reliable?
   A. The passenger car model because 3.86 > 1.93.
   B. The motorcycle model because 1.93 < 3.86.
   C. The passenger car model because 0.758 > 0.676.

5. What is the appropriate alternative hypothesis to test the statistical significance of the intercept term in the following regression?

   $Y = a_1 + a_2(X) + \varepsilon$

   A. $H_A: a_1 \neq 0$.
   B. $H_A: a_1 > 0$.
   C. $H_A: a_2 \neq 0$.

Video covering this content is available online.

MODULE 1.3: PREDICTING DEPENDENT VARIABLES AND FUNCTIONAL FORMS

LOS 1.g: Calculate and interpret the predicted value for the dependent variable, and a prediction interval for it, given an estimated linear regression model and a value for the independent variable.

CFA® Program Curriculum, Volume 1, page 37

Predicted values are values of the dependent variable based on the estimated regression coefficients and a prediction about the value of the independent variable. They are the values that are *predicted* by the regression equation, given an estimate of the independent variable.

For a simple regression, the predicted (or forecast) value of *Y* is:

$$\hat{Y} = \hat{b}_0 + \hat{b}_1 X_p$$

where:
$\hat{Y}$ = predicted value of the dependent variable
X_p = forecasted value of the independent variable

> **EXAMPLE: Predicting the dependent variable**
>
> Given the ABC regression equation:
>
> $$\widehat{ABC} = -2.3\% + (0.64)(\widehat{S\&P\ 500})$$
>
> Calculate the predicted value of ABC excess returns if forecasted S&P 500 excess returns are 10%.
>
> **Answer:**
>
> The predicted value for ABC excess returns is determined as follows:
>
> $$\widehat{ABC} = -2.3\% + (0.64)(10\%) = 4.1\%$$

Confidence Intervals for Predicted Values

The equation for the confidence interval for a predicted value of *Y* is:

$$\hat{Y} \pm \left(t_c \times s_f\right) \Rightarrow \left[\hat{Y} - \left(t_c \times s_f\right) < Y < \hat{Y} + \left(t_c \times s_f\right)\right]$$

where:
t_c = two-tailed critical *t*-value at the desired level of significance with df = n − 2
s_f = standard error of the forecast

The challenge with computing a confidence interval for a predicted value is calculating s_f. It's highly unlikely that you will have to calculate the standard error of the forecast (it will probably be provided if you need to compute a confidence interval for the dependent variable). However, if you do need to calculate s_f it can be done with the following formula for the variance of the forecast:

$$s_f^2 = SEE^2 \left[1 + \frac{1}{n} + \frac{(X - \overline{X})^2}{(n-1)s_x^2} \right]$$

where:
SEE^2 = variance of the residuals = the square of the standard error of estimate
s_x^2 = variance of the independent variable
X = value of the independent variable for which the forecast was made

---

EXAMPLE: Confidence interval for a predicted value

Calculate a 95% prediction interval on the predicted value of ABC excess returns from the previous example. Suppose the standard error of the forecast is 3.67, and the forecasted value of S&P 500 excess returns is 10%.

Answer:

The predicted value for ABC excess returns is:

$$\widehat{ABC} = -2.3\% + (0.64)(10\%) = 4.1\%$$

The 5% two-tailed critical t-value with 34 degrees of freedom is 2.03. The prediction interval at the 95% confidence level is:

$$\widehat{ABC} \pm \left(t_c \times s_f \right) \Rightarrow [4.1\% \pm (2.03 \times 3.67\%)] = 4.1\% \pm 7.5\%$$

or –3.4% to 11.6%

This range can be interpreted as, given a forecasted value for S&P 500 excess returns of 10%, we can be 95% confident that the ABC excess returns will be between –3.4% and 11.6%.

LOS 1.h: Describe different functional forms of simple linear regressions.

CFA® Program Curriculum, Volume 1, page 37

One of the assumptions of linear regression is that the relationship between X and Y is linear. However, what if that assumption is violated? Consider Y = EPS for a company and X = the time index. Suppose that EPS is growing at approximately 10% annually. Figure 1.8 shows the plot of actual EPS versus linear OLS fitted values.

Figure 1.8:   Nonlinear Relationship

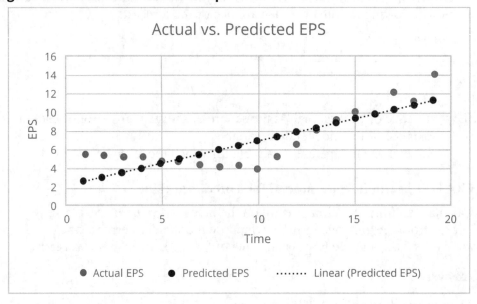

As shown, when the relationship is nonlinear, the fitted values will be biased downward in some cases and upward in other cases, resulting in a poor fit. In such a situation, transforming one or both the variables can produce a linear relationship. Depending on the characteristics of the data, several modification approaches (e.g., taking natural log) can be used, yielding different functional forms of the model.

- **Log-lin model**. If the dependent variable is logarithmic while the independent variable is linear.

- **Lin-log model**. If the dependent variable is linear while the independent variable is logarithmic.

- **Log-log model**. Both the dependent variable and the independent variable are logarithmic.

Log-Lin Model

Taking the natural logarithm of the dependent variable, our model now becomes:

$$\ln Y_i = b_0 + b_1 X_i + \varepsilon_i$$

In this model, the slope coefficient is interpreted as the *relative* change in the dependent variable for an absolute change in the independent variable. Figure 1.9 shows the results after taking the natural log of EPS, and fitting that data using a log-lin model.

Figure 1.9: Log-Lin Model, EPS Data

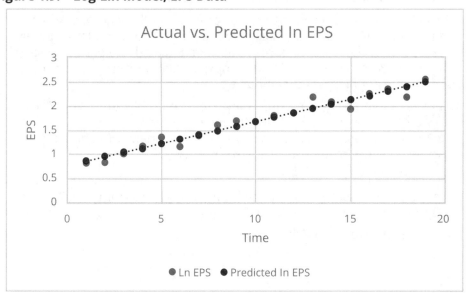

Lin-Log Model

Taking the natural logarithm of the independent variable, our model now becomes:

$$Y_i = b_0 + b_1 \ln(X)_i + \varepsilon_i$$

In this model, the slope coefficient is interpreted as the *absolute* change in the dependent variable for a *relative* change in the independent variable.

Log-Log Model

Taking the natural logarithm of both variables, our model now becomes:

$$\ln Y_i = b_0 + b_1 \ln(X)_i + \varepsilon_i$$

In this model, the slope coefficient is interpreted as the relative change in the dependent variable for a relative change in the independent variable. As such, this model is useful in calculating elasticities.

Selection of Functional Form

Selecting the correct functional form involves determining the nature of the variables and evaluating the goodness-of-fit measures (e.g., R^2, SEE, *F*-stat).

MODULE QUIZ 1.3

To best evaluate your performance, enter your quiz answers online.

1. The variation in the dependent variable explained by the independent variable is measured by:
    A. the mean squared error.
    B. the sum of squared errors.
    C. the regression sum of squares.

Use the following information for Questions 2 through 6.

Bill Coldplay, CFA, is analyzing the performance of the Vigorous Growth Index Fund (VIGRX) over the past three years. The fund employs a passive management investment approach designed to track the performance of the MSCI US Prime Market Growth Index, a broadly diversified index of growth stocks of large U.S. companies.

Coldplay estimates a regression using excess monthly returns on VIGRX (exVIGRX) as the dependent variable and excess monthly returns on the S&P 500 Index (exS&P500) as the independent variable. The data are expressed in decimal terms (e.g., 0.03, not 3%).

$$exVIGRX_t = b_0 + b_1(exS\&P500_t) + \varepsilon_t$$

A scatter plot of excess returns for both return series from June 2014 to May 2017 are shown in the following figure.

Analysis of Large-Cap Growth Fund

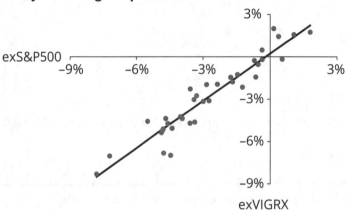

Results from that analysis are presented in the following figures.

Coefficient	Coefficient Estimate	Standard Error
b_0	0.0023	0.0022
b_1	1.1163	0.0624

Partial ANOVA Table

Source of Variation	Sum of Squares
Regression (explained)	0.0228
Error (unexplained)	0.0024

2. Are the intercept term and the slope coefficient statistically significantly different from zero at the 5% significance level?

Intercept term significant?	Slope coefficient significant?
A. Yes	Yes
B. Yes	No
C. No	Yes

3. Coldplay would like to test the following hypothesis: H_0: $b_1 \leq 1$ versus H_1: $b_1 > 1$ at the 1% significance level. The calculated t-statistic and the appropriate conclusion are:

Calculated t-statistic	Appropriate conclusion
A. 1.86	Reject H_0
B. 1.86	Fail to reject H_0
C. 2.44	Reject H_0

4. Coldplay forecasts the excess return on the S&P 500 for June 2017 to be 5% and the 95% confidence interval for the predicted value of the excess return on VIGRX for June 2017 to be 3.9% to 7.7%. The standard error of the forecast is *closest* to:
    A. 0.0080.
    B. 0.0093.
    C. 0.0111.

5. The R^2 from the regression is *closest* to:
    A. 0.095.
    B. 0.295.
    C. 0.905.

6. The standard error of estimate (SEE) is *closest* to:
    A. 0.008.
    B. 0.014.
    C. 0.049.

KEY CONCEPTS

LOS 1.a

Linear regression provides an estimate of the linear relationship between an independent variable (the explanatory variable) and a dependent variable (the predicted variable).

LOS 1.b

The general form of a simple linear regression model is $Y_i = b_0 + b_1 X_i + \varepsilon_i$.

The least-squares model minimizes the sum of squared errors.

- $\hat{b}_0 = \overline{Y} - \hat{b}_1 \overline{X}$ = fitted intercept

- $\hat{b}_1$ = fitted slope coefficient = cov (X,Y) / variance of X

The estimated intercept, $\hat{b}_0$, represents the value of the dependent variable at the point of intersection of the regression line and the axis of the dependent variable (usually the vertical axis). The estimated slope coefficient, $\hat{b}_1$, is interpreted as the change in the dependent variable for a one-unit change in the independent variable.

LOS 1.c

Assumptions made regarding simple linear regression include the following:

1. A linear relationship exists between the dependent and the independent variable.

2. The variance of the residual term is constant (homoskedasticity).

3. The residual term is free from serial correlation.

4. The residual term is normally distributed.

LOS 1.d

The standard error of the estimate in a simple linear regression is calculated as:

$$SEE = \sqrt{\frac{SSE}{n-2}}$$

The coefficient of determination, R^2, is the proportion of the total variation of the dependent variable explained by the regression:

$$R^2 = \frac{RSS}{SST} = \frac{SST - SSE}{SST}$$

In simple linear regression, because there is only one independent variable (k = 1), the *F*-test tests the same null hypothesis as testing the statistical significance of b_1 using the *t*-test: $H_0: b_1 = 0$ versus $H_a: b_1 \neq 0$. With only one independent variable, *F* is calculated as:

$$F\text{-stat} = \frac{MSR}{MSE} \text{ with 1 and n} - 2 \text{ degrees of freedom}$$

In fact, in simple linear regression, $F = t_{b_1}^2$.

LOS 1.e

ANOVA Table for Simple Linear Regression (k = 1)

Source of Variation	Degrees of Freedom	Sum of Squares	Mean Sum of Squares
Regression (explained)	1	RSS	$MSR = \dfrac{RSS}{k} = \dfrac{RSS}{1} = RSS$
Error (unexplained)	n − 2	SSE	$MSE = \dfrac{SSE}{n-2}$
Total	n − 1	SST	

LOS 1.f

We can assess a regression model by testing whether the population value of a regression coefficient is equal to a specific hypothesized value.

A *t*-test with n − 2 degrees of freedom is used to conduct hypothesis tests of the estimated regression parameters:

$$t = \frac{\hat{b}_1 - b_1}{s_{\hat{b}_1}}$$

LOS 1.g

A predicted value of the dependent variable, $\hat{Y}$, is determined by inserting the predicted value of the independent variable, X_p, in the regression equation and calculating $\hat{Y}_p = \hat{b}_0 + \hat{b}_1 X_p$.

The confidence interval for a predicted *Y*-value is $[\hat{Y} - (t_c \times s_f) < Y < \hat{Y} + (t_c \times s_f)]$, where s_f is the standard error of the forecast.

LOS 1.h

If the relationship between the independent variable and the dependent variable is not linear, we can perform a logarithmic transform on one (or both) of these variables to convert the relationship to a linear form, which then makes it possible to use simple linear regression.

Dependent Variable	Independent Variable	Model	Slope Interpretation
Logarithmic	Linear	Log-lin	*Relative* change in dependent variable for an absolute change in the independent variable
Linear	Logarithmic	Lin-log	*Absolute* change in dependent variable for a relative change in the independent variable
Logarithmic	Logarithmic	Log-log	*Relative* change in dependent variable for a *relative* change in the independent variable

ANSWER KEY FOR MODULE QUIZZES

Module Quiz 1.1

1. **C** The model does not assume that the dependent variable is uncorrelated with the residuals. It does assume that the independent variable is uncorrelated with the residuals. (LOS 1.b)

2. **B** The slope coefficient is best interpreted as the predicted change in the dependent variable for a 1-unit change in the independent variable. If the slope coefficient estimate is 10.0 and the independent variable changes by 1 unit, the dependent variable is expected to change by 10 units. The intercept term is best interpreted as the value of the dependent variable when the independent variable is equal to zero. (LOS 1.b)

Module Quiz 1.2

1. **B** The R^2 is computed as the correlation squared: $(0.9757)^2 = 0.952$.

   The interpretation of this R^2 is that 95.2% of the variation in Company XYZ's sales is explained by the variation in industry sales. (Module 1.2, LOS 1.c)

2. **B** The slope coefficient of 0.2796 indicates that a $1 million increase in industry sales will result in an increase in firm sales of approximately 28% of that amount ($279,600). (Module 1.1, LOS 1.b)

3. **B** The slope coefficient is 1.93, indicating that each additional kilometer increases travel time by 1.93 minutes:

   $$1.93 \times 8 = 15.44$$

   (Module 1.1, LOS 1.b)

4. **C** The higher R^2 for the passenger car model indicates that regression results are more reliable. Distance is a better predictor of travel time for cars. Perhaps the aggressiveness of the driver is a bigger factor in travel time for motorcycles than it is for autos. (Module 1.2, LOS 1.c)

5. **A** In this regression, a_1 is the intercept term. To test the statistical significance means to test the null hypothesis that a_1 is equal to zero, versus the alternative that a_1 is not equal to zero. (Module 1.2, LOS 1.d)

Module Quiz 1.3

1. **C** The regression sum of squares measures the amount of variation in the dependent variable explained by the independent variable (i.e., the explained variation). The sum of squared errors measures the variation in the dependent variable *not* explained by the independent variable. The

mean squared error is equal to the sum of squared errors divided by its degrees of freedom. (Module 1.2, LOS 1.e)

2. **C**   The critical two-tailed 5% *t*-value with 34 degrees of freedom is approximately 2.03. The calculated *t*-statistics for the intercept term and slope coefficient are, respectively, 0.0023 / 0.0022 = 1.05 and 1.1163 / 0.0624 = 17.9. Therefore, the intercept term is not statistically different from zero at the 5% significance level, while the slope coefficient is. (Module 1.2, LOS 1.f)

3. **B**   Notice that this is a one-tailed test. The critical one-tailed 1% *t*-value with 34 degrees of freedom is approximately 2.44. The calculated *t*-statistic for the slope coefficient is $(1.1163 - 1) / 0.0624 = 1.86$. Therefore, the slope coefficient is not statistically different from one at the 1% significance level and Coldplay should fail to reject the null hypothesis. (Module 1.2, LOS 1.f)

4. **B**   This is a tricky question because you are given the confidence interval and its midpoint, and are asked to solve for the standard error of the forecast (s_f). Remember to convert the percentages to decimals. The critical two-tailed 5% *t*-value with 34 degrees of freedom is approximately 2.03. The midpoint, or predicted value, is $0.0023 + 1.1163 \times 0.05 = 0.058$. Therefore, $0.058 +/- (2.03)(s_f)$ is equivalent to 0.039 to 0.077 and solving for s_f yields $s_f = 0.0093$. (Module 1.3, LOS 1.g)

5. **C**   SST is equal to the sum of RSS and SSE: $0.0228 + 0.0024 = 0.0252$. $R^2 = $ RSS / SST $= 0.0228 / 0.0252 = 0.905$. (Module 1.2, LOS 1.e)

6. **A**   Because n = 36, and the degrees of freedom for the sum of squared errors (SSE) is $n - 2$ in simple linear regression, the degrees of freedom for SSE is 34, and the mean squared error is SSE / 34. The standard error of estimate (SEE) is equal to the square root of the mean squared error:

$$SEE = \sqrt{\frac{0.0024}{34}} = 0.008$$

(Module 1.2, LOS 1.e)

READING
2

Multiple Regression

EXAM FOCUS

Multiple regression is the centerpiece of the quantitative methods topic at Level II. It is a useful analysis tool that closely relates to the multifactor models that appear later in the Level II curriculum, in the Equity and Portfolio Management Study Sessions. Know this material well.

You should know how to use a *t*-test to assess the significance of the individual regression parameters and an *F*-test to assess the effectiveness of the model as a whole in explaining the dependent variable. You should understand the effect that heteroskedasticity, serial correlation, and multicollinearity have on regression results. Also be able to identify the common model misspecifications.

Focus on interpretation of the regression equation and the test statistics. Remember that most of the test and descriptive statistics discussed (e.g., *t*-stat, *F*-stat, and R^2) are provided in the output of statistical software. Hence, application and interpretation of these measurements are more likely than actual computations on the exam.

WARM-UP: MULTIPLE REGRESSION BASICS

Multiple regression is regression analysis with more than one independent variable. It is used to quantify the influence of two or more independent variables on a dependent variable. For instance, simple (or univariate) linear regression explains the variation in stock returns in terms of the variation in systematic risk as measured by beta. With multiple regression, stock returns can be regressed against beta and against additional variables, such as firm size, equity, and industry classification, that might influence returns.

The general multiple linear regression model is:

$$Y_i = b_0 + b_1 X_{1i} + b_2 X_{2i} + \ldots + b_k X_{ki} + \varepsilon_i$$

where:

Y_i = ith observation of the dependent variable Y, i = 1, 2, …, n
X_j = independent variables, j = 1, 2, …, k
X_{ji} = ith observation of the jth independent variable
b_0 = intercept term
b_j = slope coefficient for each of the independent variables
ε_i = error term for the ith observation
n = number of observations
k = number of independent variables

The multiple regression methodology estimates the intercept and slope coefficients such that the sum of the squared error terms, $\sum_{i=1}^{n} \varepsilon_i^2$, is minimized. The result of this procedure is the following regression equation:

$$\hat{Y}_i = \hat{b}_0 + \hat{b}_1 X_{1i} + \hat{b}_2 X_{2i} + \ldots + \hat{b}_k X_{ki}$$

where the "^" indicates an estimate for the corresponding regression coefficient

The residual, $\hat{\varepsilon}_i$, is the difference between the observed value, Y_i, and the predicted value from the regression, $\hat{Y}_i$:

$$\hat{\varepsilon}_i = Y_i - \hat{Y}_i = Y_i - \left(\hat{b}_0 + \hat{b}_1 X_{1i} + \hat{b}_2 X_{2i} + \ldots + \hat{b}_k X_{ki} \right)$$

MODULE 2.1: MULTIPLE REGRESSION: INTRODUCTION

Video covering this content is available online.

LOS 2.a: Formulate a multiple regression equation to describe the relation between a dependent variable and several independent variables, and determine the statistical significance of each independent variable.

CFA® Program Curriculum, Volume 1, page 70

PROFESSOR'S NOTE

Testing the statistical significance of the regression coefficients means conducting a *t*-test with a null hypothesis that the regression coefficient is equal to zero. Rather than cover that concept here, even though it is mentioned in this LOS, we will cover it in detail in a later LOS as part of our general discussion of hypothesis testing.

Let's illustrate multiple regression using research by Arnott and Asness (2003).[1] As part of their research, the authors test the hypothesis that future 10-year real

---

1. Arnott, Robert D., and Clifford S. Asness. 2003. "Surprise! Higher Dividends = Higher Earnings Growth." *Financial Analysts Journal*, vol. 59, no. 1 (January/February): 70–87.

earnings growth in the S&P 500 (EG10) can be explained by the trailing dividend payout ratio of the stocks in the index (PR) and the yield curve slope (YCS). YCS is calculated as the difference between the 10-year T-bond yield and the 3-month T-bill yield at the start of the period. All three variables are measured in percent.

Formulating the Multiple Regression Equation

The authors formulate the following regression equation using annual data (46 observations):

$$EG10 = b_0 + b_1 PR + b_2 YCS + \varepsilon$$

The results of this regression are shown in Figure 2.1.

Figure 2.1:   Coefficient and Standard Error Estimates for Regression of EG10 on PR and YCS

	Coefficient	Standard Error
Intercept	–11.6%	1.657%
PR	0.25	0.032
YCS	0.14	0.280

LOS 2.b: Interpret estimated regression coefficients and their *p*-values.

CFA® Program Curriculum, Volume 1, page 70

PROFESSOR'S NOTE
We will defer a discussion of *p*-values to a later LOS.

Interpreting the Multiple Regression Results

The interpretation of the estimated regression coefficients from a multiple regression is the same as in simple linear regression for the intercept term but significantly different for the slope coefficients:

■ The **intercept term** is the value of the dependent variable when the independent variables are all equal to zero.

■ Each slope coefficient is the estimated change in the dependent variable for a one-unit change in that independent variable, *holding the other independent variables constant*. That's why the slope coefficients in a multiple regression are sometimes called **partial slope coefficients**.

For example, in the real earnings growth example, we can make these interpretations:

■ *Intercept term*: If the dividend payout ratio is zero and the slope of the yield curve is zero, we would expect the subsequent 10-year real earnings growth rate to be –11.6%.

- *PR coefficient*: If the payout ratio increases by 1%, we would expect the subsequent 10-year earnings growth rate to increase by 0.25%, *holding YCS constant*.

- *YCS coefficient*: If the yield curve slope increases by 1%, we would expect the subsequent 10-year earnings growth rate to increase by 0.14%, *holding PR constant*.

Let's discuss the interpretation of the multiple regression slope coefficients in more detail. Suppose we run a regression of the dependent variable Y on a single independent variable $X1$ and get the following result:

$$Y = 2.0 + 4.5X1$$

The appropriate interpretation of the estimated slope coefficient is that if $X1$ increases by 1 unit, we would expect Y to increase by 4.5 units.

Now suppose we add a second independent variable $X2$ to the regression and get the following result:

$$Y = 1.0 + 2.5X1 + 6.0X2$$

Notice that the estimated slope coefficient for $X1$ changed from 4.5 to 2.5 when we added $X2$ to the regression. We would expect this to happen most of the time when a second variable is added to the regression, unless $X2$ is uncorrelated with $X1$, because if $X1$ increases by 1 unit, then we would expect $X2$ to change as well. The multiple regression equation captures this relationship between $X1$ and $X2$ when predicting Y.

Now the interpretation of the estimated slope coefficient for $X1$ is that if $X1$ increases by 1 unit, we would expect Y to increase by 2.5 units, *holding X2 constant*.

Video covering this content is available online.

MODULE 2.2: HYPOTHESIS TESTS AND PREDICTED VALUES

LOS 2.c: Formulate a null and an alternative hypothesis about the population value of a regression coefficient, calculate the value of the test statistic, and determine whether to reject the null hypothesis at a given level of significance.

LOS 2.d: Interpret the results of hypothesis tests of regression coefficients.

CFA® Program Curriculum, Volume 1, page 70

Hypothesis Testing of Regression Coefficients

As with simple linear regression, the magnitude of the coefficients in a multiple regression tells us nothing about the importance of the independent variable in explaining the dependent variable. Thus, we must conduct hypothesis testing on the estimated slope coefficients to determine if the independent variables make a significant contribution to explaining the variation in the dependent variable.

The *t*-statistic used to test the significance of the individual coefficients in a multiple regression is calculated using the same formula that is used with simple linear regression:

$$t = \frac{\hat{b}_j - b_j}{s_{\hat{b}_j}} = \frac{\text{estimated regression coefficient} - \text{hypothesized value}}{\text{coefficient standard error of } b_j}$$

The *t*-statistic has $n - k - 1$ degrees of freedom.

PROFESSOR'S NOTE

An easy way to remember the number of degrees of freedom for this test is to recognize that "k" is the number of regression coefficients in the regression, and the "1" is for the intercept term. Therefore, the degrees of freedom is the number of observations minus k minus 1.

Determining Statistical Significance

The most common hypothesis test done on the regression coefficients is to test statistical significance, which means testing the null hypothesis that the coefficient is zero versus the alternative that it is not:

"testing statistical significance" $\Rightarrow H_0: b_j = 0$ versus $H_a : b_j \neq 0$

EXAMPLE: Testing the statistical significance of a regression coefficient

Test the statistical significance of the independent variable PR in the real earnings growth example at the 10% significance level. The results of that regression are reproduced in the following figure.

Coefficient and Standard Error Estimates for Regression of EG10 on PR and YCS

	Coefficient	Standard Error
Intercept	–11.6%	1.657%
PR	0.25	0.032
YCS	0.14	0.280

Answer:

We are testing the following hypothesis:

H_0: PR = 0 versus H_a: PR ≠ 0

The 10% two-tailed critical *t*-value with $46 - 2 - 1 = 43$ degrees of freedom is approximately 1.68. We should reject the null hypothesis if the *t*-statistic is greater than 1.68 or less than –1.68.

The *t*-statistic is:

$$t = \frac{0.25}{0.032} = 7.8$$

> Therefore, because the t-statistic of 7.8 is greater than the upper critical t-value of 1.68, we can reject the null hypothesis and conclude that the PR regression coefficient is statistically significantly different from zero at the 10% significance level.

Interpreting *p*-Values

The p-value is the smallest level of significance for which the null hypothesis can be rejected. An alternative method of doing hypothesis testing of the coefficients is to compare the p-value to the significance level:

- If the p-value is less than significance level, the null hypothesis can be rejected.

- If the p-value is greater than the significance level, the null hypothesis cannot be rejected.

EXAMPLE: Interpreting *p*-values

Given the following regression results, determine which regression parameters for the independent variables are statistically significantly different from zero at the 1% significance level, assuming the sample size is 60.

Variable	Coefficient	Standard Error	t-Statistic	p-Value
Intercept	0.40	0.40	1.0	0.3215
X1	8.20	2.05	4.0	0.0002
X2	0.40	0.18	2.2	0.0319
X3	−1.80	0.56	−3.2	0.0022

Answer:

The independent variable is statistically significant if the p-value is less than 1%, or 0.01. Therefore $X1$ and $X3$ are statistically significantly different from zero.

Figure 2.2 shows the results of the t-tests for each of the regression coefficients of our 10-year earnings growth example, including the p-values.

Figure 2.2: Regression Results for Regression of EG10 on PR and YCS

	Coefficient	Standard Error	t-statistic	p-value
Intercept	−11.6%	1.657%	−7.0	< 0.0001
PR	0.25	0.032	7.8	< 0.0001
YCS	0.14	0.280	0.5	0.62

As we determined in a previous example, we can reject the null hypothesis and conclude that PR is statistically significant. We can also draw the same conclusion for the intercept term because −7.0 is less than the lower critical value of −1.68 (because it is a two-tailed test). However, we fail to reject the null hypothesis for

YCS, so we cannot conclude that YCS has a statistically significant effect on the dependent variable, EG10, when PR is also included in the model. The *p*-values tell us exactly the same thing (as they always will): the intercept term and PR are statistically significant at the 10% level because their *p*-values are less than 0.10, while YCS is not statistically significant because its *p*-value is greater than 0.10.

Other Tests of the Regression Coefficients

You should also be prepared to formulate one- and two-tailed tests in which the null hypothesis is that the coefficient is equal to some value other than zero, or that it is greater than or less than some value.

EXAMPLE: Testing regression coefficients (two-tail test)

Using the data from Figure 2.2, test the null hypothesis that PR is equal to 0.20 versus the alternative that it is not equal to 0.20 using a 5% significance level.

Answer:

We are testing the following hypothesis:

H_0: PR = 0.20 versus H_a: PR ≠ 0.20

The 5% two-tailed critical *t*-value with $46 - 2 - 1 = 43$ degrees of freedom is approximately 2.02. We should reject the null hypothesis if the *t*-statistic is greater than 2.02 or less than −2.02.

The *t*-statistic is:

$$t = \frac{0.25 - 0.20}{0.032} = 1.56$$

Therefore, because the *t*-statistic of 1.56 is between the upper and lower critical *t*-values of −2.02 and 2.02, we cannot reject the null hypothesis and must conclude that the PR regression coefficient is not statistically significantly different from 0.20 at the 5% significance level.

EXAMPLE: Testing regression coefficients (one-tail test)

Using the data from Figure 2.2, test the null hypothesis that the intercept term is greater than or equal to −10.0% versus the alternative that it is less than −10.0% using a 1% significance level.

Answer:

We are testing the following hypothesis:

H_0: Intercept ≥ −10.0% versus H_a: Intercept < −10.0%

The 1% **one**-tailed critical *t*-value with $46 - 2 - 1 = 43$ degrees of freedom is approximately 2.42. We should reject the null hypothesis if the *t*-statistic is less than −2.42.

The *t*-statistic is:

$$t = \frac{-11.6\% - (-10.0\%)}{1.657\%} = -0.96$$

Therefore, because the *t*-statistic of –0.96 is not less than –2.42, we cannot reject the null hypothesis.

LOS 2.e: Calculate and interpret a predicted value for the dependent variable, given an estimated regression model and assumed values for the independent variables.

CFA® Program Curriculum, Volume 1, page 70

PREDICTING THE DEPENDENT VARIABLE

We can use the regression equation to make predictions about the dependent variable *based on forecasted values of the independent variables*. The process is similar to forecasting with simple linear regression, only now we need predicted values for more than one independent variable. The predicted value of dependent variable *Y* is:

$$\hat{Y}_i = \hat{b}_0 + \hat{b}_1 \hat{X}_{1i} + \hat{b}_2 \hat{X}_{2i} + ... + \hat{b}_k \hat{X}_{ki}$$

where:

$\hat{Y}_i$ = the predicted value of the dependent variable

$\hat{b}_j$ = the estimated slope coefficient for the *j*th independent variable

$\hat{X}_{ji}$ = the forecast of the *j*th independent variable, j = 1, 2, ..., *k*

PROFESSOR'S NOTE

The prediction of the dependent variable uses the estimated intercept and all of the estimated slope coefficients, regardless of whether the estimated coefficients are statistically significantly different from zero. For example, suppose you estimate the following regression equation: $\hat{Y} = 6 + 2X_1 + 4X_2$, and you determine that only the first independent variable (X_1) is statistically significant (i.e., you rejected the null that $b_1 = 0$). To predict Y given forecasts of $X_1 = 0.6$ and $X_2 = 0.8$, you would use the complete model: $\hat{Y} = 6 + (2 \times 0.6) + (4 \times 0.8) = 10.4$. Alternatively, you could drop X_2 and reestimate the model using just X_1, but remember that the coefficient on X_1 will probably change.

EXAMPLE: Calculating a predicted value for the dependent variable

An analyst would like to use the estimated regression equation from the previous example to calculate the predicted 10-year real earnings growth for the S&P 500, assuming the payout ratio of the index is 50%. He observes that the slope of the yield curve is currently 4%.

©2021 Kaplan, Inc.

Answer:

$$\widehat{EG10} = -11.6\% + 0.25(50\%) + 0.14(4\%) = 1.46\%$$

The model predicts a 1.46% real earnings growth rate for the S&P 500, assuming a 50% payout ratio, when the slope of the yield curve is 4%.

MODULE 2.3: ANOVA AND THE *F*-TEST

LOS 2.g: Calculate and interpret the *F*-statistic, and describe how it is used in regression analysis.

Video covering this content is available online.

Reading 2

CFA® Program Curriculum, Volume 1, page 82

THE *F*-STATISTIC

An *F*-test assesses how well the set of independent variables, as a group, explains the variation in the dependent variable. That is, the *F*-statistic is used to test whether *at least one* of the independent variables explains a significant portion of the variation of the dependent variable.

For example, if there are four independent variables in the model, the hypotheses are structured as:

$H_0: b_1 = b_2 = b_3 = b_4 = 0$ versus H_a: at least one $b_j \neq 0$

The *F*-statistic, *which is always a one-tailed test*, is calculated as:

$$F = \frac{MSR}{MSE} = \frac{RSS/k}{SSE/n - k - 1}$$

where:
RSS = regression sum of squares
SSE = sum of squared errors
MSR = mean regression sum of squares
MSE = mean squared error

PROFESSOR'S NOTE

Recall from the previous topic review that the regression sum of squares and the sum of squared errors are found in an ANOVA table. We analyze an ANOVA table from a multiple regression later in this topic review.

To determine whether at least one of the coefficients is statistically significant, the calculated *F*-statistic is compared with the **one-tailed** critical *F*-value, F_c, at the appropriate level of significance. The degrees of freedom for the numerator and denominator are:

$$df_{numerator} = k$$
$$df_{denominator} = n - k - 1$$

where:
n = number of observations
k = number of independent variables

The decision rule for the *F*-test is:

Decision rule: reject H_0 if F (test-statistic) > F_c (critical value)

Rejection of the null hypothesis at a stated level of significance indicates that at least one of the coefficients is significantly different than zero, which is interpreted to mean that at least one of the independent variables in the regression model makes a significant contribution to the explanation of the dependent variable.

PROFESSOR'S NOTE

It may have occurred to you that an easier way to test all of the coefficients simultaneously is to just conduct all of the individual *t*-tests and see how many of them you can reject. This is the wrong approach, however, because if you set the significance level for each *t*-test at 5%, for example, the significance level from testing them all simultaneously is NOT 5%, but rather some higher percentage. Just remember to use the *F*-test on the exam if you are asked to test all of the coefficients simultaneously.

EXAMPLE: Calculating and interpreting the *F*-statistic

An analyst runs a regression of monthly value-stock returns on five independent variables over 60 months. The total sum of squares is 460, and the sum of squared errors is 170. Test the null hypothesis at the 5% significance level that all five of the independent variables are equal to zero.

Answer:

The null and alternative hypotheses are:

$H_0: b_1 = b_2 = b_3 = b_4 = b_5 = 0$ versus H_a: at least one $b_j \neq 0$

$RSS = SST - SSE = 460 - 170 = 290$

$$MSR = \frac{290}{5} = 58.0$$

$$MSE = \frac{170}{60 - 5 - 1} = 3.15$$

$$F = \frac{58.0}{3.15} = 18.41$$

The critical *F*-value for 5 and 54 degrees of freedom at a 5% significance level is approximately 2.40. Remember, it's a **one-tailed** test, so we use the

5% *F*-table! Therefore, we can reject the null hypothesis and conclude that at least one of the five independent variables is significantly different than zero.

PROFESSOR'S NOTE

When testing the hypothesis that all the regression coefficients are simultaneously equal to zero, the *F*-test is always a one-tailed test, despite the fact that it looks like it should be a two-tailed test because there is an equal sign in the null hypothesis. This is a common source of confusion among Level II candidates; make sure you don't make that mistake on the exam.

LOS 2.i: Evaluate how well a regression model explains the dependent variable by analyzing the output of the regression equation and an ANOVA table.

CFA® Program Curriculum, Volume 1, page 70

ANOVA TABLES

Analysis of variance (ANOVA) is a statistical procedure that provides information on the explanatory power of a regression. We first discussed the use of ANOVA tables in the previous topic review of simple linear regression. Once again, the interpretation is the same in multiple regression.

The results of the ANOVA procedure are presented in an ANOVA table, which accompanies the multiple regression results from a statistical analysis or spreadsheet software program. An example of a generic ANOVA table is presented in Figure 2.3.

Figure 2.3: ANOVA Table

Source	df (Degrees of Freedom)	SS (Sum of Squares)	MS (Mean Square = SS/df)
Regression	k	RSS	MSR
Error	n − k − 1	SSE	MSE
Total	n − 1	SST	

The information in an ANOVA table is used to attribute the total variation of the dependent variable to one of two sources: the regression model or the residuals. This is indicated in the first column in the table, where the "source" of the variation is listed.

The information in an ANOVA table can be used to calculate R^2, the *F*-statistic, and the standard error of estimate (SEE). That is:

$$R^2 = \frac{RSS}{SST}$$

$$F = \frac{MSR}{MSE} \text{ with k and n − k − 1 degrees of freedom}$$

$$SEE = \sqrt{MSE}$$

Reading 2

PROFESSOR'S NOTE

R^2, F, and SEE are provided along with the standard ANOVA table produced by most statistical software packages. On the exam, be prepared to fill in "missing data" from an ANOVA output.

Let's look at an example to tie all of this together.

EXAMPLE: Using an ANOVA table with regression output

In an attempt to estimate a regression equation that can be used to forecast BuildCo's future sales, 22 years of BuildCo's annual sales were regressed against two independent variables:

GDP   = the level of gross domestic product

ΔI = changes in 30-year mortgage interest rates (expressed in percentage terms)

The output from a common statistical software package is contained in the following table.

Regression Results for BuildCo Sales Data

	Coefficient	Standard Error	t-Statistic	p-Value
Intercept	6.000	4.520	1.327	0.20
Level of gross domestic product (GDP)	0.004	0.003	?	0.20
Changes in 30-year mortgage rates (ΔI)	−20.500	3.560	?	< 0.001

ANOVA	df	SS	MS	F	Significance F
Regression	?	236.30	?	?	p < 0.005
Error	?	116.11	?		
Total	?	?			
R^2	?				
R_a^2	?				

Based on the output in the table, the regression equation can be stated as:

$$\widehat{\text{BuildCo Sales}} = 6.000 + 0.004(\text{GDP}) - 20.500(\Delta I)$$

Fill in the missing data and interpret the results of the regression at a 5% level of significance with respect to:

■ The significance of the individual independent variables.

■ The utility of the model as a whole.

Answer:

Step 1: Fill in the missing data.

The computed test statistics for the regression coefficients are:

$$t_{GDP} = \frac{0.004}{0.003} = 1.333$$

$$t_{\Delta I} = \frac{-20.500}{3.560} = -5.758$$

Degrees of freedom are:

$$df_{regression} = k = 2$$
$$df_{error} = n - k - 1 = 22 - 2 - 1 = 19$$
$$df_{total} = n - 1 = 22 - 1 = 21$$

Other calculations:

$$SST = RSS + SSE = 236.30 + 116.11 = \textbf{352.41}$$

$$MSR = \frac{RSS}{k} = \frac{236.30}{2} = \textbf{118.15}$$

$$MSE = \frac{SSE}{n - k - 1} = \frac{116.11}{19} = \textbf{6.11}$$

$$F = \frac{MSR}{MSE} = \frac{118.15}{6.11} = \textbf{19.34}$$

$$R^2 = \frac{RSS}{SST} = \frac{236.30}{352.41} = \textbf{67.05\%}$$

$$R_a^2 = 1 - \left(\frac{n-1}{n-k-1}\right)(1 - R^2) = 1 - \left(\frac{21}{19}\right)(1 - 0.6705) = \textbf{63.58\%}$$

The following table shows what the complete ANOVA table looks like.

Regression Results for BuildCo Sales Data

	Coefficient	Standard Error	*t*-Statistic	*p*-Value
Intercept	6.000	4.520	1.327	0.20
Level of gross domestic product (GDP)	0.004	0.003	**1.333**	0.20
Changes in 30-year mortgage rates (ΔI)	−20.500	3.560	**−5.758**	< 0.001

ANOVA	*df*	*SS*	*MS*	*F*	*Significance F*
Regression	2	236.30	**118.15**	**19.34**	p < 0.005
Error	19	116.11	**6.11**		
Total	21	352.41			
R^2	**67.05%**				
R_a^2	**63.58%**				

Reading 2

Step 2: Determine the significance of the individual independent variables.

The contribution of the individual variables, as indicated by the significance of their slope coefficients, can be tested using *t*-tests. However, since the *p*-values are included with the regression output, as is usually the case, the level of significance can be observed directly. Just for practice, let's test for significance of the individual coefficients using *t*-tests *and p*-values.

- Using *p*-values. Only the *p*-value of the coefficient for ΔI is less than the 5% level of significance, so we conclude that only ΔI contributes significantly to the level of BuildCo's annual sales.
- Using *t*-statistics. The hypothesis test structure is:

$H_0 : b_j = 0$ versus $H_a : b \neq 0$

The critical two-tailed *t*-values with df = 19 are ±2.093.

The decision rule is reject H_0 if is greater than 2.093 or less than –2.093.

Since $t_{GDP} = 1.33$ does not fall in the rejection region, we cannot reject the null for GDP, and we conclude that the level of GDP does not make a statistically significant contribution to the variation in sales at the 5% level.

Since $(t_{\Delta I} = -5.758) < (t_c = -2.093)$, we conclude that changes in mortgage rates make a significant contribution to the variation in sales at the 5% level.

PROFESSOR'S NOTE

The use of *p*-values or *t*-tests will always result in the same conclusions about the statistical significance of the slope estimate (i.e., coefficients on the independent variables). On the exam, use the *p*-value if it is provided!

Step 3: Determine the utility of the model as a whole.

The overall utility of the model can be generally assessed with the coefficient of determination, R^2. The R^2 value indicates that GDP and ΔI explain 67.05% of the variation in BuildCo's annual sales.

Tests of significance for the set of independent variables should be performed using the *F*-test. The hypotheses for the one-sided *F*-test can be structured as:

$H_0: b_{\Delta I} = b_{GDP} = 0$ versus $H_a: b_{\Delta I} \neq 0$, or $b_{GDP} \neq 0$

F_c at the 5% significance level with $df_{numerator} = 2$ and $df_{denominator} = 19$ is 3.52. Remember, this is a one-tailed test.

The decision rule is reject H_0 if F is greater than 3.52.

Since F > 3.52, the null hypothesis can be rejected and we can conclude that at least one of the independent variables significantly contributes to the dependent variable. That is, changes in mortgage rates *and* the level of GDP together explain a significant amount of the variation in BuildCo's annual sales at the 5% significance level. Notice that we could have reached this conclusion by observing that the ANOVA table reports that F is significant at a level less than 0.5%.

MODULE QUIZ 2.1, 2.2, 2.3

To best evaluate your performance, enter your quiz answers online.

Use the following information to answer Questions 1 and 2.

An analyst evaluates the sum of squared error and total sum of squares from a multiple regression with four independent variables to be 4,320 and 9,105 respectively. There are 65 observations in the sample.

1. The *F*-statistic is *closest* to:
   A. 13.54.
   B. 13.77.
   C. 16.61.

2. The critical *F*-value for testing $H_0 = b_1 = b_2 = b_3 = b_4 = 0$ vs. H_a: at least one $b_j \ne 0$ at the 5% significance level is *closest* to:
   A. 2.37.
   B. 2.53.
   C. 2.76.

Use the following ANOVA table for Questions 3 through 5.

Source	Sum of Squares (SS)	Degrees of Freedom
Regression	1,025	5
Error	925	25

3. The number of sample observations in the regression estimation is *closest* to:
   A. 29.
   B. 30.
   C. 31.

4. The mean squared error (MSE) is *closest* to:
   A. 37.
   B. 82.
   C. 205.

5. The *F*-statistic is *closest* to:
   A. 1.1.
   B. 3.3.
   C. 5.5.

Reading 2

Video covering this content is available online.

MODULE 2.4: COEFFICIENT OF DETERMINATION AND ADJUSTED R-SQUARED

LOS 2.h: Contrast and interpret the R^2 and adjusted R^2 in multiple regression.

CFA® Program Curriculum, Volume 1, page 82

COEFFICIENT OF DETERMINATION, R^2

In addition to an *F*-test, the multiple coefficient of determination, R^2, can be used to test the overall effectiveness of the entire set of independent variables in explaining the dependent variable. Its interpretation is similar to that for simple linear regression: the percentage of variation in the dependent variable that is *collectively* explained by all of the independent variables. For example, an R^2 of 0.63 indicates that the model, as a whole, explains 63% of the variation in the dependent variable.

R^2 is also calculated the same way as in simple linear regression.

$$R^2 = \frac{\text{total variation} - \text{unexplained variation}}{\text{total variation}} =$$

$$\frac{\text{SST} - \text{SSE}}{\text{SST}} = \frac{\text{explained variation}}{\text{total variation}} = \frac{\text{RSS}}{\text{SST}}$$

PROFESSOR'S NOTE

Regression output often includes multiple R, which is the correlation between actual values of y and forecasted values of y. Multiple R is the square root of R^2. For a regression with one independent variable, the correlation between the independent variable and dependent variable is the same as multiple R (with the same sign as the sign of the slope coefficient).

Adjusted R^2

Unfortunately, R^2 by itself *may not be a reliable measure of the explanatory power of the multiple regression model*. This is because R^2 almost always increases as variables are added to the model, even if the marginal contribution of the new variables is not statistically significant. Consequently, a relatively high R^2 may reflect the impact of a large set of independent variables rather than how well the set explains the dependent variable. This problem is often referred to as overestimating the regression.

To overcome the problem of overestimating the impact of additional variables on the explanatory power of a regression model, many researchers recommend adjusting R^2 for the number of independent variables. The *adjusted R^2* value is expressed as:

$$R_a^2 = 1 - \left[\left(\frac{n-1}{n-k-1} \right) \times (1 - R^2) \right]$$

where:
n = number of observations
k = number of independent variables
R_a^2 = adjusted R^2

R_a^2 will always be less than or equal to R^2. So while adding a new independent variable to the model will increase R^2, it may either increase *or decrease* the R_a^2. If the new variable has only a small effect on R^2, the value of R_a^2 may decrease. In addition, R_a^2 may be less than zero if the R^2 is low enough.

EXAMPLE: Calculating R^2 and adjusted R^2

An analyst runs a regression of monthly value-stock returns on five independent variables over 60 months. The total sum of squares for the regression is 460, and the sum of squared errors is 170. Calculate the R^2 and adjusted R^2.

Answer:

$$R^2 = \frac{460 - 170}{460} = 0.630 = 63.0\%$$

$$R_a^2 = 1 - \left[\left(\frac{60-1}{60-5-1} \right) \times (1 - 0.63) \right] = 0.596 = 59.6\%$$

The R^2 of 63% suggests that the five independent variables together explain 63% of the variation in monthly value-stock returns. The R_a^2 is, as expected, a somewhat lower value.

EXAMPLE: Interpreting adjusted R^2

Suppose the analyst now adds four more independent variables to the regression, and the R^2 increases to 65.0%. Identify which model the analyst would most likely prefer.

Answer:

With nine independent variables, even though the R^2 has increased from 63% to 65%, the adjusted R^2 has decreased from 59.6% to 58.7%:

$$R_a^2 = 1 - \left[\left(\frac{60-1}{60-9-1} \right) \times (1 - 0.65) \right] = 0.587 = 58.7\%$$

The analyst would prefer the first model because the adjusted R^2 is higher and the model has five independent variables as opposed to nine.

MODULE QUIZ 2.4

To best evaluate your performance, enter your quiz answers online.

1. Which of the following situations is *least likely* the result of a multiple regression analysis with more than 50 observations?

	R^2	Adjusted R^2
A.	71%	69%
B.	83%	86%
C.	10%	–2%

MODULE 2.5: DUMMY VARIABLES

Video covering this content is available online.

LOS 2.j: Formulate and interpret a multiple regression, including qualitative independent variables.

CFA® Program Curriculum, Volume 1, page 85

Observations for most independent variables (e.g., firm size, level of GDP, and interest rates) can take on a wide range of values. However, there are occasions when the independent variable is binary in nature—it is either "on" or "off." Independent variables that fall into this category are called **dummy variables** and are often used to quantify the impact of qualitative events.

Dummy variables are assigned a value of "0" or "1." For example, in a time series regression of monthly stock returns, you could employ a "January" dummy variable that would take on the value of "1" if a stock return occurred in January and "0" if it occurred in any other month. The purpose of including the January dummy variable would be to see if stock returns in January were significantly different than stock returns in all other months of the year. Many "January Effect" anomaly studies employ this type of regression methodology.

The estimated regression coefficient for dummy variables indicates the difference in the dependent variable for the category represented by the dummy variable and the average value of the dependent variable for all classes except the dummy variable class. For example, testing the slope coefficient for the January dummy variable would indicate whether, and by how much, security returns are different in January as compared to the other months.

An important consideration when performing multiple regression with dummy variables is the choice of the number of dummy variables to include in the model. Whenever we want to distinguish between *n* classes, we must use n – 1 dummy variables. Otherwise, the regression assumption of no exact linear relationship between independent variables would be violated.

Dummy variables can be intercept dummies, slope dummies, or a combination.

Consider a regression with one continuous X variable and one dummy variable (an intercept dummy):

$$Y = b_0 + d_0 D + b_1 X + \varepsilon$$

This regression becomes:

$$Y = b_0 + b_1X + \varepsilon \qquad \text{(if D = 0)}$$

$$Y = (b_0 + d_0) + b_1X + \varepsilon \qquad \text{(if D = 1)}$$

In other words, the intercept shifts from b_0 to $(b_0 + d_0)$ if D = 1. The value of this shift (d_0) can be positive or negative.

A slope dummy, on the other hand, changes the slope of the regression equation:

$$Y = b_0 + b_1X + d_1(D \times X) + \varepsilon$$

And the regression then becomes:

$$Y = b_0 + b_1X + \varepsilon \qquad \text{(if D = 0)}$$

$$Y = b_0 + (b_1 + d_1)X + \varepsilon \qquad \text{(if D = 1)}$$

Finally, we could have dummies in both intercept and slope:

$$Y = b_0 + d_0D + b_1X + d_1(D \times X) + \varepsilon$$

Which becomes:

$$Y = b_0 + b_1X + \varepsilon \qquad \text{(if D = 0)}$$

$$Y = (b_0 + d_0) + (b_1 + d_1)X + \varepsilon \qquad \text{(if D = 1)}$$

Interpreting the Coefficients in a Dummy Variable Regression

Consider the following regression equation for explaining quarterly EPS in terms of the quarter of their occurrence:

$$EPS_t = b_0 + b_1Q_{1t} + b_2Q_{2t} + b_3Q_{3t} + \varepsilon_t$$

where:
EPS_t = a quarterly observation of earnings per share
Q_{1t} = 1 if period t is the first quarter, Q_{1t} = 0 otherwise
Q_{2t} = 1 if period t is the second quarter, Q_{2t} = 0 otherwise
Q_{3t} = 1 if period t is the third quarter, Q_{3t} = 0 otherwise

The intercept term, b_0, represents the average value of *EPS* for the fourth quarter. The slope coefficient on each dummy variable estimates the *difference* in earnings per share (on average) between the respective quarter (i.e., quarter 1, 2, or 3) and the omitted quarter (the fourth quarter in this case). *Think of the omitted class as the reference point.*

For example, suppose we estimate the quarterly EPS regression model with 10 years of data (40 quarterly observations) and find that b_0 = 1.25, b_1 = 0.75, b_2 = –0.20, and b_3 = 0.10:

$$\widehat{EPS}_t = 1.25 + 0.75Q_{1t} - 0.20Q_{2t} + 0.10Q_{3t}$$

We can use the equation to determine the average EPS in each quarter over the past 10 years:

average fourth quarter EPS	= 1.25
average first quarter EPS	= 1.25 + 0.75 = 2.00
average second quarter EPS	= 1.25 − 0.20 = 1.05
average third quarter EPS	= 1.25 + 0.10 = 1.35

These are also the model's predictions of future EPS in each quarter of the following year. For example, to use the model to predict EPS in the first quarter of the next year, set $\widehat{Q}_1 = 1$, $\widehat{Q}_2 = 0$, and $\widehat{Q}_3 = 0$. Then $\widehat{EPS}_{Q1} = 1.25 + 0.75(1) − 0.20(0) + 0.10(0) = 2.00$. This simple model uses average EPS for any specific quarter over the past 10 years as the forecast of EPS in its respective quarter of the following year.

As with all multiple regression results, the F-statistic for the set of coefficients and the R^2 should be evaluated to determine if the quarters, individually or collectively, contribute to the explanation of quarterly EPS.

We can also test whether the average EPS in each of the first three quarters is equal to the fourth quarter EPS (the omitted quarter) by testing the individual slope coefficients using the following null hypotheses:

H_0: $b_1 = 0$ tests whether fourth quarter EPS = first quarter EPS
H_0: $b_2 = 0$ tests whether fourth quarter EPS = second quarter EPS
H_0: $b_3 = 0$ tests whether fourth quarter EPS = third quarter EPS

As before, the t-statistic for each test is equal to the coefficient divided by its standard error, and the critical t-value is a two-tailed value with $n − k − 1 = 40 − 3 − 1 = 36$ degrees of freedom.

EXAMPLE: Hypothesis testing with dummy variables

The standard error of the coefficient b_1 is equal to 0.15 from the EPS regression model. Test whether first quarter EPS is equal to fourth quarter EPS at the 5% significance level.

Answer:

We are testing the following hypothesis:

H_0: $b_1 = 0$ vs. H_A: $b_1 \neq 0$

The t-statistic is 0.75 / 0.15 = 5.0 and the two-tail 5% critical value with 36 degrees of freedom is approximately 2.03. Therefore, we should reject the null and conclude that first quarter EPS is statistically significantly different than fourth quarter EPS at the 5% significance level.

Example of Regression Application With Dummy Variables

Mazumdar and Sengupta (2005)[2] provide a more complex example of an investment application of multiple regression using dummy variables. They determine that loan spreads relative to LIBOR on private debt contracts are negatively associated with measures of the quality of the company's financial disclosures.

The dependent variable (SPREAD) is the quoted spread in basis points over LIBOR on the first year of the loan. The independent variables include a number of quantitative variables, including, for example, average total disclosure score (DISC), standard deviation of daily stock returns (STDRETN), current ratio (CRATIO), and market to book ratio (MKBK). The authors also include three dummy variables in the regression:

- SECURE, which is equal to one if the loan is collateralized, and equal to zero otherwise.

- BID, which is equal to one if the loan contained the option to price the loan relative to a different index, and equal to zero otherwise.

- RESTRUC, which is equal to one if the loan was a result of corporate restructuring, and equal to zero otherwise.

In the model both SECURE and RESTRUC are positive and statistically significantly different from zero, while BID is not. The proper interpretation is that the loan spreads on private debt contracts are higher for collateralized loans than for uncollateralized loans, and higher for loans used for corporate restructuring than for loans used for other purposes, *after controlling for the other independent variables in the model.*

WARM-UP: WHY MULTIPLE REGRESSION ISN'T AS EASY AS IT LOOKS

Regression analysis relies on the assumptions listed earlier in this topic review. When these assumptions are violated, the inferences drawn from the model are questionable. There are three primary assumption violations that you will encounter: (1) heteroskedasticity, (2) serial correlation (i.e., autocorrelation), and (3) multicollinearity.

On exam day, you must be able to answer the following four questions about each of the three assumption violations:

- What is it?
- What is its effect on regression analysis?
- How do we detect it?
- How do we correct for it?

---

2. Mazumdar, S. and P. Sengupta. 2005. "Disclosure of the Loan Spread on Private Debt." *Financial Analysts Journal*, vol. 61, no. 3 (May/June): 83–95.

Recall that the calculated test statistic for the estimated regression coefficient on the jth independent variable is:

$$t = \frac{\hat{b}_j - b_j}{s_{\hat{b}_j}}$$

Note that the denominator in the test statistic equation above, $s_{\hat{b}_j}$, is the standard error for coefficient j. Without getting into the math, suffice it to say that the coefficient standard error is calculated using the standard error of estimate (SEE), which is the standard deviation of the error term. Any violation of an assumption that affects the error term will ultimately affect the coefficient standard error. Consequently, this will affect the t-statistic and F-statistic and any conclusions drawn from hypothesis tests involving these statistics.

MODULE QUIZ 2.5

To best evaluate your performance, enter your quiz answers online.

Use the following information for Questions 1 and 2.

Phil Ohlmer estimates a cross sectional regression in order to predict price to earnings ratios (P/E) with fundamental variables that are related to P/E, including dividend payout ratio (DPO), growth rate (G), and beta (B). In addition, all 50 stocks in the sample come from two industries, electric utilities or biotechnology. He defines the following dummy variable:

IND   = 0 if the stock is in the electric utilities industry, or

            = 1 if the stock is in the biotechnology industry

The results of his regression are shown in the following table.

Variable	Coefficient	*t*-Statistic
Intercept	6.75	3.89*
IND	8.00	4.50*
DPO	4.00	1.86
G	12.35	2.43*
B	–0.50	1.46

*significant at the 5% level

1. Based on these results, it would be *most appropriate* to conclude that:
   A. biotechnology industry PEs are statistically significantly larger than electric utilities industry PEs.
   B. electric utilities PEs are statistically significantly larger than biotechnology industry PEs, holding DPO, G, and B constant.
   C. biotechnology industry PEs are statistically significantly larger than electric utilities industry PEs, holding DPO, G, and B constant.

2. Ohlmer is valuing a biotechnology stock with a dividend payout ratio of 0.00, a beta of 1.50, and an expected earnings growth rate of 0.14. The predicted P/E on the basis of the values of the explanatory variables for the company is *closest* to:
   A. 7.7.
   B. 15.7.
   C. 17.2.

MODULE 2.6: ASSUMPTIONS: HETEROSKEDASTICITY

Video covering this content is available online.

LOS 2.f: Explain the assumptions of a multiple regression model.

CFA® Program Curriculum, Volume 1, page 70

As with simple linear regression, most of the assumptions made with the multiple regression pertain to ε, the model's error term:

- A linear relationship exists between the dependent and independent variables. In other words, the model on the first page of this topic review correctly describes the relationship.

- The independent variables are not random, and there is no exact linear relation between any two or more independent variables.

- The expected value of the error term, conditional on the independent variable, is zero [i.e., $E(\varepsilon \,|\, X_1, X_2, ..., X_k) = 0$].

- The variance of the error terms is constant for all observations [i.e., $E(\varepsilon_i^2) = \sigma_\varepsilon^2$].

- The error term for one observation is not correlated with that of another observation [i.e., $E(\varepsilon_i \varepsilon_j) = 0, j \neq i$].

- The error term is normally distributed.

LOS 2.k: Explain the types of heteroskedasticity and how heteroskedasticity and serial correlation affect statistical inference.

CFA® Program Curriculum, Volume 1, page 92

WHAT IS HETEROSKEDASTICITY?

Recall that one of the assumptions of multiple regression is that the variance of the residuals is constant across observations. **Heteroskedasticity** occurs when the variance of the residuals is not the same across all observations in the sample. This happens when there are subsamples that are more spread out than the rest of the sample.

Unconditional heteroskedasticity occurs when the heteroskedasticity is not related to the level of the independent variables, which means that it doesn't systematically increase or decrease with changes in the value of the independent variable(s). While this is a violation of the equal variance assumption, *it usually causes no major problems with the regression*.

Conditional heteroskedasticity is heteroskedasticity that is related to the level of (i.e., conditional on) the independent variables. For example, conditional heteroskedasticity exists if the variance of the residual term increases as the value of the independent variable increases, as shown in Figure 2.4. Notice in this figure that the residual variance associated with the larger values of the independent variable, X, is larger than the residual variance associated with the smaller values of X. Conditional heteroskedasticity *does create significant problems for statistical inference*.

Reading 2

Figure 2.4: Conditional Heteroskedasticity

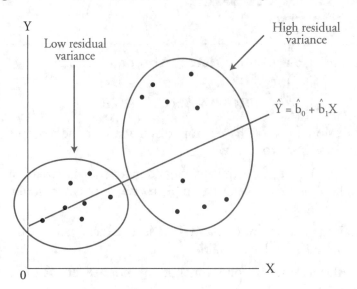

Effect of Heteroskedasticity on Regression Analysis

There are four effects of heteroskedasticity you need to be aware of:

■ The standard errors are usually unreliable estimates.

■ The coefficient estimates (the $\hat{b}_j$) aren't affected.

■ If the standard errors are too small, but the coefficient estimates themselves are not affected, the *t*-statistics will be too large and the null hypothesis of no statistical significance is rejected too often. The opposite will be true if the standard errors are too large.

■ The *F*-test is also unreliable.

Detecting Heteroskedasticity

There are two methods to detect heteroskedasticity: examining scatter plots of the residuals and using the Breusch-Pagan chi-square (χ^2) test. A scatter plot of the residuals versus one or more of the independent variables can reveal patterns among observations.

EXAMPLE: Detecting heteroskedasticity with a residual plot

You have been studying the monthly returns of a mutual fund over the past five years, hoping to draw conclusions about the fund's average performance. You calculate the mean return, the standard deviation, and the portfolio's beta by regressing the fund's returns on S&P 500 index returns (the independent variable). The standard deviation of returns and the fund's beta don't seem to fit the firm's stated risk profile. For your analysis, you have prepared a scatter plot of the error terms (actual return – predicted return) for the regression using five years of returns, as shown in the following figure. Determine whether the residual plot indicates that there may be a problem with the data.

Residual Plot

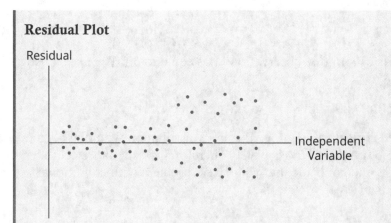

Answer:

The residual plot in the previous figure indicates the presence of conditional heteroskedasticity. Notice how the variation in the regression residuals increases as the independent variable increases. This indicates that the variance of the fund's returns about the mean is related to the level of the independent variable.

The more common way to detect conditional heteroskedasticity is the *Breusch-Pagan test*, which calls for the regression of the squared residuals on the independent variables. If conditional heteroskedasticity is present, the independent variables will significantly contribute to the explanation of the squared residuals. The test statistic for the Breusch-Pagan test, which has a chi-square (χ^2) distribution, is calculated as:

$$\text{BP chi-square test} = n \times R^2_{\text{resid}} \text{ with } k \text{ degrees of freedom}$$

where:

n $\quad$ = the number of observations

R^2_{resid} = R^2 from a second regression of the squared residuals from the first regression on the independent variables

k $\quad$ = the number of independent variables

PROFESSOR'S NOTE

The R^2 used in the BP test is the R^2 from a second regression, NOT the original regression.

This is a one-tailed test because heteroskedasticity is only a problem if the R^2 and the BP test statistic are too large.

EXAMPLE: The Breusch-Pagan test

The residual plot of mutual fund returns over time shows evidence of heteroskedasticity. To confirm your suspicions, you regress the squared residuals from the original regression on the independent variable, S&P 500 index returns. The R^2 from that regression is 8%. Use the Breusch-Pagan test to determine whether heteroskedasticity is present at the 5% significance level.

Reading 2

Answer:

With five years of monthly observations, n is equal to 60. The test statistic is:

$$n \times R^2 = 60 \times 0.08 = 4.8$$

The one-tailed critical value for a chi-square distribution with one degree of freedom and α equal to 5% is 3.841. Therefore you should reject the null hypothesis and conclude that you have a problem with conditional heteroskedasticity.

Correcting Heteroskedasticity

The most common remedy and the one recommended in the CFA curriculum is to calculate *robust standard errors* (also called White-corrected standard errors or heteroskedasticity-consistent standard errors). These robust standard errors are then used to recalculate the t-statistics using the original regression coefficients. On the exam, use robust standard errors to calculate t-statistics if there is evidence of heteroskedasticity. A second method to correct for heteroskedasticity is the use of *generalized least squares*, which attempts to eliminate the heteroskedasticity by modifying the original equation.

EXAMPLE: Using White-corrected standard errors

An analyst runs a regression of annualized Treasury bill rates (the dependent variable) on annual inflation rates (the independent variable) using monthly data for 10 years. The results of the regression are shown in the following table.

Regression of T-Bill Rates on Inflation Rates

Variable	Coefficient	Standard Error	t-Statistic	p-Value
Intercept	4.82	0.85	5.67	< 0.0001
Inflation	0.60	0.28	2.14	0.0340

He determines using the Breusch-Pagan test that heteroskedasticity is present, so he also estimates the White-corrected standard error for the coefficient on inflation to be 0.31. The critical two-tail 5% t-value for 118 degrees of freedom is 1.98. Is inflation statistically significant at the 5% level?

Answer:

The t-statistic should be recalculated using the White-corrected standard error as:

$$t = \frac{0.60}{0.31} = 1.94$$

This is less than the critical t-value of 1.98, which means after correcting for heteroskedasticity, the null hypothesis that the inflation coefficient is

©2021 Kaplan, Inc.

zero cannot be rejected. Therefore, inflation is not statistically significant. Notice that because the coefficient estimate of 0.60 was not affected by heteroskedasticity, but the original standard error of 0.28 was too low, the original t-statistic of 2.14 was too high. After using the higher White-corrected standard error of 0.31, the t-statistic fell to 1.94.

MODULE QUIZ 2.6
To best evaluate your performance, enter your quiz answers online.

1. Assumptions underlying a multiple regression are *most likely* to include:
   A. The expected value of the error term is 0.00 < i < 1.00.
   B. Linear and non-linear relationships exist between the dependent and independent variables.
   C. The error for one observation is not correlated with that of another observation.

MODULE 2.7: SERIAL CORRELATION

WHAT IS SERIAL CORRELATION?

Video covering this content is available online.

Serial correlation, also known as **autocorrelation**, refers to the situation in which the residual terms are correlated with one another. Serial correlation is a relatively common problem with time series data.

■ *Positive serial correlation* exists when a positive regression error in one time period increases the probability of observing a positive regression error for the next time period.

■ *Negative serial correlation* occurs when a positive error in one period increases the probability of observing a negative error in the next period.

Effect of Serial Correlation on Regression Analysis

Because of the tendency of the data to cluster together from observation to observation, positive serial correlation typically results in coefficient standard errors that are too small, even though the estimated coefficients are consistent. These small standard error terms will cause the computed t-statistics to be larger than they should be, which will cause too many Type I errors: the rejection of the null hypothesis when it is actually true. The F-test will also be unreliable because the MSE will be underestimated leading again to too many Type I errors.

PROFESSOR'S NOTE
Positive serial correlation is much more common in economic and financial data, so we focus our attention on its effects. Additionally, if one of the independent variables in the regression is a lagged value of the dependent variable, it may make the parameter estimates inconsistent. This is discussed in our topic review on Time Series Analysis.

Detecting Serial Correlation

There are two methods that are commonly used to detect the presence of serial correlation: residual plots and the Durbin-Watson statistic.

A scatter plot of residuals versus time, like those shown in Figure 2.5, can reveal the presence of serial correlation. Figure 2.5 illustrates examples of positive and negative serial correlation.

Figure 2.5: Residual Plots for Serial Correlation

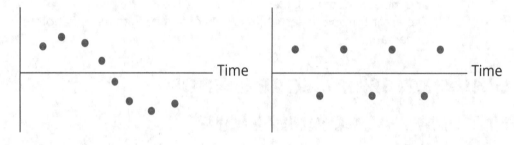

The more common method is to use the **Durbin-Watson statistic** (DW) to detect the presence of serial correlation. It is calculated as:

$$DW = \frac{\sum_{t=2}^{T}(\hat{\varepsilon}_t - \hat{\varepsilon}_{t-1})^2}{\sum_{t=1}^{T}\hat{\varepsilon}_t^2}$$

where:
$\hat{\varepsilon}_t$ = residual for period t

If the sample size is very large:

$DW \approx 2(1 - r)$

where:
r = correlation coefficient between residuals from one period and those from the previous period

You can see from the approximation that the Durbin-Watson test statistic is approximately equal to 2 if the error terms are homoskedastic and not serially correlated (r = 0). DW < 2 if the error terms are positively serially correlated (r > 0), and DW > 2 if the error terms are negatively serially correlated (r < 0). But how much below the magic number 2 is statistically significant enough to reject the null hypothesis of no positive serial correlation?

There are tables of DW statistics that provide upper and lower critical DW-values (d_u and d_l, respectively) for various sample sizes, levels of significance, and numbers of degrees of freedom against which the computed DW test statistic can be compared. The DW-test procedure for positive serial correlation is as follows:

H_0: the regression has *no* positive serial correlation

The decision rules are rather complicated because they allow for rejecting the null in favor of either positive or negative correlation. The test can also be inconclusive, which means we neither accept nor reject (See Figure 2.6).

- If DW < d_l, the error terms are *positively* serially correlated (i.e., reject the null hypothesis of no positive serial correlation).

- If d_l < DW < d_u, the test is inconclusive.

- If DW > d_u, there is *no* evidence that the error terms are positively correlated. (i.e., fail to reject the null of no positive serial correlation).

Figure 2.6: Durbin-Watson Decision Rule

(H_0: No positive serial correlation)

Reject H_0, conclude Positive Serial Correlation	Inconclusive	Do not reject H_0
0	d_l	d_u

EXAMPLE: The Durbin-Watson test for serial correlation

Suppose you have a regression output which includes three independent variables that provide you with a DW statistic of 1.23. Also suppose that the sample size is 40. At a 5% significance level, determine if the error terms are serially correlated.

Answer:

From a 5% DW table with n = 40 and k = 3, the upper and lower critical DW values are found to be d_l = 1.34 and d_u = 1.66, respectively. Since DW < d_l (i.e., 1.23 < 1.34), you should reject the null hypothesis and conclude that the regression has positive serial correlation among the error terms.

Correcting Serial Correlation

Possible remedies for serial correlation include:

- *Adjust the coefficient standard errors*, which is the method recommended in the CFA curriculum, using the Hansen method. The Hansen method also corrects for conditional heteroskedasticity. These adjusted standard errors, which are sometimes called serial correlation consistent standard errors or Hansen-White standard errors, are then used in hypothesis testing of the regression coefficients. Only use the Hansen method if serial correlation is a problem. The White-corrected standard errors are preferred if only heteroskedasticity is a problem. If both conditions are present, use the Hansen method.

- *Improve the specification of the model*. The best way to do this is to explicitly incorporate the time-series nature of the data (e.g., include a seasonal term). This can be tricky.

MODULE QUIZ 2.7

To best evaluate your performance, enter your quiz answers online.

1. What condition is the Durbin-Watson statistic designed to detect in multiple regression, and what is the *most appropriate* remedy to correct for that condition?

	Condition	Remedy
A.	Serial correlation	Use the Hansen method
B.	Autocorrelation	Use generalized least squares
C.	Heteroskedasticity	Use generalized least squares

Video covering this content is available online.

MODULE 2.8: MULTICOLLINEARITY

LOS 2.1: Describe multicollinearity, and explain its causes and effects in regression analysis.

CFA® Program Curriculum, Volume 1, page 102

Multicollinearity refers to the condition when two or more of the independent variables, or linear combinations of the independent variables, in a multiple regression are highly correlated with each other. This condition distorts the standard error of estimate and the coefficient standard errors, leading to problems when conducting *t*-tests for statistical significance of parameters.

Effect of Multicollinearity on Regression Analysis

Even though multicollinearity does not affect the consistency of slope coefficients, such coefficients themselves tend to be *unreliable*. Additionally, the standard errors of the slope coefficients are artificially inflated. Hence, there is a *greater probability that we will incorrectly conclude that a variable is not statistically significant* (i.e., a Type II error). Multicollinearity is likely to be present to some extent in most economic models. The issue is whether the multicollinearity has a significant effect on the regression results.

Detecting Multicollinearity

The most common way to detect multicollinearity is the situation where *t*-tests indicate that none of the individual coefficients is significantly different than zero, while the *F*-test is statistically significant and the R^2 is high. This suggests that the variables together explain much of the variation in the dependent variable, but the individual independent variables don't. The only way this can happen is when the independent variables are highly correlated with each other, so while their common source of variation is explaining the dependent variable, the high degree of correlation also "washes out" the individual effects.

High correlation among independent variables is sometimes suggested as a sign of multicollinearity. In fact, answers to some old CFA questions suggest the following general rule of thumb: If the absolute value of the sample correlation between any two independent variables in the regression is greater than 0.7, multicollinearity is a potential problem.

However, this only works if there are exactly two independent variables. If there are more than two independent variables, while individual variables may not be highly correlated, linear combinations might be, leading to multicollinearity. High correlation among the independent variables suggests the possibility of multicollinearity, but low correlation among the independent variables *does not necessarily* indicate multicollinearity is *not* present.

EXAMPLE: Detecting multicollinearity

Bob Watson, CFA, runs a regression of mutual fund returns on average P/B, average P/E, and average market capitalization, with the following results:

Variable	Coefficient	p-Value
Average P/B	3.52	0.15
Average P/E	2.78	0.21
Market Cap	4.03	0.11
F-test	34.6	< 0.001
R^2	89.6%	

Determine whether or not multicollinearity is a problem in this regression.

Answer:

The R^2 is high and the F-test is statistically significant, which suggest that the three variables as a group do an excellent job of explaining the variation in mutual fund returns. However, none of the independent variables individually is statistically significant to any reasonable degree, since the p-values are larger than 10%. This is a classic indication of multicollinearity.

Correcting Multicollinearity

The most common method to correct for multicollinearity is to omit one or more of the correlated independent variables. Unfortunately, it is not always an easy task to identify the variable(s) that are the source of the multicollinearity. There are statistical procedures that may help in this effort, like stepwise regression, which systematically remove variables from the regression until multicollinearity is minimized.

WARM-UP: MODEL SPECIFICATION

Regression model specification is the selection of the explanatory (independent) variables to be included in the regression and the transformations, if any, of those explanatory variables.

For example, suppose we're trying to predict a P/E ratio using a cross-sectional regression with fundamental variables that are related to P/E. Valuation theory tells us that the stock's dividend payout ratio (DPO), growth rate (G), and beta (B) are associated with P/E. One specification of the model would be:

Specification 1: $P/E = b_0 + b_1DPO + b_2G + b_3B + \varepsilon$

If we also decide that market capitalization (M) is related to P/E ratio, we would create a second specification of the model by including M as an independent variable:

Specification 2: $P/E = a_0 + a_1DPO + a_2G + a_3B + a_4M + \varepsilon$

Finally, suppose we conclude that market cap is not linearly related to P/E, but the natural log of market cap is linearly related to P/E. Then, we would transform M by taking its natural log and creating a new variable lnM. Thus, our third specification would be:

Specification 3: $P/E = c_0 + c_1DPO + c_2G + c_3B + c_4lnM + \varepsilon$

PROFESSOR'S NOTE

Notice that we used "a" instead of "b" in Specification 2 and "c" in Specification 3. We must do that to recognize that when we change the specifications of the model, the regression parameters change. For example, we wouldn't expect the intercept in Specification 1 (b_0) to be the same as in Specification 2 (a_0) or the same as in Specification 3 (c_0).

Video covering this content is available online.

MODULE 2.9: MODEL MISSPECIFICATION, AND QUALITATIVE DEPENDENT VARIABLES

LOS 2.m: Describe how model misspecification affects the results of a regression analysis, and describe how to avoid common forms of misspecification.

CFA® Program Curriculum, Volume 1, page 105

There are three broad categories of *model misspecification*, or ways in which the regression model can be specified incorrectly, each with several subcategories:

1. The functional form can be misspecified.

   - Important variables are omitted.

   - Variables should be transformed.

   - Data is improperly pooled.

2. Explanatory variables are correlated with the error term in time series models.

   - A lagged dependent variable is used as an independent variable.

   - A function of the dependent variable is used as an independent variable ("forecasting the past").

   - Independent variables are measured with error.

3. Other time-series misspecifications that result in nonstationarity.

PROFESSOR'S NOTE

We'll focus on the first two categories because nonstationarity in time series regressions is covered in the next topic review.

The *effects of the model misspecification on the regression results*, as shown in Figure 2.7, are basically the same for all of the misspecifications we will discuss: regression coefficients are often biased and/or inconsistent, which means we can't have any confidence in our hypothesis tests of the coefficients or in the predictions of the model.

Figure 2.7:   Effects of Model Misspecification

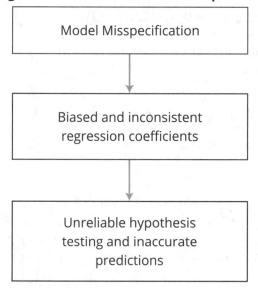

PROFESSOR'S NOTE

Recall the definitions of unbiased and consistent estimators from the Level I curriculum:

■ An unbiased estimator is one for which the expected value of the estimator is equal to the parameter you are trying to estimate. For example, because the expected value of the sample mean is equal to the population mean, the sample mean is an unbiased estimator of the population mean.

■ A consistent estimator is one for which the accuracy of the parameter estimate increases as the sample size increases. As the sample size increases, the standard error of the sample mean falls, and the sampling distribution bunches more closely around the population mean. In fact, as the sample size approaches infinity, the standard error approaches zero.

EXAMPLES OF MISSPECIFICATION OF FUNCTIONAL FORM

Let's start with a regression in which we're trying to predict monthly returns on portfolios of Chinese stocks (R) using four independent variables: portfolio beta (B), the natural log of market capitalization (lnM), the natural log of the price-to-book ratio ln(PB), and free float (FF). Free float is equal to the ratio of shares available to be traded by the investing public to total company shares. The regression is estimated with 72 monthly observations from July 1996 to June 2002. The *correct* specification of the model is as follows:

$$R = b_0 + b_1B + b_2lnM + b_3lnPB + b_4FF + \varepsilon$$

Suppose we determine in this specification that both lnM and FF are statistically significant at the 1% level.

PROFESSOR'S NOTE

The correct regression model specification is based on a study by Wang and Xu (2004).[3] The incorrect specifications that follow are designed to illustrate examples of common misspecifications, but they are not included in the Wang and Xu study.

Misspecification #1: Omitting a Variable

Suppose we do not include lnM in the regression model:

$$R = a_0 + a_1B + a_2lnPB + a_3FF + \varepsilon$$

If lnM is correlated with any of the remaining independent variables (B, lnPB, or FF), then the error term is also correlated with the same independent variables and the resulting regression coefficients (the estimates of a_0, a_1, and a_2) are biased and inconsistent. That means our hypothesis tests and predictions using the model are unreliable.

PROFESSOR'S NOTE

Omission of a variable in this context means that the variable should be included in the model but is not. Absence of a variable in the model does not necessarily imply omission.

Just because a variable is highly correlated with an independent variable does not mean it has to be included in the model to avoid omission error.

Misspecification #2: Variable Should Be Transformed

Regression assumes that the dependent variable is linearly related to each of the independent variables. Typically, however, market capitalization is not linearly related to portfolio returns, but rather the natural log of market cap is linearly related. If we include market cap in the regression without transforming it by taking the natural log—if we use M and not ln(M)—we've misspecified the model.

$$R = c_0 + c_1B + c_2M + c_3lnPB + c_4FF + \varepsilon$$

Other examples of transformations include squaring the variable or taking the square root of the variable. If financial statement data are included in the regression

3. Fenghua Wang and Yexiao Xu. "What Determines Chinese Stock Returns." *Financial Analysts Journal* no. 6 (November/December 2004): 65–77.

model, a common transformation is to standardize the variables by dividing by sales (for income statement or cash flow items) or total assets (for balance sheet items). You should recognize these as items from *common-size financial statements*.

Misspecification #3: Incorrectly Pooling Data

Suppose the relationship between returns and the independent variables during the first three years is actually different than the relationship in the second 3-year period (i.e., the regression coefficients are different from one period to the next). By pooling the data and estimating one regression over the entire period, rather than estimating two separate regressions over each of the subperiods, we have misspecified the model and our hypothesis tests and predictions of portfolio returns will be misleading.

Misspecification #4: Using a Lagged Dependent Variable as an Independent Variable

A lagged variable in a time series regression is the value of a variable from a prior period. In our example, the dependent variable is portfolio return in month t, so a lagged dependent variable would be the portfolio return in the previous period, month $t - 1$ (which is denoted as R_{t-1}).

$$R = d_0 + d_1B + d_2\ln M + d_3\ln PB + d_4FF + d_5R_{t-1} + \varepsilon$$

If the error term in the regression model is serially correlated as a result of inclusion of the lagged dependent variable (which is common in time series regressions), then this model misspecification will result in biased and inconsistent regression estimates and unreliable hypothesis tests and return predictions.

PROFESSOR'S NOTE

In the reading on time series analysis, AR models are introduced which rely exclusively on lagged dependent variables. The difference relates to the data set: if lagged dependent variables help *explain (and NOT cause)* serial correlation in residuals, they are okay!

Misspecification #5: Forecasting the Past

The proper specification of the model mentioned previously will measure the dependent variable as returns during a particular month (say July 1996), and the independent variable ln(M) as the natural log of market capitalization *at the beginning* of July. Remember that market cap is equal to shares outstanding times price per share. If we measure market cap *at the end* of July and use it in our regression, we're naturally going to conclude that stocks with higher market cap at the end of July had higher returns during July. In other words, our model is misspecified because it is forecasting the past: we're using variables measured at the *end* of July to predict a variable measured *during* July.

Misspecification #6: Measuring Independent Variables With Error

The free float (FF) independent variable is actually trying to capture the relationship between corporate governance quality and portfolio returns. However, because we can't actually measure "corporate governance quality," we have to use a proxy variable. Wang and Xu used free float to proxy for corporate governance quality. The presumption is that the higher the level of free float, the more influence the capital markets have on management's decision-making process and the more effective the corporate governance structure. However, because we're using free float as a proxy, we're actually measuring the variable we want to include in our regression—corporate governance quality—with error. Once again our regression estimates will be biased and inconsistent and our hypothesis testing and predictions unreliable.

PROFESSOR'S NOTE

For more information on corporate governance and the valuation implications of effective corporate governance practices, see the topic review of corporate governance.

Another common example when an independent variable is measured with error is when we want to use *expected* inflation in our regression but use *actual* inflation as a proxy.

LOS 2.n: Interpret an estimated logistic regression.

CFA® Program Curriculum, Volume 1, page 118

Financial analysis often calls for the use of a model that has a **qualitative dependent variable**, a dummy variable that takes on a value of either zero or one. An example of an application requiring the use of a qualitative dependent variable is a model that attempts to predict when a bond issuer will default. In this case, the dependent variable may take on a value of one in the event of default and zero in the event of no default. An ordinary regression model is not appropriate for situations that require a qualitative dependent variable. The **logit model** is most commonly used in such a situation.

A logit model assumes that residuals have a logistic distribution, which is similar to a normal distribution but with fatter tails. Logit models are used to estimate the probability of a discrete outcome, such as the probability of default. The maximum likelihood methodology is used to estimate coefficients for logit models. These coefficients relate the independent variables to the likelihood of an event occurring, such as a merger, bankruptcy, or default. The slope coefficient in a logit model is interpreted as the change in the "log odds" of the event occurring per one unit change in the independent variable, holding all other independent variables constant.

The analysis of regression models with qualitative dependent variables is the same as we have been discussing all through this topic review. Examine the individual coefficients using t-tests, determine the validity of the model with the F-test and the R^2, and look out for heteroskedasticity, serial correlation, and multicollinearity.

LOS 2.o: Evaluate and interpret a multiple regression model and its results.

CFA® Program Curriculum, Volume 1, page 70

The economic meaning of the results of a regression estimation focuses primarily on the slope coefficients. For example, suppose that we run a regression using a cross section of stock returns (in percent) as the dependent variable, and the stock betas (CAPM) and market capitalizations (in $ billions) as our independent variables. The slope coefficients indicate the expected change in the stock returns for a one unit change in beta or market capitalization. The estimated regression equation is:

$$return = 5.0 + 4.2 \text{ beta} - 0.05 \text{ market cap} + \varepsilon$$

Furthermore, assume that these coefficient estimates are significantly different from zero in a statistical sense. The economic meaning of these results is that, on average, a one unit increase in beta risk is associated with a 4.2% *increase* in return, while a $1 billion increase in market capitalization implies a 0.05% *decrease* in return.

As is always the case with statistical inferences, it is possible to identify a relationship that has statistical significance without having any economic significance. For instance, a study of dividend announcements may identify a statistically significant abnormal return following the announcement, but these returns may not be sufficient to cover transactions costs.

ASSESSING A MULTIPLE REGRESSION MODEL— PUTTING IT ALL TOGETHER

The flow chart in Figure 2.8 will help you evaluate a multiple regression model and grasp the "big picture" in preparation for the exam.

Figure 2.8:   Assessment of a Multiple Regression Model

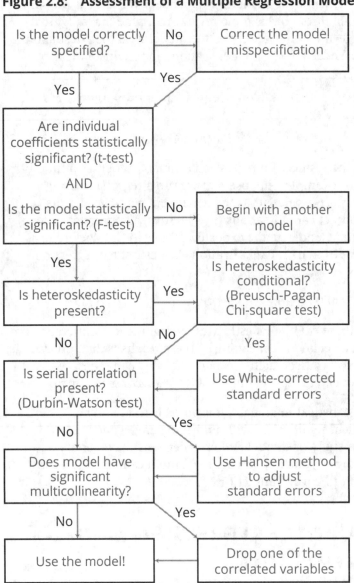

MODULE QUIZ 2.8, 2.9

To best evaluate your performance, enter your quiz answers online.

Use the following information to answer Questions 1 through 5.

Multiple regression was used to explain stock returns using the following variables:

Dependent variable:

RET = annual stock returns (%)

Independent variables:

MKT = Market capitalization = Market capitalization / $1.0 million

IND = Industry quartile ranking (IND = 4 is the highest ranking)

FORT = Fortune 500 firm, where {FORT = 1 if the stock is that of a Fortune 500 firm, FORT = 0 if not a Fortune 500 stock}

The regression results are presented in the tables below.

	Coefficient	Standard Error	*t*-Statistic	*p*-Value
Intercept	0.5220	1.2100	0.430	0.681
Market Capitalization	0.0460	0.0150	3.090	0.021
Industry Ranking	0.7102	0.2725	2.610	0.040
Fortune 500	0.9000	0.5281	1.700	0.139

ANOVA	df	SS	MSS	F	Significance F
Regression	3	20.5969	6.8656	12.100	0.006
Error	6	3.4031	0.5672		
Total	9	24.0000			

Test	Test-Statistic
Breusch-Pagan	17.7
Durbin-Watson	1.8

1. Based on the results in the table, which of the following *most accurately* represents the regression equation for annual stock percentage returns?
   A. 1.21 + 0.0150(MKT) + 0.2725(IND) + 0.5281(FORT)
   B. 0.5220(INT) + 0.0460(MKT) + 0.7102(IND) + 0.9000(FORT)
   C. 0.0460(MKT) + 0.7102(IND) + 0.9(FORT) + 0.522

2. Relative to a non-Fortune 500 company, the expected extra annual stock return attributable to being a Fortune 500 stock is *closest* to:
   A. 0.522.
   B. 0.139.
   C. 0.900.

3. The expected return on the stock of a firm that is not in the Fortune 500, has a market capitalization of $5 million, and is in an industry with a rank of 3 is *closest* to:
   A. 2.88%.
   B. 3.98%.
   C. 1.42%.

4. Does being a Fortune 500 stock contribute significantly to stock returns?
   A. Yes, at a 10% level of significance.
   B. Yes, at a 5% level of significance.
   C. No, not at a reasonable level of significance.

5. The *p*-value of the Breusch-Pagan test is 0.0005. The lower and upper limits for the Durbin-Watson test are 0.40 and 1.90, respectively. Based on this data and the information in the tables, there is evidence of:
   A. only serial correlation.
   B. serial correlation and heteroskedasticity.
   C. only heteroskedasticity.

6. Which of the following situations is *least likely* to result in the misspecification of a regression model with monthly returns as the dependent variable?
   A. Failing to include an independent variable that is related to monthly returns.
   B. Using leading P/E from the previous period as an independent variable.
   C. Using actual inflation as an independent variable to proxy for expected inflation.

7. The *least likely* result of regression model misspecification is:
   A. unreliable hypothesis tests of the regression coefficients.
   B. inconsistent regression coefficients.
   C. unbiased regression coefficients.

8. Phil Ohlmer is developing a regression model to predict returns on a hedge fund composite index using several different independent variables. Which of the following list of independent variables, if included in the model, is *most likely* to lead to biased and inconsistent regression coefficients and why?
   A. Small-cap index returns, high-yield bond index returns, and emerging market index returns; because small-cap returns and hedge fund index returns are likely to be correlated.
   B. Small-cap index returns, high-yield bond index returns, and emerging market index returns; because small-cap returns and emerging market index returns are likely to be correlated.
   C. Small-cap index returns, previous period hedge fund composite index returns, high-yield bond index returns, and emerging market index returns; because the regression model is likely to be misspecified.

9. Qualitative dependent variables should be verified using:
   A. a dummy variable based on the logistic distribution.
   B. a discriminant model using a linear function for ranked observations.
   C. tests for heteroskedasticity, serial correlation, and multicollinearity.

KEY CONCEPTS

LOS 2.a

The multiple regression equation specifies a dependent variable as a linear function of two or more independent variables:

$$Y_i = b_0 + b_1 X_{1i} + b_2 X_{2i} + \ldots + b_k X_{ki} + \varepsilon_i$$

The intercept term is the value of the dependent variable when the independent variables are equal to zero. Each slope coefficient is the estimated change in the dependent variable for a one-unit change in that independent variable, holding the other independent variables constant.

LOS 2.b

The *p*-value is the smallest level of significance for which the null hypothesis can be rejected.

- If the *p*-value is less than the significance level, the null hypothesis can be rejected.

- If the *p*-value is greater than the significance level, the null hypothesis cannot be rejected.

LOS 2.c

A *t*-test is used for hypothesis testing of regression parameter estimates:

$$t_{b_j} = \frac{\hat{b}_j - b_j}{s_{\hat{b}_j}} \text{ with } n - k - 1 \text{ degrees of freedom}$$

Testing for statistical significance means testing $H_0: b_j = 0$ vs. $H_a: b_j \neq 0$.

LOS 2.d

For a two-tailed test of a regression coefficient, if the *t*-statistic is between the upper and lower critical *t*-values, we cannot reject the null hypothesis. We cannot conclude that the regression coefficient is statistically significantly different from the null hypothesis value at the chosen significance level.

If the *t*-statistic is greater than the upper critical *t*-value or lower than the lower critical *t*-value, we can reject the null hypothesis and conclude that the regression coefficient is statistically significantly different from the null hypothesis value at the specified significance level.

LOS 2.e

The value of dependent variable Y is predicted as:

$$\hat{Y} = \hat{b}_0 + \hat{b}_1 X_1 + \hat{b}_2 X_2 + \ldots + \hat{b}_k X_k$$

LOS 2.f

Assumptions of multiple regression mostly pertain to the error term, ε_i.

- A linear relationship exists between the dependent and independent variables.

- The independent variables are not random, and there is no exact linear relation between any two or more independent variables.
- The expected value of the error term is zero.
- The variance of the error terms is constant.
- The error for one observation is not correlated with that of another observation.
- The error term is normally distributed.

LOS 2.g

The *F*-distributed test statistic can be used to test the significance of all (or any subset of) the independent variables (i.e., the overall fit of the model) using a one-tailed test:

$$F = \frac{MSR}{MSE} = \frac{RSS/k}{SSE/n-k-1} \text{ with k and n} - \text{k} - 1 \text{ degrees of freedom}$$

LOS 2.h

The coefficient of determination, R^2, is the percentage of the variation in Y that is explained by the set of independent variables.

- R^2 increases as the number of independent variables increases—this can be a problem.
- The adjusted R^2 adjusts the R^2 for the number of independent variables.
- $R_a^2 = 1 - \left[\left(\frac{n-1}{n-k-1}\right) \times \left(1 - R^2\right)\right]$

LOS 2.i

An ANOVA table is used to assess the usefulness of a regression model's independent variable(s) in explaining the dependent variable:

Source	df (Degrees of Freedom)	SS (Sum of Squares)	MS Mean Square = (SS/df)
Regression	k	RSS	MSR
Error	n − k −1	SSE	MSE
Total	n − 1	SST	

$$MSE = \frac{SSE}{n-k-1}; \ MSR = \frac{RSS}{k}; \ R^2 = \frac{RSS}{SST}; \ F = \frac{MSR}{MSE}; \ SEE = \sqrt{MSE}$$

LOS 2.j

Qualitative independent variables (dummy variables) capture the effect of a binary independent variable:

- Slope coefficient is interpreted as the change in the dependent variable for the case when the dummy variable is one.
- Use one less dummy variable than the number of categories.

LOS 2.k, 2.l

Summary of what you need to know regarding violations of the assumptions of multiple regression:

Violation	Conditional Heteroskedasticity	Serial Correlation	Multicollinearity
What is it?	Residual variance related to level of independent variables	Residuals are correlated	Two or more independent variables are correlated
Effect?	Coefficients are consistent. Standard errors are underestimated. Too many Type I errors.	Coefficients are consistent. Standard errors are underestimated. Too many Type I errors (positive correlation).	Coefficients are consistent (but unreliable). Standard errors are overestimated. Too many Type II errors.
Detection?	Breusch-Pagan chi-square test $= n \times R^2$	Durbin-Watson test $\approx 2(1 - r)$	Conflicting t and F statistics; correlations among independent variables if $k = 2$
Correction?	Use White-corrected standard errors	Use the Hansen method to adjust standard errors	Drop one of the correlated variables

LOS 2.m

There are six common misspecifications of the regression model that you should be aware of and able to recognize:

- Omitting a variable.
- Variable should be transformed.
- Incorrectly pooling data.
- Using lagged dependent variable as independent variable.
- Forecasting the past.
- Measuring independent variables with error.

The effects of the model misspecification on the regression results are basically the same for all of the misspecifications: regression coefficients are biased and inconsistent, which means we can't have any confidence in our hypothesis tests of the coefficients or in the predictions of the model.

LOS 2.n

Qualitative dependent variables (e.g., bankrupt versus non-bankrupt) require methods other than ordinary least squares (e.g., logit analysis).

LOS 2.o

The values of the slope coefficients suggest the economic meaning of the relationship between the independent and dependent variables, but it is important for the analyst to keep in mind that a regression may have statistical significance even when there is no practical economic significance in the relationship.

Reading 2

ANSWER KEY FOR MODULE QUIZZES

Module Quiz 2.1, 2.2, 2.3

1. **C** RSS = 9,105 − 4,320 = 4,785

$$F = \frac{\dfrac{4,785}{4}}{\dfrac{4,320}{65-4-1}} = \frac{1,196.25}{72} = 16.61$$

(Module 2.3, LOS 2.g)

2. **B** This is a one-tailed test, so the critical F-value at the 5% significance level with 4 and 60 degrees of freedom is approximately 2.53. (Module 2.3, LOS 2.g)

3. **C** k = 5 and n − 5 − 1 = 25, so n = 31
(Module 2.3, LOS 2.g)

4. **A** $MSE = \dfrac{SSE}{df_{error}} = \dfrac{925}{25} = 37$
(Module 2.3, LOS 2.g)

5. **C** $F = \dfrac{MSR}{MSE} = \dfrac{\dfrac{RSS}{df_{regression}}}{\dfrac{SSE}{df_{error}}} = \dfrac{\dfrac{1,025}{5}}{\dfrac{925}{25}} = \dfrac{205}{37} = 5.5$
(Module 2.3, LOS 2.g)

Module Quiz 2.4

1. **B** Adjusted R^2 must be less than or equal to R^2. However, if R^2 is low enough and the number of independent variables is large, adjusted R^2 may be negative. (LOS 2.h)

Module Quiz 2.5

1. **C** The t-statistic tests the null that industry PEs are equal. The dummy variable is significant and positive, and the dummy variable is defined as being equal to one for biotechnology stocks, which means that biotechnology PEs are statistically significantly larger than electric utility PEs. Remember, however, this is only accurate if we hold the other independent variables in the model constant. (LOS 2.j)

2. **B** Note that IND = 1 because the stock is in the biotech industry. Predicted
P/E = 6.75 + (8.00 × 1) + (4.00 × 0.00) + (12.35 × 0.14) – (0.50 × 1.5) =
15.7. (LOS 2.j)

Module Quiz 2.6

1. **C** Assumptions underlying a multiple regression include: the error for one
observation is not correlated with that of another observation; the expected
value of the error term is zero; a linear relationship exists between the
dependent and independent variables; the variance of the error terms is
constant. (LOS 2.f)

Module Quiz 2.7

1. **A** The Durbin-Watson statistic tests for serial correlation of the residuals. The
appropriate remedy if serial correlation is detected is to use the Hansen
method. (LOS 2.k)

Module Quiz 2.8, 2.9

1. **C** The coefficients column contains the regression parameters. The
regression equation is thus RET = 0.522 + 0.0460(MKT) + 0.7102(IND) +
0.9(FORT). (Module 2.9, LOS 2.o)

2. **C** The coefficient on FORT is the amount of the return attributable to the
stock of a Fortune 500 firm. Other things equal, the return on a Fortune
500 company is expected to exceed the return on a non-Fortune 500
company by 0.9% annually. (Module 2.2, LOS 2.d)

3. **A** The regression equation is 0.522 + 0.0460(MKT) + 0.7102(IND) +
0.9(FORT), so RET = 0.522 + 0.0460(5) + 0.7102(3) + 0.900(0) = 2.88%.
(Module 2.1, LOS 2.b)

4. **C** The p-value = 0.139, or 13.9%, which is not a reasonable level of
significance. (Module 2.2, LOS 2.d)

5. **C** The Breusch-Pagan test is statistically significant at any reasonable level
of significance, which indicates heteroskedasticity. The Durbin-Watson
statistic is greater than the lower limit, but less than the upper limit, which
places it in the "inconclusive" area. Thus, we are unable to reject the null
hypothesis that there is no serial correlation present. (Module 2.7, LOS 2.k)

6. **B** Using leading P/E from a prior period as an independent variable in
the regression is unlikely to result in misspecification because it is not
related to any of the six types of misspecifications previously discussed.
We're not forecasting the past because leading P/E is calculated using
beginning-of-period stock price and a forecast of earnings for the next
period. Also, because the dependent variable is monthly returns and not
leading P/E, there is no concern about inclusion of a lagged dependent

variable in the model. Omitting a relevant independent variable from the regression and using actual instead of expected inflation (measuring the independent variable in error) are likely to result in model misspecification. (Module 2.9, LOS 2.m)

7. **C**   The effects of the model misspecification on the regression results are basically the same for all of the misspecifications: regression coefficients are biased and inconsistent, which means we can't have any confidence in our hypothesis tests of the coefficients or in the predictions of the model. Notice that choice C states that model misspecification will result in "unbiased" regression coefficients, while in fact model misspecification is most likely to result in "biased" regression coefficients. (Module 2.9, LOS 2.m)

8. **C**   Including a lagged dependent variable (previous period hedge fund composite index returns) in the list of independent variables is likely to lead to model misspecification and biased and inconsistent regression coefficients.

    The fact that an independent variable (small-cap returns) and the dependent variable (hedge fund index returns) are correlated is not a problem for the regression model; we would expect that if the model has predictive power, the dependent variable would be correlated with the independent variables. The fact that two independent variables (small-cap returns and emerging market index returns) are correlated is not a problem of model misspecification, but potentially one of multicollinearity. Without additional information, we can't draw any conclusions concerning whether multicollinearity is a problem (remember "most likely"). (Module 2.9, LOS 2.m)

9. **C**   All qualitative dependent variable models must be tested for heteroskedasticity, serial correlation, and multicollinearity. Each of the alternatives are potential examples of a qualitative dependent variable model, but none are universal elements of all qualitative dependent variable models. (Module 2.9, LOS 2.n)

READING

3

Time-Series Analysis

EXAM FOCUS

A time series is a set of observations of a random variable spaced evenly through time (e.g., quarterly sales revenue for a company over the past 60 quarters). For the exam, given a regression output, identifying violations such as heteroskedasticity, nonstationarity, serial correlation, etc., will be important, as well as being able to calculate a predicted value given a time-series model. Know why a log-linear model is sometimes used; understand the implications of seasonality and how to detect and correct it, as well as the root mean squared error (RMSE) criterion.

MODULE 3.1: LINEAR AND LOG-LINEAR TREND MODELS

▶

Video covering this content is available online.

LOS 3.a: Calculate and evaluate the predicted trend value for a time series, modeled as either a linear trend or a log-linear trend, given the estimated trend coefficients.

CFA® Program Curriculum, Volume 1, page 171

A **time series** is a set of observations for a variable over successive periods of time (e.g., monthly stock market returns for the past ten years). The series has a **trend** if a consistent pattern can be seen by plotting the data (i.e., the individual observations) on a graph. For example, a seasonal trend in sales data is easily detected by plotting the data and noting the significant jump in sales during the same month(s) each year.

Linear Trend Model

A **linear trend** is a time series pattern that can be graphed using a straight line. A downward sloping line indicates a negative trend, while an upward-sloping line indicates a positive trend.

The simplest form of a linear trend is represented by the following linear trend model:

$$y_t = b_0 + b_1(t) + \varepsilon_t$$

where:
y_t = the value of the time series (the dependent variable) at time t
b_0 = intercept at the vertical axis (y-axis)
b_1 = slope coefficient (or trend coefficient)
ε_t = error term (or residual term or disturbance term)
t = time (the independent variable); t = 1, 2, 3...T

Ordinary least squares (OLS) regression is used to estimate the coefficient in the trend line, which provides the following prediction equation:

$$\hat{y}_t = \hat{b}_0 + \hat{b}_1(t)$$

where:
$\hat{y}_t$ = the predicted value of y (the dependent variable) at time t

$\hat{b}_0$ = the estimated value of the intercept term

$\hat{b}_1$ = the estimated value of the slope coefficient

Don't let this model confuse you. It's very similar to the simple linear regression model we covered previously; only here, (t) takes on the value of the time period. For example, in period 2, the equation becomes:

$$\hat{y}_2 = \hat{b}_0 + \hat{b}_1(2)$$

And, likewise, in period 3:

$$\hat{y}_3 = \hat{b}_0 + \hat{b}_1(3)$$

This means $\hat{y}$ increases by the value of $\hat{b}_1$ each period.

> **EXAMPLE: Using a linear trend model**
>
> Suppose you are given a linear trend model with $\hat{b}_0 = 1.70$ and $\hat{b}_1 = 3.0$.
>
> Calculate $\hat{y}_t$ for t = 1 and t = 2.
>
> **Answer:**
>
> When t = 1, $\hat{y}_1 = 1.70 + 3.0(1) = 4.70$
>
> When t = 2, $\hat{y}_2 = 1.70 + 3.0(2) = 7.70$
>
> Note that the difference between $\hat{y}_1$ and $\hat{y}_2$ is 3.0, or the value of the trend coefficient b_1.

EXAMPLE: Trend analysis

Consider hypothetical time series data for manufacturing capacity utilization.

Manufacturing Capacity Utilization

Quarter	Time (t)	Manufacturing Capacity Utilization (in %)	Quarter	Time (t)	Manufacturing Capacity Utilization (in %)
2013.1	1	82.4	2014.4	8	80.9
2013.2	2	81.5	2015.1	9	81.3
2013.3	3	80.8	2015.2	10	81.9
2013.4	4	80.5	2015.3	11	81.7
2014.1	5	80.2	2015.4	12	80.3
2014.2	6	80.2	2016.1	13	77.9
2014.3	7	80.5	2016.2	14	76.4

Applying the OLS methodology to fit the linear trend model to the data produces the results shown below.

Time Series Regression Results for Manufacturing Capacity Utilization

Regression model: $y_t = b_0 + b_1 t + \varepsilon_t$			
R square	0.346		
Adjusted R square	0.292		
Standard error	1.334		
Observations	14		

	Coefficients	Standard Error	t-Statistic
Intercept	82.137	0.753	109.066
Manufacturing utilization	−0.223	0.088	−2.534

Based on this information, predict the projected capacity utilization for the time period involved in the study (i.e., in-sample estimates).

Answer:

As shown in the regression output, the estimated intercept and slope parameters for our manufacturing capacity utilization model are $\hat{b}_0 =$ 82.137 and $\hat{b}_1 = -0.223$, respectively. This means that the prediction equation for capacity utilization can be expressed as:

$$\hat{y}_t = 82.137 - 0.223t$$

With this equation, we can generate estimated values for capacity utilization, $\hat{y}_t$, for each of the 14 quarters in the time series. For example, using the model capacity utilization for the first quarter of 2013 is estimated at 81.914:

$$\hat{y}_t = 82.137 - 0.223(1) = 82.137 - 0.223 = 81.914$$

Note that the estimated value of capacity utilization in that quarter (using the model) is not exactly the same as the actual, measured capacity utilization for that quarter (82.4). The difference between the two is the error or residual term associated with that observation:

Residual (error) = actual value – predicted value $\approx 82.4 - 81.914 = 0.486$

Note that since the actual, measured value is greater than the predicted value of y for 2013.1, the error term is positive. Had the actual, measured value been less than the predicted value, the error term would have been negative.

The projections (i.e., values generated by the model) for all quarters are compared to the actual values below.

Projected Versus Actual Capacity Utilization

Quarter	Time	$\hat{y}_t$	y_t	Quarter	Time	$\hat{y}_t$	y_t
2013.1	1	81.914	82.4	2014.4	8	80.353	80.9
2013.2	2	81.691	81.5	2015.1	9	80.130	81.3
2013.3	3	81.468	80.8	2015.2	10	79.907	81.9
2013.4	4	81.245	80.5	2015.3	11	79.684	81.7
2014.1	5	81.022	80.2	2015.4	12	79.460	80.3
2014.2	6	80.799	80.2	2016.1	13	79.237	77.9
2014.3	7	80.576	80.5	2016.2	14	79.014	76.4

The following graph shows visually how the predicted values compare to the actual values, which were used to generate the regression equation. The **residuals**, or **error terms**, are represented by the distance between the predicted (straight) regression line and the actual data plotted in blue. For example, the residual for t = 10 is $81.9 - 79.907 = 1.993$

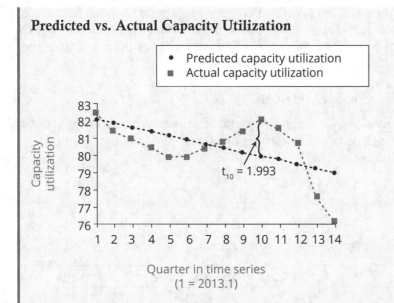

Predicted vs. Actual Capacity Utilization

Since we utilized a linear regression model, the predicted values will by definition fall on a straight line. Since the raw data does not display a linear relationship, the model will probably not do a good job of predicting future values.

Log-Linear Trend Models

Time series data, particularly financial time series, often display *exponential growth* (growth with continuous compounding). Positive exponential growth means that the random variable (i.e., the time series) tends to increase at some constant rate of growth. If we plot the data, the observations will form a convex curve. Negative exponential growth means that the data tends to decrease at some constant rate of decay, and the plotted time series will be a concave curve.

When a series exhibits exponential growth, it can be modeled as:

$$y_t = e^{b_0 + b_1(t)}$$

where:
y_t = the value of the dependent variable at time t
b_0 = the intercept term
b_1 = the constant rate of growth
e = the base of the natural logarithm
t = time = 1, 2, 3...T

This model defines *y*, the dependent variable, as an *exponential* function of time, the independent variable. Rather than try to fit the nonlinear data with a linear (straight line) regression, we take the natural log of both sides of the equation and arrive at the *log-linear* model. This is frequently used when time series data exhibit exponential growth.

$$\ln(y_t) = \ln(e^{b_0 + b_1(t)}) \Rightarrow \ln(y_t) = b_0 + b_1(t)$$

Reading 3

Now that the equation has been transformed from an exponential to a linear function, we can use a linear regression technique to model the series. The use of the transformed data produces a *linear* trend line with a better fit for the data and increases the predictive ability of the model.

> **EXAMPLE: Log-linear trend model**
>
> An analyst estimates a log-linear trend model using quarterly revenue data (in millions of $) from the first quarter of 2005 to the fourth quarter of 2016 for JP Northfield, Inc.:
>
> $$\ln \text{revenue}_t = b_0 + b_1(t) + \varepsilon_t$$
>
> $$t = 1, 2, \ldots, 48$$
>
> The results are shown in the following table.
>
> | | Coefficient | Standard Error | *t*-statistic |
> |---|---|---|---|
> | Intercept | 4.00 | 0.05 | 80.0 |
> | Trend | 0.09 | 0.01 | 9.0 |
>
> Calculate JP Northfield's predicted revenues in the first quarter of 2017.
>
> **Answer:**
>
> In the first quarter of 2017, *t* is equal to 49 because the sample has 48 observations.
>
> $$\ln \text{revenue}_{49} = 4.00 + 0.09(49) = 8.41$$
>
> $$\text{revenue}_{49} = e^{\ln \text{revenue}_{49}} = e^{8.41} = \$4{,}492 \text{ million}$$
>
> The first answer you get in this calculation is the natural log of the revenue forecast. In order to turn the natural log into a revenue figure, you use the 2nd function of the LN key (e^x) on your BA II Plus: enter 8.41 and press [2nd] e^x = 4,492 million.

LOS 3.b: Describe factors that determine whether a linear or a log-linear trend should be used with a particular time series and evaluate limitations of trend models.

CFA® Program Curriculum, Volume 1, page 174

FACTORS THAT DETERMINE WHICH MODEL IS BEST

To determine if a linear or log-linear trend model should be used, the analyst should plot the data. A *linear trend model* may be appropriate if the data points appear to be equally distributed above and below the regression line. Inflation rate data can often be modeled with a linear trend model.

If, on the other hand, the data plots with a non-linear (curved) shape, then the residuals from a linear trend model will be persistently positive or negative for a period of time. In this case, the *log-linear model* may be more suitable. In other words, when the residuals from a linear trend model are serially correlated, a log-linear trend model may be more appropriate. By taking the log of the *y* variable, a regression line can better fit the data. Financial data (e.g., stock indices and stock prices) and company sales data are often best modeled with log-linear models.

Figure 3.1 shows a time series that is best modeled with a log-linear trend model rather than a linear trend model.

Figure 3.1: Linear vs. Log-Linear Trend Models

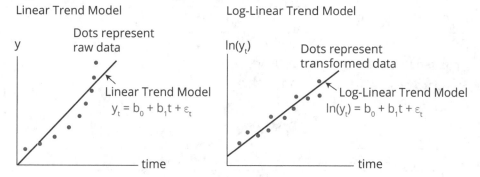

The left panel is a plot of data that exhibits exponential growth along with a linear trend line. The panel on the right is a plot of the natural logs of the original data and a representative log-linear trend line. The log-linear model fits the transformed data better than the linear trend model and, therefore, yields more accurate forecasts.

The bottom line is that when a variable grows at a constant *rate*, a log-linear model is most appropriate. When the variable increases over time by a constant *amount*, a linear trend model is most appropriate.

LIMITATIONS OF TREND MODELS

Recall from the previous two topic reviews that one of the assumptions underlying linear regression is that the residuals are uncorrelated with each other. A violation of this assumption is referred to as autocorrelation. In this case, the residuals are persistently positive or negative for periods of time and it is said that the data exhibit serial correlation. This is a significant limitation, as it means that the model is not appropriate for the time series and that we should not use it to predict future values.

In the preceding discussion, we suggested that a log-linear trend model would be better than a linear trend model when the variable exhibits a constant growth rate. However, it may be the case that even a log-linear model is not appropriate in the presence of serial correlation. In this case, we will want to turn to an autoregressive model.

Recall from the previous topic review that the Durbin Watson statistic (DW) is used to detect autocorrelation. For a time series model without serial correlation

DW should be approximately equal to 2.0. A DW significantly different from 2.0 suggests that the residual terms are correlated.

MODULE QUIZ 3.1

To best evaluate your performance, enter your quiz answers online.

Use the following data to answer Questions 1 through 5.

Consider the results of the regression of monthly real estate loans (RE) in billions of dollars by commercial banks over the period January 2013 through September 2016 in the following table:

Time Series Regression Results for Real Estate Loans

Model: $RE_t = b_0 + b_1 t + \varepsilon_t$	$t = 1, 2, ..., 45$
R^2	0.967908
Adjusted R^2	0.9671617
Standard error	29.587649
Observations	45
Durbin-Watson	0.601

	Coefficients	Standard Error
Intercept	1195.6241	8.9704362
b_1	12.230448	0.3396171

1. The regression of real estate loans against time is a(an):
   A. trend model.
   B. AR model.
   C. ARCH model.

2. The results of the estimation indicate a(an):
   A. upward trend.
   B. AR(2) model.
   C. ARCH system.

3. Are the intercept and slope coefficient significantly different from zero at the 5% level of significance?
   A. Both are statistically significant.
   B. One is, but the other is not.
   C. Neither of them is statistically significant.

4. The forecasted value of real estate loans for October 2016 is *closest* to:
   A. $1,733.764 billion.
   B. $1,745.990 billion.
   C. $1,758.225 billion.

5. Based on the time series regression results, is there evidence of serial correlation of the residuals?
   A. Yes, there is evidence of presence of serial correlation.
   B. No, serial correlation is not present.
   C. The test for serial correlation is inconclusive.

6. An analyst has determined that monthly sport utility vehicle (SUV) sales in the United States have been increasing over the last ten years, but the growth rate over that period has been relatively constant. Which model is *most appropriate* to predict future SUV sales?

   A. $SUVsales_t = b_0 + b_1(t) + e_t$.

   B. $lnSUVsales_t = b_0 + b_1(t) + e_t$.

   C. $lnSUVsales_t = b_0 + b_1(SUVsales_{t-1}) + e_t$.

MODULE 3.2: AUTOREGRESSIVE (AR) MODELS

Video covering this content is available online.

LOS 3.c: Explain the requirement for a time series to be covariance stationary and describe the significance of a series that is not stationary.

CFA® Program Curriculum, Volume 1, page 181

When the dependent variable is regressed against one or more lagged values of itself, the resultant model is called as an **autoregressive model** (AR). For example, the sales for a firm could be regressed against the sales for the firm in the previous month.

Consider:

$$x_t = b_0 + b_1 x_{t-1} + \varepsilon_t$$

where:

x_t = value of time series at time t

b_0 = intercept at the vertical axis (y-axis)

b_1 = slope coefficient

x_{t-1} = value of time series at time $t - 1$

ε_t = error term (or residual term or disturbance term)

t = time; t = 1, 2, 3...T

In an autoregressive time series, past values of a variable are used to predict the current (and hence future) value of the variable.

Statistical inferences based on ordinary least squares (OLS) estimates for an AR time series model may be invalid unless the time series being modeled is **covariance stationary.**

A time series is covariance stationary if it satisfies the following three conditions:

1. *Constant and finite expected value.* The expected value of the time series is constant over time. (Later, we will refer to this value as the mean-reverting level.)

2. *Constant and finite variance.* The time series' volatility around its mean (i.e., the distribution of the individual observations around the mean) does not change over time.

3. *Constant and finite covariance between values at any given lag.* The covariance of the time series with leading or lagged values of itself is constant.

LOS 3.d: Describe the structure of an autoregressive (AR) model of order p and calculate one- and two-period-ahead forecasts given the estimated coefficients.

CFA® Program Curriculum, Volume 1, page 183

The following model illustrates how variable x would be regressed on itself with a lag of one and two periods:

$$x_t = b_0 + b_1 x_{t-1} + b_2 x_{t-2} + \varepsilon_t$$

Such a model is referred to as a *second-order* autoregressive model, or an AR(2) model. In general, an AR model of order p, AR(p), is expressed as:

$$x_t = b_0 + b_1 x_{t-1} + b_2 x_{t-2} + \ldots + b_p x_{t-p} + \varepsilon_t$$

where p indicates the number of lagged values that the autoregressive model will include as independent variables.

Forecasting With an Autoregressive Model

Autoregressive time series model forecasts are calculated in the same manner as those for other regression models, but since the independent variable is a lagged value of the dependent variable, it is necessary to calculate a one-step-ahead forecast before a two-step-ahead forecast can be calculated. The calculation of successive forecasts in this manner is referred to as the **chain rule of forecasting**.

A one-period-ahead forecast for an AR(1) model is determined in the following manner:

$$\hat{x}_{t+1} = \hat{b}_0 + \hat{b}_1 x_t$$

Likewise, a two-step-ahead forecast for an AR(1) model is calculated as:

$$\hat{x}_{t+2} = \hat{b}_0 + \hat{b}_1 \hat{x}_{t+1}$$

Note that the ^ symbol above the variables in the equations indicates that the inputs used in multi-period forecasts are actually forecasts (estimates) themselves. This implies that multi-period forecasts are more uncertain than single-period forecasts. For example, for a two-step-ahead forecast, there is the usual uncertainty associated with forecasting x_{t+1} using x_t, plus the additional uncertainty of forecasting x_{t+2} using the forecasted value for x_{t+1}.

> **EXAMPLE: Forecasting**
>
> Suppose that an AR(1) model has been estimated and has produced the following prediction equation: $x_t = 1.2 + 0.45 x_{t-1}$. Calculate a two-step-ahead forecast if the current value of x is 5.0.

Answer:

One-step-ahead forecast: If $x_t = 5$, then $\hat{x}_{t+1} = 1.2 + 0.45(5) = 3.45$.

Two-step-ahead forecast: If $\hat{x}_{t+1} = 3.45$, then $\hat{x}_{t+2} = 1.2 + 0.45(3.45) = 2.75$.

LOS 3.e: Explain how autocorrelations of the residuals can be used to test whether the autoregressive model fits the time series.

CFA® Program Curriculum, Volume 1, page 183

Autocorrelation & Model Fit

When an AR model is correctly specified, the residual terms will not exhibit *serial correlation*. Serial correlation (or autocorrelation) means the error terms are positively or negatively correlated. When the error terms are correlated, standard errors are unreliable and *t*-tests of individual coefficients can incorrectly show statistical significance or insignificance.

If the residuals have significant autocorrelation, the AR model that produced the residuals is not the best model for the time series being analyzed. The procedure to test whether an AR time series model is correctly specified involves three steps:

Step 1: **Estimate** the AR model being evaluated using linear regression:
Start with a first-order AR model [i.e., AR(1)] using $x_t = b_0 + b_1 x_{t-1} + \varepsilon_t$.

Step 2: **Calculate** the autocorrelations of the model's residuals (i.e., the level of correlation between the forecast errors from one period to the next).

Step 3: **Test** whether the autocorrelations are significantly different from zero:

If the model is correctly specified, none of the autocorrelations will be statistically significant. To test for significance, a *t*-test is used to test the hypothesis that the correlations of the residuals are zero. The *t*-statistic is the estimated autocorrelation divided by the standard error. The standard error is $1/\sqrt{T}$, where T is the number of observations, so the test statistic for each autocorrelation is $t = \dfrac{\rho_{\varepsilon_t, \varepsilon_{t-k}}}{1/\sqrt{T}}$ with $(T-2)$ degrees of freedom and $\rho_{\varepsilon_t, \varepsilon_{t-k}}$ is the correlation of error term t with the kth lagged error term.

PROFESSOR'S NOTE

The Durbin-Watson test that we used with trend models is not appropriate for testing for serial correlation of the error terms in an autoregressive model. Use this *t*-test instead.

EXAMPLE: Testing an AR model for proper specification

The correlations of the error terms from the estimation of an AR(1) model using a sample with 102 observations are presented in the following figure. Determine whether the model is correctly specified.

Autocorrelation Analysis

Model: $y_t = b_0 + b_1 y_{t-1} + \varepsilon_t$

Lag	Autocorrelation	t-Statistic	Lag	Autocorrelation	t-Statistic
1	0.0616114	0.622245	7	–0.010146	–0.102470
2	0.0843368	0.851760	8	0.0211711	0.213818
3	0.0258823	0.261398	9	–0.0959502	–0.969050
4	0.0188928	0.190808	10	0.0389730	0.393608
5	0.1001404	1.011368	11	–0.0677132	–0.683870
6	–0.0638219	–0.644570	12	–0.0122798	–0.124020

Answer:

In this example, the standard error is $1/\sqrt{102}$ or 0.099. The *t*-statistic for Lag 2 is then computed as 0.0843368 / 0.099 = 0.8518.

The critical two-tail *t*-value at the 5% significance level and 100 degrees of freedom is 1.98. The *t*-statistics indicate that none of the autocorrelations of the residuals in the previous figure is statistically different from zero because their absolute values are less than 1.98. Thus, there is sufficient reason to believe that the error terms from the AR(1) model are not serially correlated.

If the *t*-tests indicate that any of the correlations computed in Step 2 are statistically significant (i.e., $t \geq 1.98$), the AR model is not specified correctly. Additional lags are included in the model and the correlations of the residuals (error terms) are checked again. This procedure will be followed until all autocorrelations are insignificant.

LOS 3.f: Explain mean reversion and calculate a mean-reverting level.

CFA® Program Curriculum, Volume 1, page 186

A time series exhibits **mean reversion** if it has a tendency to move toward its mean. In other words, the time series has a tendency to decline when the current value is above the mean and rise when the current value is below the mean. If a time series is at its mean-reverting level, the model predicts that the next value of the time series will be the same as its current value (i.e., $\hat{x}_t = x_{t-1}$ when a time series is at its mean-reverting level).

For an AR(1) model, $x_t = b_0 + b_1 x_{t-1}$, the above equality implies that $x_t = b_0 + b_1 x_t$. Solving for x_t, the mean-reverting level is expressed as $x_t = \dfrac{b_0}{(1 - b_1)}$.

So, if $x_t > \dfrac{b_0}{(1 - b_1)}$, the AR(1) model predicts that $x_{t + 1}$ will be lower than x_t, and

if $x_t < \dfrac{b_0}{1 - b_1}$, the model predicts that $x_{t + 1}$ will be higher than x_t.

EXAMPLE: Mean-reverting time series

Calculate the mean-reverting level for the manufacturing capacity utilization time series using the following regression results:

Time Series Regression Results for Manufacturing Capacity Utilization

Regression model: $x_t = b_0 + b_1 x_{t-1}$

R square	0.346508
Adjusted R square	0.29205
Standard error	1.333885
Observations	14

	Coefficients	Standard Error	t-Statistic
Intercept	82.137	0.753	109.080
Manufacturing utilization	–0.223	0.0884	–2.522

Answer:

$b_0 = 82.137$ and $b_1 = -0.223$, so the mean-reverting level, $b_0 / (1 - b_1)$, is computed as: mean-reverting level $= \dfrac{82.137}{[1 - (-0.223)]} = 67.16$

This means that if the current level of manufacturing capacity utilization is above 67.16, it is expected to fall in the next period, and if manufacturing capacity utilization is below 67.16 in the current period, it is expected to rise in the next period.

All covariance stationary time series have a finite mean-reverting level. An AR(1) time series will have a finite mean-reverting level when the absolute value of the lag coefficient is less than 1 (i.e., $|b_1| < 1$).

LOS 3.g: Contrast in-sample and out-of-sample forecasts and compare the forecasting accuracy of different time-series models based on the root mean squared error criterion.

CFA® Program Curriculum, Volume 1, page 190

In-sample forecasts $(\hat{y}_t)$ are *within* the range of data (i.e., time period) used to estimate the model, which for a time series is known as the sample or test period. In-sample forecast errors are $(y_t - \hat{y}_t)$, where *t* is an observation within the sample period. In other words, we are comparing how accurate our model is in forecasting the actual data we used to develop the model. The Predicted vs. Actual Capacity Utilization figure in our Trend Analysis example shows an example of values predicted by the model compared to the values used to generate the model.

Out-of-sample forecasts are made *outside* of the sample period. In other words, we compare how accurate a model is in forecasting the *y* variable value for a time period outside the period used to develop the model. Out-of-sample forecasts are important because they provide a test of whether the model adequately describes the time series and whether it has relevance (i.e., predictive power) in the real world. Nonetheless, an analyst should be aware that most published research employs in-sample forecasts only.

The **root mean squared error** criterion (RMSE) is used to compare the accuracy of autoregressive models in forecasting out-of-sample values. For example, a researcher may have two autoregressive (AR) models: an AR(1) model and an AR(2) model. To determine which model will more accurately forecast future values, we calculate the RMSE (the square root of the average of the squared errors) for the out-of-sample data. Note that the model with the lowest RMSE for in-sample data may not be the model with the lowest RMSE for out-of-sample data.

For example, imagine that we have 60 months of historical unemployment data. We estimate both models over the first 36 of 60 months. To determine which model will produce better (i.e., more accurate) forecasts, we then forecast the values for the last 24 of 60 months of historical data. Using the actual values for the last 24 months as well as the values predicted by the models, we can calculate the RMSE for each model.

The model with the lower RMSE for the out-of-sample data will have lower forecast error and will be expected to have better predictive power in the future.

In addition to examining the RMSE criteria for a model, we will also want to examine the stability of regression coefficients, which we discuss in the following.

LOS 3.h: Explain the instability of coefficients of time-series models.

CFA® Program Curriculum, Volume 1, page 192

Financial and economic time series inherently exhibit some form of *instability* or *nonstationarity*. This is because financial and economic conditions are dynamic, and the estimated regression coefficients in one period may be quite different from those estimated during another period.

Models estimated with shorter time series are usually more stable than those with longer time series because a longer sample period increases the chance that the underlying economic process has changed. Thus, there is a tradeoff between the increased statistical reliability when using longer time periods and the increased stability of the estimates when using shorter periods.

The primary concern when selecting a time series sample period is the underlying economic processes. Have there been regulatory changes? Has there been a dramatic change in the underlying economic environment?

If the answer is yes, then the historical data may not provide a reliable model. Merely examining the significance of the autocorrelation of the residuals will not indicate whether the model is valid. We must also examine whether the data is covariance stationary.

MODULE QUIZ 3.2

To best evaluate your performance, enter your quiz answers online.

1. Is the time series shown in the following figure likely to be covariance stationary?

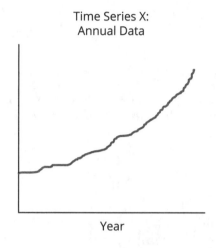

Time Series X:
Annual Data

Year

    A. X is not covariance stationary due to homoskedasticity.
    B. X is not covariance stationary due to non-constant mean.
    C. X is covariance stationary.

2. Given the prediction equation: $\hat{x}_t = 5 + 1.75x_{t-1}$, what is the forecast value of x_{t+2} if x_{t-1} is 16.5?
    A. 64.28.
    B. 117.49.
    C. 210.61.

3. When evaluating a time series model's real-world ability to forecast, we would have the most confidence in a model with small:
    A. in-sample forecast error.
    B. out-of-sample forecast error.
    C. residuals.

MODULE 3.3: RANDOM WALKS AND UNIT ROOTS

Video covering this content is available online.

LOS 3.i: Describe characteristics of random walk processes and contrast them to covariance stationary processes.

CFA® Program Curriculum, Volume 1, page 194

Random walk. If a time series follows a random walk process, the predicted value of the series (i.e., the value of the dependent variable) in one period is equal to the value of the series in the previous period plus a random error term.

A time series that follows a simple random walk process is described in equation form as $x_t = x_{t-1} + \varepsilon_t$, where the best forecast of x_t is x_{t-1} and:

1. $E(\varepsilon_t) = 0$: The expected value of each error term is zero.

2. $E(\varepsilon_t^2) = \sigma^2$: The variance of the error terms is constant.

3. $E(\varepsilon_i \varepsilon_j) = 0$; if $i \neq j$: There is no serial correlation in the error terms.

Reading 3

Random Walk with a Drift. If a time series follows a random walk *with a drift*, the intercept term is not equal to zero. That is, in addition to a random error term, the time series is expected to increase or decrease by a constant amount each period. A random walk with a drift can be described as:

$$x_t = b_0 + b_1 x_{t-1} + \varepsilon_t$$

where:
b_0 = the constant drift
b_1 = 1

Covariance Stationarity. Neither a random walk nor a random walk with a drift exhibits covariance stationarity. To show this, let's start by expressing a random walk as:

$$x_t = b_0 + b_1 x_{t-1} + \varepsilon_t$$

where:
b_0 = 0 (for a random walk without a drift)
$b_0 \neq 0$ (for a random walk with a drift)
b_1 = 1 (for a random walk with or without a drift)

In either case (with or without a drift), the mean-reverting level is $\dfrac{b_0}{1-b_1} = \dfrac{b_0}{0}$ (the division of any number by zero is undefined), and as we stated earlier, a time series must have a **finite mean-reverting level** to be covariance stationary. Thus, a random walk, with or without a drift, is not covariance stationary, and exhibits what is known as a **unit root** ($b_1 = 1$). For a time series that is not covariance stationary, the least squares regression procedure that we have been using to estimate an AR(1) model will not work without transforming the data. We discuss unit roots and how they are handled in the next section.

LOS 3.j: Describe implications of unit roots for time-series analysis, explain when unit roots are likely to occur and how to test for them, and demonstrate how a time series with a unit root can be transformed so it can be analyzed with an AR model.

LOS 3.k: Describe the steps of the unit root test for nonstationarity and explain the relation of the test to autoregressive time-series models.

CFA® Program Curriculum, Volume 1, page 198

As we discussed in the previous LOS, if the coefficient on the lag variable is 1, the series is not covariance stationary. If the value of the lag coefficient is equal to one, the time series is said to have a **unit root** and will follow a random walk process. Since a time series that follows a random walk is not covariance stationary, modeling such a time series in an AR model can lead to incorrect inferences.

Unit Root Testing for Nonstationarity

To determine whether a time series is covariance stationary, we can (1) run an AR model and examine autocorrelations, or (2) perform the Dickey Fuller test.

In the first method, an AR model is estimated and the statistical significance of the autocorrelations at various lags is examined. A stationary process will usually have residual autocorrelations insignificantly different from zero at all lags or residual autocorrelations that decay to zero as the number of lags increases.

A more definitive test for unit root is the Dickey Fuller test. For statistical reasons, you cannot directly test whether the coefficient on the independent variable in an AR time series is equal to 1. To compensate, **Dickey and Fuller** created a rather ingenious test for a unit root. Remember, if an AR(1) model has a coefficient of 1, it has a unit root and no finite mean reverting level (i.e., it is not covariance stationary). Dickey and Fuller (DF) transform the AR(1) model to run a simple regression. To transform the model, they (1) start with the basic form of the AR(1) model and (2) subtract x_{t-1} from both sides:

(1) $x_t = b_0 + b_1 x_{t-1} + \varepsilon$

(2) $x_t - x_{t-1} = b_0 + b_1 x_{t-1} - x_{t-1} + \varepsilon \rightarrow$

$$x_t - x_{t-1} = b_0 + (b_1 - 1)x_{t-1} + \varepsilon$$

Then, rather than directly testing whether the original coefficient is different from 1, they test whether the new, transformed coefficient $(b_1 - 1)$ is different from zero using a modified t-test. If $(b_1 - 1)$ is not significantly different from zero, they say that b_1 must be equal to 1.0 and, therefore, the series must have a unit root.

PROFESSOR'S NOTE

In their actual test, Dickey and Fuller use the variable g, which equals $(b_1 - 1)$. The null hypothesis is g = 0 (i.e., the time series has a unit root). For the exam, understand how the test is conducted and be able to interpret its results. For example, if on the exam you are told the null (g = 0) cannot be rejected, your answer is that the time series has a unit root. If the null is rejected, the time series does not have a unit root.

FIRST DIFFERENCING

If we believe a time series is a random walk (i.e., has a unit root), we can transform the data to a covariance stationary time series using a procedure called **first differencing**. The first differencing process involves subtracting the value of the time series (i.e., the dependent variable) in the immediately preceding period from the current value of the time series to define a new dependent variable, y. Note that by taking first differences, you model the **change** in the value of the dependent variable

So, if the original time series of x has a unit root, the change in x, $x_t - x_{t-1} = \varepsilon_t$, is just the error term. This means we can define y_t as:

$$y_t = x_t - x_{t-1} \Rightarrow y_t = \varepsilon_t$$

Then, stating y in the form of an AR(1) model:

$$y_t = b_0 + b_1 y_{t-1} + \varepsilon_t$$
where:
$$b_0 = b_1 = 0$$

This transformed time series has a finite mean-reverting level of $\dfrac{0}{1-0} = 0$ and is, therefore, covariance stationary.

> **EXAMPLE: Unit root**
>
> Suppose we decide to model the capacity utilization data. Using an AR(1) model, the results indicate that the capacity utilization time series probably contains a unit root and is, therefore, not covariance stationary. Discuss how this time series can be transformed to be covariance stationary.
>
> **Answer:**
>
> Covariance stationarity can often be achieved by transforming the data using first differencing and modeling the first-differenced time series as an autoregressive time series.

> **EXAMPLE: First differencing**
>
> The next figure contains the first-differences of our manufacturing capacity utilization time series for the period 2013.1 through 2016.3. The first two columns contain the original time series. The first differences of the original series are contained in the third column of the table, and the one-period lagged values on the first-differences are presented in the fourth column of the table. Note that the first differences in this example represent the *change* in manufacturing capacity from the preceding period and are designated as y_t and y_{t-1}.

©2021 Kaplan, Inc.

First-Differenced Manufacturing Capacity Utilization Data

Quarter	Capacity	Change in Capacity $y_t = x_t - x_{t-1}$	Lagged Change in Capacity $y_{t-1} = x_{t-1} - x_{t-2}$
2013.1	82.4		
2013.2	81.5	–0.9	
2013.3	80.8	–0.7	–0.9
2013.4	80.5	–0.3	–0.7
2014.1	80.2	–0.3	–0.3
2014.2	80.2	0.0	–0.3
2014.3	80.5	0.3	0.0
2014.4	80.9	0.4	0.3
2015.1	81.3	0.4	0.4
2015.2	81.9	0.6	0.4
2015.3	81.7	–0.2	0.6
2015.4	80.3	–1.4	–0.2
2016.1	77.9	–2.4	–1.4
2016.2	76.4	–1.5	–2.4
2016.3	76.4	0.0	–1.5

After this transformation, it is appropriate to regress the AR(1) model, $y_t = b_0 + b_1 y_{t-1}$. The regression results for the first-differenced time series are presented in the next figure, where it can be seen that the estimated coefficient on the lag variable is statistically significant at 5% level of significance.

Regression Output for First-Differenced Manufacturing Capacity

Change in Capacity Utilization

AR(1) Model $y_t = b_0 + b_1 y_{t-1} + \varepsilon_t$

R^2		0.430869388		
Adjusted R^2		0.379130241		
Standard error		0.699210366		
Observations		13		
	Coefficients	*Standard Error*	*t-Statistic*	*p-Value*
Intercept	–0.090014589	0.220409703	–0.4084	0.69082
Lag 1	0.65496839	0.226964091	2.885780	0.0148

MODULE QUIZ 3.3

To best evaluate your performance, enter your quiz answers online.

Use the following data to answer Questions 1 and 2.

The results of the estimation of monthly revolving credit outstanding (RCO) on the one-period lagged values for RCO from January 2013 through December 2015 are presented in the following table.

Regression Results for Outstanding Revolving Credit Study

Model: $RCO_t = b_0 + b_1 RCO_{t-1} + \varepsilon_t$

R^2	0.952643			
Adjusted R^2	0.951208			
Standard error	9.261452			
Observations	35			

	Coefficients	Standard Error	t-Statistic	p-Value
Intercept	–34.0019	24.19417	–1.40537	0.169255
Lag 1	1.065697	0.041362	25.76512	< 0.0001

1. What type of time-series model was used to produce the regression results in the table? A(n):
   A. AR model.
   B. heteroskedasticity (H) model.
   C. trend model with a drift.

2. An approach that may work in the case of modeling a time series that has a unit root is to:
   A. use an ARCH model.
   B. use a trend model.
   C. model the first differences of the time series.

3. Which of the following will always have a finite mean-reverting level?
   A. A covariance-stationary time series.
   B. A random-walk-with-drift time series.
   C. A time series with unit root.

4. Which of the following statements is *most accurate*? A random walk process:
   A. is nonstationary.
   B. has a finite mean-reverting level.
   C. can be appropriately fit as an AR(1) model.

5. Which of the following is not correct about the Dickey-Fuller unit root test for nonstationarity?
   A. The null hypothesis is that the time series has a unit root.
   B. A hypothesis test is conducted using critical values computed by Dickey and Fuller in place of conventional *t*-test values.
   C. If the test statistic is significant, we conclude that the times series is nonstationary.

MODULE 3.4: SEASONALITY

LOS 3.l: Explain how to test and correct for seasonality in a time-series model and calculate and interpret a forecasted value using an AR model with a seasonal lag.

Video covering this content is available online.

CFA® Program Curriculum, Volume 1, page 207

Seasonality in a time-series is a pattern that tends to repeat from year to year. One example is monthly sales data for a retailer. Given that sales data normally vary according to the time of year, we might expect this month's sales (x_t) to be related to sales for the same month last year (x_{t-12}).

When seasonality is present, modeling the associated time series data would be misspecified unless the AR model incorporates the effects of the seasonality.

EXAMPLE: Detecting seasonality

You are interested in predicting occupancy levels for a resort hotel chain and have obtained the chain's quarterly occupancy levels for the most recent 40 quarters (10 years). You decide to model the quarterly occupancy time-series using the AR(1) model:

$$\ln x_t = b_0 + b_1 \ln x_{t-1} + \varepsilon_t$$

Determine whether seasonality exists using the results presented in the following example.

Autoregression Output for Log-Quarterly Hotel Occupancy

Resort Occupancy Levels			
AR(1) Model: $\ln x_t = b_0 + b_1 \ln x_{t-1} + \varepsilon_t$			
R^2	0.7929		
Standard error	0.1952		
Observations	39		
	Coefficients	*Standard Error*	*t-Statistic*
Intercept	0.0375	0.0274	1.369
Lag 1	0.5318	0.1635	3.2526

Autocorrelation of Residuals			
Residual Lag	Autocorrelation	Standard Error	*t*-Statistic
1	−0.0615	0.1601	−0.3841
2	−0.0121	0.1601	−0.0756
3	−0.0212	0.1601	−0.1324
4	0.8719	0.1601	5.4460

Reading 3

Answer:

The bottom part of the table contains the residual autocorrelations for the first four lags of the time series. What stands out is the relatively large autocorrelation and t-statistic for the fourth lag. With 39 observations and two parameters, (b_0 and b_1), there are 37 degrees of freedom. At a significance level of 5%, the critical t-value is 2.026.

The t-statistics indicate that none of the first three lagged autocorrelations is significantly different from zero. However, the t-statistic at Lag 4 is 5.4460, which means that we must reject the null hypothesis that the Lag 4 autocorrelation is zero and conclude that seasonality is present in the time-series. Thus, we conclude that this model is misspecified and will be unreliable for forecasting purposes. We need to include a seasonality term to make the model more correctly specified.

PROFESSOR'S NOTE

The reason 40 quarters of data only produces 39 observations is because we're analyzing the difference from one quarter to the next; 40 data points yields 39 differences.

Correcting for seasonality. The interpretation of seasonality in the previous example is that occupancy in any quarter is related to occupancy in the previous quarter and the same quarter in the previous year. For example, fourth quarter 2015 occupancy is related to third quarter 2015 occupancy as well as fourth quarter 2014 occupancy.

To adjust for seasonality in an AR model, an additional lag of the *dependent* variable (corresponding to the same period in the previous year) is added to the original model as another *independent* variable. For example, if quarterly data are used, the **seasonal lag** is 4; if monthly data are used the seasonal lag is 12; and so on.

EXAMPLE: Correcting for seasonality in a time-series model

We continue with our resort occupancy level example, where the significant residual correlation at Lag 4 indicates seasonality in the quarterly time series. By testing the correlations of the error terms, it appears that occupancy levels in each quarter are related not only to the previous quarter, but also to the corresponding quarter in the previous year. To adjust for this problem, we add a lagged value of the dependent variable to the original model that corresponds to the seasonal pattern.

To model the autocorrelation of the same quarters from year to year, we use an AR(1) model with a seasonal lag: $\ln x_t = b_0 + b_1(\ln x_{t-1}) + b_2(\ln x_{t-4}) + \varepsilon_t$. Note that this specification, the inclusion of a seasonal lag, does not result in an AR(2) model. It results in an AR(1) model incorporating a seasonal lag term.

The results obtained when this model is fit to the natural logarithm of the time series are presented in the following. Determine whether the model is specified correctly.

Log-Resort Hotel Occupancy

AR(1) Model with a Seasonal Lag: $\ln x_t = b_0 + b_1 (\ln x_{t-1}) + b_2(\ln x_{t-4}) + \varepsilon_t$

R^2	0.948983874		
Standard error	0.3754		
Observations	36		

	Coefficients	Standard Error	t-Statistic
Intercept	0.0085	0.0049	1.7347
Lag 1	0.2598	0.0527	4.9298
Lag 4	0.7921	0.2166	3.6570

Autocorrelation of Residuals

Residual Lag	Autocorrelation	Standard Error	t-Statistic
1	−0.0526	0.1667	−0.3156
2	0.0715	0.1667	0.4290
3	−0.0241	0.1667	−0.1446
4	−0.0435	0.1667	−0.2610

Answer:

Notice in the bottom of the table that the fourth-lag residual autocorrelation has dropped substantially and is, in fact, no longer statistically significant. Also notable in these results is the improvement in the R-square for the adjusted model (94.9%) compared to the R-square from the original model (79.3%). The results shown in the figure indicate that, by incorporating a seasonal lag term, the model is now specified correctly.

FORECASTING WITH AN AR MODEL WITH A SEASONAL LAG

EXAMPLE: Forecasting with an autoregressive model

Based on the regression results from the previous example and the occupancy levels over the past year (presented below), forecast the level of hotel occupancy for the first quarter of 2016.

Quarterly Hotel Occupancy Levels

Quarter	2015.1	2015.2	2015.3	2015.4
Occupancy Level	250,000	750,000	450,000	600,000

Answer:

We express the seasonally adjusted forecasting equation as:

$$\ln x_t = 0.0085 + 0.2598(\ln x_{t-1}) + 0.7921(\ln x_{t-4})$$

where x_t is the occupancy level for the tth quarter.

To forecast the occupancy level for the hotel chain for the first quarter of 2016 (i.e., 2016.1), the following computation is made:

$$\ln y_{2016.1} = 0.0085 + 0.2598(\ln y_{2015.4}) + 0.7921(\ln y_{2015.1})$$

$$\ln y_{2016.1} = 0.0085 + 0.2598(\ln 600{,}000) + 0.7921(\ln 250{,}000)$$

$$\ln y_{2016.1} = 0.0085 + 0.2598(13.3047) + 0.7921(12.4292)$$

$$\ln y_{2016.1} = 13.3103$$

Since $y = e^{\ln(y)}$, $y_{2016.1} = e^{13.3103} = 603{,}378.52$

The forecasted level of hotel occupancy for the first quarter of 2016 is 603,379, a significant increase over the same quarter the previous year.

 PROFESSOR'S NOTE

Once again, the first answer you get in this calculation is the natural log of the occupancy forecast. In order to turn the natural log into an occupancy figure, you use the 2nd function of the LN key (e^x) on your BA II Plus: enter 13.3103 and press [2nd] e^x = 603,378.52.

 MODULE QUIZ 3.4

To best evaluate your performance, enter your quiz answers online.

Use the following data to answer Questions 1 through 3.

Regression Results for Monthly Cash Flow Study

	Coefficients	Standard Error	t-Statistic	p-Value
Intercept	26.8625	12.15146	2.210639	0.035719
Lag 1	0.7196	0.042584	16.89837	< 0.0001

Autocorrelation of the Residual				
Lag	Autocorrelation	Standard Error	t-Statistic	p-Value
12	–0.0254	0.0632	–0.4019	0.5612

1. The number of observations in the time series used to estimate the model represented in the table above is *closest* to:
   A. 16.
   B. 50.
   C. 250.

2. Based on the information given, what type of model was used?
   A. AR(1).
   B. AR(2).
   C. AR(12).

3. At a 5% level of significance, does the information indicate the presence of seasonality?
    A. No, because the lag-12 autocorrelation of the residual is not significant.
    B. Yes, because the lag-12 autocorrelation of the residual is significantly different than one.
    C. There is not enough information provided; the autocorrelation for the first lag is also needed to detect seasonality.

4. A time-series model that uses quarterly data exhibits seasonality if the fourth autocorrelation of the error term:
    A. differs significantly from 0.
    B. does not differ significantly from 0.
    C. does not differ significantly from the first autocorrelation of the error term.

5. In an autoregressive time-series model, seasonality may be corrected by:
    A. excluding one or more of the lagged variables until the seasonality disappears.
    B. transforming the time series using first-differencing.
    C. adding an additional variable that reflects an appropriate lag of the time series.

6. Which of the following AR models is *most appropriate* for a time series with annual seasonality using quarterly observations?
    A. $b_1 x_{t-1} + b_2 x_{t-12} + \varepsilon_t$.
    B. $b_0 + b_1 x_{t-1} + b_2 x_{t-4} + \varepsilon_t$.
    C. $b_0 + b_1 x_{t-4} + b_2 x_{t-12} + \varepsilon_t$.

MODULE 3.5: ARCH AND MULTIPLE TIME SERIES

LOS 3.m: Explain autoregressive conditional heteroskedasticity (ARCH) and describe how ARCH models can be applied to predict the variance of a time series.

Video covering this content is available online.

CFA® Program Curriculum, Volume 1, page 213

When examining a single time series, such as an AR model, **autoregressive conditional heteroskedasticity (ARCH)** exists if the variance of the residuals in one period is *dependent* on the variance of the residuals in a previous period. When this condition exists, the standard errors of the regression coefficients in AR models and the hypothesis tests of these coefficients are invalid.

Using ARCH Models

An ARCH model is used to test for autoregressive conditional heteroskedasticity. Within the ARCH framework, an ARCH(1) time series is one for which the variance of the residuals in one period is dependent on (i.e., a function of) the variance of the residuals in the preceding period. To test whether a time series is ARCH(1), the squared residuals from an estimated time-series model, $\hat{\varepsilon}_t^2$, are regressed on the first lag of the squared residuals $\hat{\varepsilon}_{t-1}^2$.

The ARCH(1) regression model is expressed as:

$$\hat{\varepsilon}_t^2 = a_0 + a_1\hat{\varepsilon}_{t-1}^2 + \mu_t$$

where a_0 is the constant and μ_t is an error term.

If the coefficient, a_1, is statistically different from zero, the time series is ARCH(1).

If a time-series model has been determined to contain ARCH errors, regression procedures that correct for heteroskedasticity, such as *generalized least squares*, must be used in order to develop a predictive model. Otherwise, the standard errors of the model's coefficients will be incorrect, leading to invalid conclusions.

Predicting the Variance of a Time Series

However, if a time series has ARCH errors, an ARCH model can be used to predict the variance of the residuals in future periods. For example, if the data exhibit an ARCH(1) pattern, the ARCH(1) model can be used in period t to predict the variance of the residuals in period t + 1:

$$\hat{\sigma}_{t+1}^2 = \hat{a}_0 + \hat{a}_1\hat{\varepsilon}_t^2$$

EXAMPLE: ARCH(1) time series

The next figure contains the results from the regression of an ARCH(1) model. The squared errors for periods *t* through *T* are regressed on the squared errors for periods t – 1 through T – 1. (μ_t is the error term for the model.) Determine whether the results indicate autoregressive conditional heteroskedasticity (ARCH), and if so, calculate the predicted variance of the error terms in the next period if the current period squared error is 0.5625.

ARCH (1) Regression Results

Model: $\hat{\varepsilon}_t^2 = a_0 + a_1\hat{\varepsilon}_{t-1}^2 + \mu_t$	Coefficients	Standard Error	t-Statistic	p-Value
Constant	5.9068	1.08631	5.4375	< 0.001
Lag 1	0.4515	0.09558	4.7238	< 0.001

Answer:

Since the *p*-value for the coefficient on the lagged variable indicates statistical significance, we can conclude that the time series is ARCH(1). As such, the variance of the error term in the next period can be computed as:

$$\hat{\sigma}_{t+1}^2 = \hat{a}_0 + \hat{a}_1\hat{\varepsilon}_t^2 = 5.9068 + 0.4515(0.5625) = 6.1608$$

 PROFESSOR'S NOTE

If the coefficient a_1 is zero, the variance is constant from period to period. If a_1 is greater than (less than) zero, the variance increases (decreases) over time (i.e., the error terms exhibit heteroskedasticity).

LOS 3.n: Explain how time-series variables should be analyzed for nonstationarity and/or cointegration before use in a linear regression.

CFA® Program Curriculum, Volume 1, page 217

Occasionally an analyst will run a regression using two time series (i.e., time series utilizing two different variables). For example, using the market model to estimate the equity beta for a stock, an analyst regresses a time series of the stock's returns (y_t) on a time series of returns for the market (x_t):

$$y_t = b_0 + b_1 x_t + e_t$$

Notice that now we are faced with two different time series (y_t and x_t), either or both of which could be subject to nonstationarity.

To test whether the two time series have unit roots, the analyst first runs separate DF tests with five possible results:

1. Both time series are covariance stationary.

2. Only the dependent variable time series is covariance stationary.

3. Only the independent variable time series is covariance stationary.

4. Neither time series is covariance stationary and the two series *are not* cointegrated.

5. Neither time series is covariance stationary and the two series *are* cointegrated.

In scenario 1 the analyst can use linear regression, and the coefficients should be statistically reliable, but regressions in scenarios 2 and 3 will not be reliable. Whether linear regression can be used in scenarios 4 and 5 depends upon whether the two time series are *cointegrated*.

Cointegration

Cointegration means that two time series are economically linked (related to the same macro variables) or follow the same trend and that relationship is not expected to change. If two time series are cointegrated, the error term from regressing one on the other is covariance stationary and the *t*-tests are reliable. This means that scenario 5 will produce reliable regression estimates, whereas scenario 4 will not.

To test whether two time series are cointegrated, we regress one variable on the other using the following model:

$$y_t = b_0 + b_1 x_t + \varepsilon$$
where:
y_t = value of time series y at time t
x_t = value of time series x at time t

The residuals are tested for a unit root using the Dickey Fuller test with critical *t*-values calculated by Engle and Granger (i.e., the DF–EG test). If the test rejects the null hypothesis of a unit root, we say the error terms generated by the two time series are covariance stationary and the two series are cointegrated. If the two series are cointegrated, we can use the regression to model their relationship.

PROFESSOR'S NOTE

For the exam, remember that the Dickey Fuller test does not use the standard critical *t*-values we typically use in testing the statistical significance of individual regression coefficients. The DF–EG test further adjusts them to test for cointegration. As with the DF test, you do not have to know critical *t*-values for the DF–EG test. Just remember that like the regular DF test, if the null is rejected, we say the series (of error terms in this case) is covariance stationary and the two time series are cointegrated.

Figure 3.2: Can Linear Regression Be Used to Model the Relationship Between Two Time Series?

		Independent Variable Time Series	
		Is Covariance Stationary	*Is NOT Covariance Stationary*
Dependent Variable Time Series	*Is Covariance Stationary*	Yes	No
	Is NOT Covariance Stationary	No	Yes, IF the two time series are cointegrated

LOS 3.o: Determine an appropriate time-series model to analyze a given investment problem and justify that choice.

CFA® Program Curriculum, Volume 1, page 221

To determine what type of model is best suited to meet your needs, follow these guidelines:

1. Determine your goal.

    ■ Are you attempting to model the relationship of a variable to other variables (e.g., cointegrated time series, cross-sectional multiple regression)?

    ■ Are you trying to model the variable over time (e.g., trend model)?

2. If you have decided on using a time series analysis for an individual variable, plot the values of the variable over time and look for characteristics that would indicate nonstationarity, such as non-constant variance (heteroskedasticity), non-constant mean, seasonality, or structural change.

    A **structural change** is indicated by a significant *shift* in the plotted data at a point in time that seems to divide the data into two or more distinct patterns. (Figure 3.3 shows a data plot that indicates a structural shift in the time series at Point a.) In this example, you have to run two different models, one incorporating the data before and one after that date, and test whether the time series has actually shifted. If the time series has shifted significantly, a single time series encompassing the entire period (i.e., both patterns) will likely produce unreliable results.

Figure 3.3: A Structural Shift in a Time Series

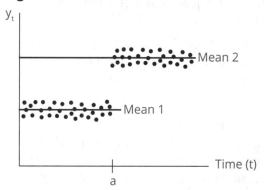

3. If there is no seasonality or structural shift, use a trend model.

   ■ If the data plot on a straight line with an upward or downward slope, use a linear trend model.

   ■ If the data plot in a curve, use a log-linear trend model.

4. Run the trend analysis, compute the residuals, and test for serial correlation using the Durbin Watson test.

   ■ If you detect no serial correlation, *you can use the model.*

   ■ If you detect serial correlation, you must use another model (e.g., AR).

5. If the data has serial correlation, reexamine the data for stationarity before running an AR model. If it is not stationary, treat the data for use in an AR model as follows:

   ■ If the data has a linear trend, first-difference the data.

   ■ If the data has an exponential trend, first-difference the natural log of the data.

   ■ If there is a structural shift in the data, run two separate models as discussed above.

   ■ If the data has a seasonal component, incorporate the seasonality in the AR model as discussed in the following.

6. After first-differencing in 5 previously, if the series is covariance stationary, run an AR(1) model and test for serial correlation and seasonality.

   ■ If there is no remaining serial correlation, *you can use the model.*

   ■ If you still detect serial correlation, incorporate lagged values of the variable (possibly including one for seasonality—e.g., for monthly data, add the 12th lag of the time series) into the AR model until you have removed (i.e., modeled) any serial correlation.

7. Test for ARCH. Regress the square of the residuals on squares of lagged values of the residuals and test whether the resulting coefficient is significantly different from zero.

   ■ If the coefficient is not significantly different from zero, *you can use the model.*

   ■ If the coefficient is significantly different from zero, ARCH is present. Correct using generalized least squares.

8. If you have developed two statistically reliable models and want to determine which is better at forecasting, calculate their out-of-sample RMSE.

MODULE QUIZ 3.5

To best evaluate your performance, enter your quiz answers online.

1. Which of the following is true of modeling a time series that contains two or more distinct periods where the data is fundamentally different?
   A. The optimal data sample period for estimating the time-series model can be calculated mathematically.
   B. To most accurately estimate the time-series model, the entire available time series data set should be used as the sample period.
   C. We have to fit two different models for each of the two distinct periods.

2. Which of the following indicates the presence of Autoregressive Conditional Heteroskedasticity (ARCH) in a time-series model?
   A. The autocorrelations of the error terms are zero at all lags.
   B. The variance of the current error depends on the variance of lagged errors.
   C. The error term shows significant serial correlation at lag 1.

3. Linear regression is least appropriate for modeling the relationship between two time series when:
   A. neither series has a unit root.
   B. one of the time series has a unit root, the other does not.
   C. both series have a unit root, and the time series are cointegrated.

KEY CONCEPTS

LOS 3.a

A time series is a set of observations for a variable over successive periods of time. A time series model captures the time series pattern and allows us to make predictions about the variable in the future.

LOS 3.b

A simple linear trend model is: $y_t = b_0 + b_1 t + \varepsilon_t$, estimated for t = 1, 2, …, T.

A log-linear trend model, $\ln(y_t) = b_0 + b_1 t + \varepsilon_t$, is appropriate for exponential data.

A plot of the data should be used to determine whether a linear or log-linear trend model should be used.

The primary limitation of trend models is that they are not useful if the residuals exhibit serial correlation.

LOS 3.c

A time series is covariance stationary if its mean, variance, and covariances with lagged and leading values do not change over time. Covariance stationarity is a requirement for using AR models.

LOS 3.d

Autoregressive time series multiperiod forecasts are calculated in the same manner as those for other regression models, but since the independent variable consists of a lagged variable, it is necessary to calculate a one-step-ahead forecast before a two-step-ahead forecast may be calculated. The calculation of successive forecasts in this manner is referred to as the chain rule of forecasting.

A one-period-ahead forecast for an AR(1) would be determined in the following manner:

$$\hat{x}_{t+1} = \hat{b}_0 + \hat{b}_1 x_t$$

A two-period-ahead forecast for an AR(1) would be determined in the following manner:

$$\hat{x}_{t+2} = \hat{b}_0 + \hat{b}_1 \hat{x}_{t+1}$$

LOS 3.e

When an AR model is correctly specified, the residual terms will not exhibit serial correlation. If the residuals possess some degree of serial correlation, the AR model that produced the residuals is not the best model for the data being studied and the regression results will be problematic. The procedure to test whether an AR time-series model is correctly specified involves three steps:

1. Estimate the AR model being evaluated using linear regression.

2. Calculate the autocorrelations of the model's residuals.

3. Test whether the autocorrelations are significant.

LOS 3.f

A time series is mean reverting if it tends towards its mean over time. The mean reverting level for an AR(1) model is $\dfrac{b_0}{(1 - b_1)}$.

LOS 3.g

In-sample forecasts are made *within* the range of data used in the estimation. Out-of-sample forecasts are made *outside* of the time period for the data used in the estimation.

The root mean squared error criterion (RMSE) is used to compare the accuracy of autoregressive models in forecasting out-of-sample values. A researcher may have two autoregressive (AR) models, both of which seem to fit the data: an AR(1) model and an AR(2) model. To determine which model will more accurately forecast future values, we calculate the square root of the mean squared error (RMSE). The model with the lower RMSE for the out-of-sample data will have lower forecast error and will be expected to have better predictive power in the future.

LOS 3.h

Most economic and financial time series data are not stationary. The degree of the nonstationarity depends on the length of the series and changes in the underlying economic environment.

LOS 3.i

A random walk time series is one for which the value in one period is equal to the value in another period, plus a random error. A random walk process does not have a mean reverting level and is not stationary.

LOS 3.j

A time series has a unit root if the coefficient on the lagged dependent variable is equal to one. A series with a unit root is not covariance stationary. Economic and finance time series frequently have unit roots. Data with a unit root must be first differenced before being used in a time series model.

LOS 3.k

To determine whether a time series is covariance stationary, we can (1) run an AR model and/or (2) perform the Dickey Fuller test.

LOS 3.l

Seasonality in a time series is tested by calculating the autocorrelations of error terms. A statistically significant lagged error term corresponding to the periodicity of the data indicates seasonality. Seasonality can be corrected by incorporating the appropriate seasonal lag term in an AR model.

If a seasonal lag coefficient is appropriate and corrects the seasonality, the AR model with the seasonal terms will have no statistically significant autocorrelations of error terms.

LOS 3.m

ARCH is present if the variance of the residuals from an AR model are correlated across time. ARCH is detected by estimating $\hat{\epsilon}_t^2 = a_0 + a_1 \hat{\epsilon}_{t-1}^2 + \mu_t$. If a_1 is significant, ARCH exists and the variance of errors can be predicted using: $\hat{\sigma}_{t+1}^2 = \hat{a}_0 + \hat{a}_1 \hat{\epsilon}_t^2$.

LOS 3.n

When working with two time series in a regression: (1) if neither time series has a unit root, then the regression can be used; (2) if only one series has a unit root, the regression results will be invalid; (3) if both time series have a unit root and are cointegrated, then the regression can be used; (4) if both time series have a unit root but are not cointegrated, the regression results will be invalid.

The Dickey Fuller test with critical *t*-values calculated by Engle and Granger is used to determine whether two times series are cointegrated.

LOS 3.o

The RMSE criterion is used to determine which forecasting model will produce the most accurate forecasts. The RMSE equals the square root of the average squared error.

Reading 3

ANSWER KEY FOR MODULE QUIZZES

Module Quiz 3.1

1. **A** With a trend model, the independent variable is time, t. (LOS 3.b)

2. **A** The slope coefficient (b_1) is positive and significantly different from zero indicating an upward trend. (LOS 3.a)

3. **A** The t-statistic to test the statistical significance of the intercept and slope coefficient is the parameter estimate divided by its standard error. We reject the null hypothesis and conclude the coefficients are statistically significant if the absolute value of the t-statistic is greater than the two-tail 5% critical t-value with 43 degrees of freedom, which is 2.02.

$$t_{b_0} = \frac{1,195.6241}{8.9704362} = 133.3$$

$$t_{b_1} = \frac{12.230448}{0.3396171} = 36.0$$

Both the intercept term and the slope coefficient are significantly different from zero at the 5% level because both t-statistics are greater than the critical t-value of 2.02. (LOS 3.a)

4. **C** $\hat{Y}_{46} = \$1,195.6241 + \$12.230448(46) = \$1,758.225$ billion

(LOS 3.a)

5. **A** The Durbin-Watson statistic is used to detect serial correlation in the residuals. The lower critical value for a DW test with one independent variable and 45 observations is 1.48 and the upper critical value is 1.57. The actual DW-statistic is 0.601, which is less than the lower critical value. This indicates the residuals are positively serially correlated. See the previous topic review for details on implementing the Durbin-Watson test. (LOS 3.b)

6. **B** A log-linear model (choice B) is most appropriate for a time series that grows at a relatively constant growth rate. Neither a linear trend model (choice A), nor an AR(1) model (choice C) are appropriate in this case. (LOS 3.b)

Module Quiz 3.2

1. **B** Time series X has a definite upward trend, which once again suggests the expected value of the time series X is not constant, and therefore it is not covariance stationary. (LOS 3.c)

2. **B** Given $x_{t-1} = 16.5$, $\hat{x}_t = 5 + 1.75(16.5) = 33.875$. So, $\hat{x}_{t+1} = 5 + 1.75\hat{x}_t$ $= 5 + 1.75(33.875) = 64.28$. So, $\hat{x}_{t+2} = 5 + 1.75\hat{x}_{t+1} = 5 + 1.75(64.28) = 117.49$. (LOS 3.d)

3. **B**   Out-of-sample performance is the most important indicator of a model's real-world forecasting ability. In-sample forecast performance is less persuasive, because forecasting the past is not difficult. The residuals from the fitted time-series model are another name for the model's in-sample forecast errors. (LOS 3.g)

Module Quiz 3.3

1. **A**   The independent variable is the dependent variable lagged one period, so the model is an AR(1) model. (Module 3.2, LOS 3.d)

2. **C**   The first-differenced series usually does not have a unit root and is, therefore, covariance stationary. (Module 3.3, LOS 3.j)

3. **A**   All random-walk time series have a unit root. Time series with unit root do not have a finite mean-reverting level. (Module 3.3, LOS 3.i)

4. **A**   A random walk process does not have a finite mean-reverting level and hence covariance nonstationary. An AR(1) model cannot be used to fit a covariance nonstationary time series. (Module 3.3, LOS 3.j)

5. **C**   For a unit root test, the null hypothesis is that the time series has a unit root. For testing for unit roots, the Dickey-Fuller (DF) test computes the conventional t-statistic, which is then compared against the revised set of critical values computed by DF. If the test statistic is significant, we reject the null hypothesis (that the time series has a unit root), implying that a unit root is not present. (Module 3.3, LOS 3.k)

Module Quiz 3.4

1. **C**   The standard error of the estimated autocorrelations is $1/\sqrt{T}$, where T is the number of observations (periods). So, if the standard error is given as 0.0632, the number of observations, T, in the time series must be $(1 / 0.0632)^2 \approx 250$. (Module 3.2, LOS 3.e)

2. **A**   The results in the table indicate that the prediction equation is $x_t = 26.8625 + 0.7196x_{t-1}$, which is estimated from an AR(1) model. (Module 3.1, LOS 3.a)

3. **A**   The autocorrelation in the twelfth month is not statistically different from zero. (p-value: $0.5612 > 0.05$) Thus, there appears to be no seasonality. (Module 3.4, LOS 3.l)

4. **A**   If the fourth autocorrelation of the error term differs significantly from 0, this is an indication of seasonality. (Module 3.4, LOS 3.l)

5. **C**   Adding an appropriate lag is an appropriate solution to seasonality. Excluding variables can sometimes be used to solve multicollinearity. Transforming using first-differencing can be a cure for nonstationarity. (Module 3.4, LOS 3.l)

Reading 3

6. **B** The seasonal (annual) lag occurs on a quarterly basis, so the appropriate model is $b_0 + b_1x_{t-1} + b_2x_{t-4} + \varepsilon_t$. The intercept b_0 should be included in the model. (Module 3.4, LOS 3.l)

Module Quiz 3.5

1. **C** To accurately model a time series that contains shifts, it may be necessary to strategically choose a longer or shorter sample period, or to use a first- or second-order autoregressive model. There is no accepted formula for estimating the optimal sample period (though a graphical inspection of the data may be helpful). (LOS 3.o)

2. **B** ARCH is present when the variance of the error depends on the variance of previous errors. A zero autocorrelation of the error term at all lags suggests that an autoregressive model is a good fit to the data. (LOS 3.m)

3. **B** If only one time series has a unit root, we should not use linear regression. If neither time series have unit root, or if both time series have unit root and the time series are cointegrated, linear regression is appropriate to use. (LOS 3.n)

READING 4

Machine Learning

EXAM FOCUS

This topic review discusses the terminology used in advanced statistical models collectively referred to as machine learning. Be familiar with this terminology and the different types of models, their applications in investment decision-making, and their limitations. Specifically, be able to identify the appropriate algorithm that is most suitable for a given problem.

MACHINE LEARNING

The statistical models we have discussed so far rely on a set of assumptions about the distribution of the underlying data. **Machine learning (ML)** requires no such assumptions. Very broadly, ML is defined as the use of algorithms to make decisions by generalizing (or finding patterns) in a given data set. ML performs better than standard statistical approaches when dealing with a large number of variables (high dimension) and when the relationships are nonlinear.

ML terms are as follows:

- **Target variable.** This is the dependent variable (i.e., the y variable). Target variables can be continuous, categorical, or ordinal.

- **Features.** These are the independent variables (i.e., the x variables).

- **Training data set.** This is the sample used to fit the model.

- **Hyperparameter.** This is a model input specified by the researcher.

Video covering this content is available online.

MODULE 4.1: TYPES OF LEARNING AND OVERFITTING PROBLEMS

LOS 4.a: Describe supervised machine learning, unsupervised machine learning, and deep learning.

CFA® Program Curriculum, Volume 1, page 254

Supervised learning uses labeled training data to guide the ML program toward superior forecasting accuracy. To identify earnings manipulators, for example, a large collection of attributes could be provided for known manipulators and for known nonmanipulators. A computer program could then be used to identify patterns that identify manipulators in another data set. Multiple regression (discussed in an earlier topic review) is an example of supervised learning. Typical tasks for supervised learning include classification and regression. If the target variable is continuous, the model involved is a regression model. Classification models are used in cases where the target variable is categorical or ordinal (e.g., ranking). Algorithms can be designed for binary classification (e.g., classifying companies as likely to default vs. not likely to default) or multicategory classification (e.g., a ratings class for bonds).

In **unsupervised learning**, the ML program is not given labeled training data; instead, inputs (i.e., features) are provided without any conclusions about those inputs. In the absence of any target variable, the program seeks out structure or interrelationships in the data. Clustering is an example of an unsupervised ML program.

Deep learning algorithms are used for complex tasks such as image recognition, natural language processing, and so on. Programs that learn from their own prediction errors are called **reinforced learning** algorithms. Both of these kinds of algorithms are based on **neural networks**, a group of ML algorithms applied to problems with significant nonlinearities. We will discuss these kinds of algorithms in detail in a later LOS.

Figure 4.1 summarizes the suitability of various ML algorithms.

Figure 4.1: ML Algorithm Types

Variables	ML Algorithm Type	
	Supervised (Target Variable)	Unsupervised (No Target Variable)
Continuous	**Regression** ■ Linear; Penalized Regression/LASSO ■ Logistic ■ Classification and Regression Tree (CART) ■ Random Forest	**Dimensionality Reduction** ■ Principal Components Analysis (PCA) **Clustering** ■ K-Means ■ Hierarchical
Categorical	**Classification** ■ Logit ■ Support Vector Machine (SVM) ■ K-Nearest Neighbor (KNN) ■ Classification and Regression Tree (CART)	**Dimensionality Reduction** ■ Principal Components Analysis (PCA) **Clustering** ■ K-Means ■ Hierarchical
Continuous or Categorical	Neural Networks Deep Learning Reinforcement Learning	Neural Networks Deep Learning Reinforcement Learning

Source: 2020 Level II CFA® Program Curriculum, Volume 1, page 468, ©2019, CFA Institute

Figure 4.2 shows the steps involved in selecting the appropriate ML algorithm to use, based on the problem to be solved and the characteristics of the data.

Figure 4.2: Choice of Appropriate ML Algorithm

Step 1: Decide if the data set is complex (too many features). If so, apply a dimension reduction algorithm before proceeding to step 2.

Step 2: Decide if the problem is that of classification. If yes, go to step 3. If no, (i.e., it is a numerical prediction problem):
   – Use penalized regression if the data is linear.
   – Or, for nonlinear and complex data, use CART, random forests, or neural networks.

Step 3: Is it supervised classification? If no, go to step 4. For supervised classification:
   – For linear data, use KNN or SVM.
   – For complex nonlinear data, use CART, random forests, or neural networks.

Step 4: For unsupervised classification:
   – For linear data, use *k*-means if the number of categories is known. If the number of categories is not known, use hierarchical clustering.
   – For complex nonlinear data, use neural networks.

We will discuss these ML algorithms in the remainder of this topic review.

Reading 4

LOS 4.b: Describe overfitting and identify methods of addressing it.

CFA® Program Curriculum, Volume 1, page 259

Overfitting is an issue with supervised ML that results when a large number of features (i.e., independent variables) are included in the data sample. Overfitting has occurred when the noise in the target variables seems to improve the model fit (i.e., randomness is misperceived to be a pattern, resulting in high in-sample R-squared). Overfitting the model will decrease the accuracy of model forecasts on other (out-of-sample) data—overfit models do not **generalize** well to new data (i.e., out-of-sample R-squared will be low).

PROFESSOR'S NOTE

When a model generalizes well, it means that the model retains its explanatory power when it is applied to new (i.e., out-of-sample) data.

To measure how well a model generalizes, data analysts create three nonoverlapping data sets: (1) **training sample** (used to develop the model), (2) **validation sample** (used for tuning the model), and (3) **test sample** (used for evaluating the model using new data). In-sample prediction errors occur with the training sample, while prediction errors in the validation and test samples are known as the out-of-sample errors. Data scientists then decompose these errors into the following:

- **Bias error**. This is the in-sample error resulting from models with a poor fit.
- **Variance error**. This is the out-of-sample error resulting from overfitted models that do not generalize well.
- **Base error**. These are residual errors due to random noise.

A **learning curve** plots the accuracy rate (i.e., 1 − error rate) in the validation or test sample versus the size of the training sample. A robust, well-generalizing model will show an improving accuracy rate as the sample size is increased, and the in-sample and out-of-sample error rates will converge toward a *desired* accuracy level, as shown in the third panel of Figure 4.3. Models with high bias error (first panel) will see the error rates converge, but far below the desired level. Models with high variance error (second panel) will see only the in-sample accuracy rate converge toward the desired level, while the out-of-sample accuracy rate lags far behind.

Figure 4.3: Accuracy Rate Patterns

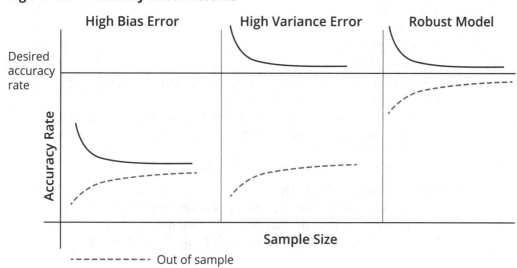

Variance error increases with model complexity, while bias error decreases with complexity. Data scientists often express this as a tradeoff between *cost* and *complexity*. An optimal level of complexity minimizes the total error and is a key part of successful model generalization.

To reduce the problem of overfitting, data scientists use complexity reduction and cross validation. In complexity reduction, a penalty is imposed to exclude features that are not meaningfully contributing to out-of-sample prediction accuracy. This penalty value increases with the number of independent variables (features) used by the model.

For a model to learn sufficiently, researchers must ensure that the training data set is both large and representative of the population. The validation sample, similarly, should be large and representative to properly test the model. A sampling technique known as **cross validation** estimates out-of-sample error rates directly from the validation sample.

In a **k-fold cross validation**, the sample is randomly divided equally into *k* parts. The training sample comprises (k − 1) parts, with one part left for validation. Error is then measured for the model in each of the parts. This process is repeated *k* times, and the average in-sample and out-of-sample error rates are compiled.

MODULE QUIZ 4.1
To best evaluate your performance, enter your quiz answers online.

1. Which statement about target variables is *most accurate*?
   A. They can be continuous, ordinal, or categorical.
   B. They are not specified for supervised learning.
   C. They refer to independent variables.

2. Which statement *most accurately* describes supervised learning?
   A. It uses labeled training data.
   B. It requires periodic human intervention.
   C. It is best suited for classification.

Reading 4

3. A model that has poor in-sample explanatory power is *most likely* to have a high:
    A. bias error.
    B. variance error.
    C. base error.

4. The problem of overfitting a model would *least appropriately* be addressed by:
    A. imposing a penalty on included features that do not add to explanatory power of the model.
    B. using cross validation.
    C. using a smaller sample.

5. Cross validation occurs when:
    A. training and validation samples change over the learning cycle.
    B. prediction is tested in another heterogeneous sample.
    C. the performance parameter is set by another algorithm.

Video covering this content is available online.

MODULE 4.2: SUPERVISED LEARNING ALGORITHMS

LOS 4.c: Describe supervised machine learning algorithms—including penalized regression, support vector machine, k-nearest neighbor, classification and regression tree, ensemble learning, and random forest—and determine the problems for which they are best suited.

CFA® Program Curriculum, Volume 1, page 264

We will now describe some of the common supervised ML algorithms and their applications:

1. **Penalized regressions.** Penalized regression models reduce the problem of overfitting by imposing a penalty based on the number of features used by the model. The penalty value increases with the number of independent variables (features) used. Imposing such a penalty can exclude features that are not meaningfully contributing to out-of-sample prediction accuracy (i.e., it makes the model more parsimonious). Penalized regression models seek to minimize the sum of square errors (SSE) *as well as* a penalty value.

    Least absolute shrinkage and selection operator (LASSO). This is a popular penalized regression model. In addition to minimizing SSE, LASSO minimizes the sum of the absolute values of the slope coefficients. In such a framework, there is a tradeoff between reducing the SSE (by increasing the number of features) and the penalty imposed on the inclusion of more features. Through optimization, LASSO automatically eliminates the least predictive features. A penalty term, λ (lambda), is the hyperparameter that determines the balance between overfitting the model and keeping it parsimonious.

    A related method to reduce statistical variability in a high dimension data estimation problem is **regularization**. Regularization forces the beta coefficients of nonperforming features toward zero.

Investment analysts use LASSO to build parsimonious models. Regularization can be applied to nonlinear models, such as the estimation of a stable covariance matrix that can be used for mean-variance optimization.

PROFESSOR'S NOTE

In everyday usage, *parsimonious* means stingy or penny-pinching. In the world of statistics, a parsimonious model is one that accomplishes the required level of explanation using as few predictor variables as possible.

2. **Support vector machine (SVM).** SVM is a linear classification algorithm that separates the data into one of two possible classifiers (e.g., sell vs. buy). Given n features, an n-dimensional hyperplane divides a sample into one of the two possible classifications. SVM maximizes the probability of making a correct prediction by determining the boundary that is farthest away from all the observations. This boundary comprises a discriminant boundary as well as margins on the side of the boundary. The margins are determined by the support vectors, observations that are closest to the boundary. Misclassified observations in the training data are handled via **soft margin classification**. This adaptation optimizes the tradeoff between a wider margin and classification error. We should note that a more complex, nonlinear model can be used for classification as opposed to SVM to reduce classification error, but this requires more features and may result in overfitting.

Applications of SVM in investment management include classifying debt issuers into likely-to-default versus not-likely-to-default issuers, stocks-to-short versus not-to-short, and even classifying text (from news articles or company press releases) as positive or negative.

3. **K-nearest neighbor (KNN).** More commonly used in classification (but sometimes in regression), this technique is used to classify an observation based on *nearness* to the observations in the training sample. The researcher specifies the value of k, the hyperparameter, triggering the algorithm to look for the k observations in the sample that are closest to the new observation that is being classified. The specification of k is important because if it is too small, it will result in a high error rate, and if it is too large, it will dilute the result by averaging across too many outcomes. Also, if k is even, there may be ties, with no clear winner. KNN is a powerful, nonparametric model, but it requires a specification of what it means to be *near*. Analysts need to have a clear understanding of the data and the underlying business to be able to specify the distance metric that needs to be optimized. Another issue with KNN is the specification of feature set; inclusion of irrelevant or correlated features can skew the results.

Investment applications of KNN include predicting bankruptcy, assigning a bond to a ratings class, predicting stock prices, and creating customized indices.

4. **Classification and regression trees (CART).** Classification trees are appropriate when the target variable is categorical, and are typically used when the target is binary (e.g., an IPO will be successful vs. not successful). Logit models, discussed in a previous reading, are also used when the target is binary, but are ill-suited when there are significant nonlinear relationships among variables. In

Reading 4

such cases, classification trees may be a viable alternative. Regression trees are appropriate when the target is continuous.

Classification trees assign observations to one of two possible classifications at each node. At the top of the tree, the top feature (i.e., the one most important in explaining the target) is selected, and a cutoff value c is estimated. Observations with feature values greater than c are assigned to one classification, and the remainder are assigned to the other classification. The resulting classes are then evaluated based on a second feature, and again divided into one of two classes. Every successive classification should result in a lower estimation error than the nodes that preceded it. The tree stops when the error cannot be reduced further, resulting in a terminal node as shown in Figure 4.4.

Figure 4.4: Classification Tree Example

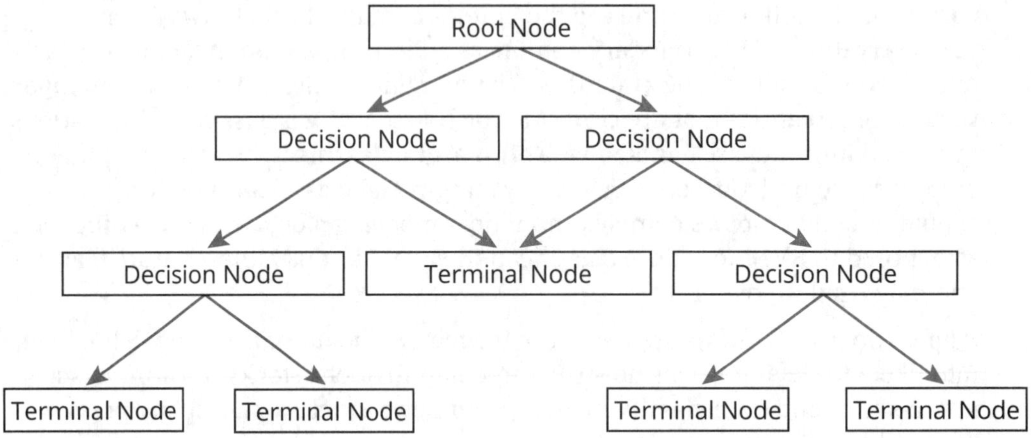

It should be noted that a feature may reappear in lower nodes of a tree with a different cutoff value if it helps in classification. The features and cutoff values are learned by the algorithm based on labeled training data.

To avoid overfitting, regularization criteria such as maximum tree depth, maximum number of decision nodes, and so on are specified by the researcher. Alternatively, sections of tree with minimal explanatory power are **pruned**.

CART is popular because it provides a visual explanation of the prediction process, compared to other algorithms that are often described as black boxes due to their opacity.

Investment applications of CART include detecting fraudulent financial statements and selecting stocks and bonds.

5. **Ensemble and Random Forest.** Ensemble learning is the technique of combining predictions from multiple models rather than a single model. The ensemble method results in a lower average error rate because the different models cancel out noise. Two kinds of ensemble methods are used: aggregation of heterogeneous learners and aggregation of homogenous learners.

Under aggregation of heterogeneous learners, different algorithms are combined together via a **voting classifier**. The different algorithms each get a vote, and then we go with whichever answer gets the most votes. Ideally, the models selected will have sufficient diversity in approach, resulting in a greater level of confidence in the predictions.

Under aggregation of homogenous learners, the same algorithm is used, but on different training data. The different training data samples (used by the same model) can be derived by **bootstrap aggregating** or **bagging**. The process relies on generating random samples (bags) with replacement from the initial training sample.

Random forest is a variant of classification trees whereby a large number of classification trees are trained using data bagged from the same data set. A randomly selected subset of features is used in creating each tree, and each tree is slightly different from the others. The process of using multiple classification trees to determine the final classification is akin to the practice of crowdsourcing. Because each tree only uses a subset of features, random forests can mitigate the problem of overfitting. Using random forests can increase the signal-to-noise ratio because errors across different trees tend to cancel each other out. A drawback of random forests is that the transparency of CART is lost, and we are back to the black-box category of algorithms.

Investment applications of random forest include factor-based asset allocation, and prediction models for the success of an IPO.

MODULE QUIZ 4.2

To best evaluate your performance, enter your quiz answers online.

1. A general linear regression model that focuses on reduction of the total number of features used is *best* described as:
   A. a clustering model.
   B. a deep learning model.
   C. a penalized regression model.

2. A machine learning technique that can be applied to predict either a categorical target variable or a continuous target variable is *most likely* to describe:
   A. a support vector machine.
   B. a classification and regression tree (CART).
   C. a logit model.

3. An algorithm to assign a bond to a credit rating category is *least likely* to use:
   A. clustering.
   B. classification and regression tree (CART).
   C. K-nearest neighbor (KNN).

4. A fixed-income analyst is designing a model to categorize bonds into one of five ratings classifications. The analyst uses 12 fundamental variables and 2 technical variables to help her in the task. The number of features used by the analyst is *closest* to:
   A. 14 features.
   B. 70 features.
   C. 120 features.

Video covering this content is available online.

MODULE 4.3: UNSUPERVISED LEARNING ALGORITHMS AND OTHER MODELS

LOS 4.d: Describe unsupervised machine learning algorithms—including principal components analysis, k-means clustering, and hierarchical clustering—and determine the problems for which they are best suited.

CFA® Program Curriculum, Volume 1, page 287

We now discuss some of the following examples of unsupervised learning and their applications in the investment field:

1. **Principal component analysis (PCA).** Problems associated with too much noise often arise when the number of features in a data set (i.e., its dimension) is excessive. Dimension reduction seeks to reduce this noise by discarding those attributes that contain little information. One method is PCA, which summarizes the information in a large number of correlated factors into a much smaller set of uncorrelated factors. These uncorrelated factors, called **eigenvectors**, are linear combinations of the original features. Each eigenvector has an **eigenvalue**—the proportion of total variance in the data set explained by the eigenvector. The first factor in PCA would be the one with the highest eigenvalue, and would represent the most important factor. The second factor is the second-most important (i.e., has the second-highest eigenvalue) and so on, up to the number of uncorrelated factors specified by the researcher. **Scree plots** show the proportion of total variance explained by each of the principal components. In practice, the smallest number of principal components that collectively capture 85%–95% of the total variance are retained. Since the principal components are linear combinations of the original data set, they cannot be easily labeled or interpreted, resulting in a black-box approach.

2. **Clustering.** Given a data set, *clustering* is the process of grouping observations into categories based on similarities in their attributes (called cohesion). For example, stocks can be assigned to different categories based on their past performance, rather than using standard sector classifiers (e.g., finance, healthcare, technology, etc.). In practice, human judgment plays a role in defining what is similar. Euclidian distance, the straight-line distance between two observations, is one common metric that is used. Common types of clustering include *k*-means clustering and hierarchical clustering.

   K-means clustering partitions observations into *k* nonoverlapping clusters, where *k* is a hyperparameter (i.e., set by the researcher). Each cluster has a centroid (the center of the cluster), and each new observation is assigned to a cluster based on its proximity to the centroid. Initially, *k* centroids are randomly selected, and clustering starts. As a new observation gets assigned to a cluster, its centroid is recalculated, which may result in reassignment of some observations, thus resulting in a new centroid and so forth until all observations are assigned and no new reassignment is made. One limitation of this type of algorithm is that the hyperparameter *k* is chosen before clustering starts, meaning that one has to have some idea about the nature of the data set. K-means clustering is used in investment management to classify thousands of securities based on patterns in high dimensional data.

Hierarchical clustering builds a hierarchy of clusters without any predefined number of clusters. In an **agglomerative** (or bottom-up) **clustering**, we start with one observation as its own cluster and add other similar observations to that group, or form another nonoverlapping cluster. A **divisive** (or top-down) **clustering** algorithm starts with one giant cluster, and then it partitions that cluster into smaller and smaller clusters.

Clustering can be used in investment management for diversification by investing in assets from multiple clusters. Clustering can also be useful in analysis of portfolio risk, as concentration is evidenced by a large portfolio allocation to one cluster. While clusters are themselves not clearly labeled or defined, clustering can be valuable in uncovering hidden structures or similarities between observations in complex data sets.

> **EXAMPLE: Application of machine learning to ESG investing**
>
> ESG (environmental, social, and governance) factor-based investing is lately becoming popular owing to changes in investor preferences. The governance factor which focuses on corporate board actions in the interests of shareholders, can be objectively observed and measured. The social and environmental impact of a company's actions is more subjective. Machine learning and artificial intelligence techniques can use natural language processors to parse through corporate disclosures in text, audio, and video formats to collate the information. For example, mentions of words such as "human capital," "living wage," and "D&I" can be collected to represent a company's response to social responsibilities. Similarly, "sustainable," "recycle," "green," and similar words could indicate the company's intentions toward environmental goals.
>
> Supervised learning algorithms such as logistic regression, SVM, CART, random forests, or neural networks can then be used to generate ESG scores.

LOS 4.e: Describe neural networks, deep learning nets, and reinforcement learning.

CFA® Program Curriculum, Volume 1, page 302

Neural Networks

Useful in supervised regression and classification models, **neural networks** (NNs), (also called artificial neural networks, or ANNs) are constructed as nodes connected by links. The input layer consists of nodes with values for the features (independent variables). These values are scaled so that the information from multiple nodes is comparable and can be used to calculate a weighted average. The input values from the nodes in the input layer connect to a second set of nodes in the hidden layer. Typically, several inputs are connected to a particular hidden node, meaning that the node receives multiple input values via the links. The nodes that follow the input variables are called **neurons** because they process the input information. These neurons comprise a **summation operator** that collates the information (as a weighted average) and passes it on to a (typically nonlinear) **activation function**, to generate a value from the input values. This value is then passed forward to other neurons in subsequent hidden layers (a process called **forward propagation**). A related process, **backward propagation**, is employed to revise the weights used in the summation operator as the network learns from its errors.

There may be multiple hidden layers with linked nodes. The multiple links between the information in the input layer and multiple nodes in the hidden layers (each with its own activation function) allow the neural network to model complex, nonlinear functions. There is typically a single node in the output layer that is the prediction of the model.

The researcher must determine the structure of the network. For example, for a network with three inputs (features), we would have three nodes in the input layer. We might specify a single hidden layer with four nodes, in addition to an output layer with a single node. This structure—3, 4, and 1—is set by the researcher, and referred to as the hyperparameters of the neural network. Hyperparameters may be revised based on the out-of-sample performance of the model.

Deep Learning Networks (DLNs)

Deep learning networks (DLNs) are neural networks with many hidden layers (often more than 20). DLNs are often used for image, pattern, and character recognition. The last layer in a DLN calculates the expected probability of an observation belonging to a category, and the observation is assigned to the category with the highest probability. Additional applications of DLNs include credit card fraud detection, autonomous cars, natural language processing, and investment decision-making.

In one study using the six input parameters of the Black-Scholes model, a DLN was able to predict option values with model R^2 of 99.8%. Other studies have used DLNs in investment decision-making using standard factors (e.g., book-to-market values, operating income to market capitalization) to beat strategies using standard factor models.

The popularity of DLNs can be linked to advances in analytical methods, increases in computing speed, and availability of large quantities of machine-readable data.

Reinforcement Learning (RL)

Reinforcement learning (RL) algorithms have an agent that seeks to maximize a defined reward given defined constraints. The RL agent does not rely on labeled training data, but rather learns based on immediate feedback from (millions of) trials. When applied to the ancient game of Go, DeepMind's AlphaGo algorithm was able to beat the reigning world champion. The efficacy of RL in investment decision-making is not yet conclusive.

MODULE QUIZ 4.3

To best evaluate your performance, enter your quiz answers online.

1. Image recognition problems are *best* suited for which category of machine learning (ML) algorithms?
   A. Hierarchical clustering.
   B. Unsupervised learning.
   C. Deep learning.

2. Which of the following is *least likely* to be described as a black-box approach to machine learning (ML)?
   A. Principal component analysis (PCA).
   B. Classification trees.
   C. Random forests.

3. An analyst wants to categorize an investment universe of 1,000 stocks into 10 dissimilar groups. The machine learning (ML) algorithm most suited for this task is:
   A. a classification and regression tree (CART).
   B. clustering.
   C. regression.

Reading 4

KEY CONCEPTS

LOS 4.a

With supervised learning, inputs and outputs are identified for the computer, and the algorithm uses this labeled training data to model relationships.

With unsupervised learning, the computer is not given labeled data; rather, it is provided unlabeled data that the algorithm uses to determine the structure of the data.

With deep learning algorithms, algorithms such as neural networks and reinforced learning learn from their own prediction errors, and they are used for complex tasks such as image recognition and natural language processing.

LOS 4.b

In supervised learning, overfitting results from a large number of independent variables (features), resulting in an overly complex model that may have generalized random noise that improves in-sample forecasting accuracy. However, overfit models do not generalize well to new data (i.e., low out-of-sample R-squared).

To reduce the problem of overfitting, data scientists use complexity reduction and cross validation. In complexity reduction, a penalty is imposed to exclude features that are not meaningfully contributing to out-of-sample prediction accuracy. This penalty value increases with the number of independent variables used by the model.

LOS 4.c

Supervised learning algorithms include:

- Penalized regression. Reduces overfitting by imposing a penalty on and reducing the nonperforming features.

- Support vector machine (SVM). A linear classification algorithm that separates the data into one of two possible classifiers based on a model-defined hyperplane.

- K-nearest neighbor (KNN). Used to classify an observation based on nearness to the observations in the training sample.

- Classification and regression tree (CART). Used for classifying categorical target variables when there are significant nonlinear relationships among variables.

- Ensemble learning. Combines predictions from multiple models, resulting in a lower average error rate.

- Random forest. A variant of the classification tree whereby a large number of classification trees are trained using data bagged from the same data set.

LOS 4.d

Unsupervised learning algorithms include:

- Principal components analysis. Summarizes the information in a large number of correlated factors into a much smaller set of uncorrelated factors, called eigenvectors.

- K-means clustering. Partitions observations into k nonoverlapping clusters; a centroid is associated with each cluster.

- Hierarchical clustering. Builds a hierarchy of clusters without any predefined number of clusters.

LOS 4.e

Neural networks comprise an input layer, hidden layers (which process the input), and an output layer. The nodes in the hidden layer are called neurons, which comprise a summation operator (that calculates a weighted average) and an activation function (a nonlinear function).

Deep learning networks are neural networks with many hidden layers (more than 20), useful for pattern, speech, and image recognition.

Reinforcement learning (RL) algorithms seek to learn from their own errors, thus maximizing a defined reward.

Reading 4

ANSWER KEY FOR MODULE QUIZZES

Module Quiz 4.1

1. **A** Target variables (i.e., dependent variables) can be continuous, ordinal, or categorical. Target variables are not specified for unsupervised learning. (LOS 4.a)

2. **A** Supervised learning uses labeled training data, and it does not need human intervention. Classification algorithms can be used for both supervised and unsupervised learning. (LOS 4.a)

3. **A** Bias error is the in-sample error resulting from models with a poor fit. (LOS 4.b)

4. **C** To reduce the problem of overfitting, data scientists use complexity reduction and cross validation. In complexity reduction, a penalty is imposed to exclude features that are not meaningfully contributing to out-of-sample prediction accuracy. (LOS 4.b)

5. **A** In cross validation, the training and validation samples are randomly generated every learning cycle. (LOS 4.b)

Module Quiz 4.2

1. **C** Penalized regression imposes a penalty based on the number of features used in a model. Penalized regression is used to construct parsimonious models. (LOS 4.c)

2. **B** Classification and regression tree (CART) is a supervised machine learning technique that can be applied to predict either a continuous target variable (producing a regression tree), or a categorical target variable (producing a classification tree). CART is most commonly applied to binary classification or regression. Support vector machines and logit models are used only for categorical target variable. (LOS 4.c)

3. **A** CART and KNN are supervised learning algorithms used for classification. Clustering is an unsupervised learning algorithm (i.e., it does not use labeled training data for ratings such as AAA, AA, etc.) for grouping similar observations. (LOS 4.c)

4. **A** The analyst is using 12 fundamental variables and 2 technical variables for a total of 14 features. (LOS 4.c)

©2021 Kaplan, Inc.

Module Quiz 4.3

1. **C** Deep learning algorithms are used for complex tasks such as image recognition and natural language processing. (LOS 4.e)

2. **B** Classification trees are popular because they provide a visual explanation of the predictive process. Random forests and PCA do not provide clear guidance about the features used to classify observations (random forests) or what the principal components represent, resulting in the black-box descriptor for both algorithms. (LOS 4.c, 4.d)

3. **B** Since the researcher is not providing any labeled training data about the 1,000 stocks, we have to use an unsupervised learning algorithm. Both regression and CART are supervised learning algorithms. Clustering, an unsupervised learning algorithm, is suitable for this task. (LOS 4.c)

Reading 4

READING

5

Big Data Projects

EXAM FOCUS

This topic review is a very broad overview of the usage of big data analysis for financial forecasting. Candidates should understand (1) the terminology used and the processes involved in big data projects, (2) the requirements and limitations of the techniques discussed, and (3) how to evaluate a model's performance.

INTRODUCTION

Big data is characterized by the three *V*s of volume, variety, and velocity:

- *Volume* refers to the quantity of data. Big data refers to a huge volume of data.

- *Variety* refers to data sources. Big data is collected from various sources: user-generated, traditional transactional, emails, images, clickstreams, and so on. The collection of various data presents tremendous opportunities as well as concerns, such as privacy protection.

- *Velocity* refers to the speed with which the data is created and collected (e.g., all the social media postings created during a specified time interval).

When used for generating inferences, an additional characteristic, the **veracity** or validity of the data, needs to be considered. Not all data sources are reliable, and the researcher has to separate quality from quantity to generate robust forecasts.

Structured data (e.g., balance sheet data for companies) is neatly organized in rows and columns. **Unstructured data** (e.g., text from SEC filings) is unorganized, and the machine learning (ML) algorithm has to sift through the noise to pick out information.

Video covering this
content is available
online.

MODULE 5.1: DATA ANALYSIS STEPS

LOS 5.a: Identify and explain steps in a data analysis project.

CFA® Program Curriculum, Volume 1, page 329

To illustrate the steps involved in analyzing data for financial forecasting, we will use an example of a consumer credit scoring model in the following five steps:

1. *Conceptualization of the modeling task.* This step requires us to define the problem at hand, the output of the model, how the model will be used and for whom, and whether the model will be embedded in existing (or new) business processes. In our example, the purpose of the model is to accurately measure the credit risk for a borrower.

2. *Data collection.* For financial forecasting, usually structured, numeric data is collected from internal and external sources. Credit scoring models may use past repayment history, employment history, income, and other relevant variables about a borrower. The researcher has to determine which sources (internal or external) to use to collect this data.

3. *Data preparation and wrangling.* This step involves cleaning the data set and preparing it for the model. Cleaning the data set includes addressing any missing values or verification of any out-of-range values. Preprocessing data may involve aggregating, filtering, or extracting relevant variables. For the credit scoring model, rules may be used to fill in the gaps where data is either missing or deemed to be inaccurate.

4. *Data exploration.* This step involves feature selection and engineering as well as initial (i.e., exploratory) data analysis. In a credit scoring model, several variables may be combined to form an ability-to-pay score.

5. *Model training.* This step involves determining the appropriate ML algorithm to use, evaluating the algorithm using a training data set, and tuning the model. The choice of the model depends on the nature of the relationship between the features and the target variable.

These five steps are iterative. Depending on the quality of the output, the researcher can go back and tweak any of the steps involved to improve the model. For example, the researcher may revisit the data exploration step to reengineer the features selected for the model.

The steps involved need to be modified in order to analyze unstructured, text-based data. For example, suppose the researcher wants to also incorporate a borrower's social media posts in the determination of credit scores. The first four steps would then be modified as follows:

1. *Text problem formulation.* The analyst will determine the problem and identify the exact inputs and output of the model. The analyst also has to determine how the output will be used.

2. *Data collection (curation).* This is determining the sources of data to be used (e.g., web scouring, specific social media sites). If using supervised learning, annotating a reliable target variable is also necessary (e.g., specifying which text is associated with negative or positive scoring of credit risk).

3. *Text preparation and wrangling.* This requires preprocessing the stream(s) of unstructured data to make it usable by traditional structured modeling methods.

4. *Text exploration.* This involves test visualization as well as text feature selection and engineering.

The output of a model using unstructured data may then be used in isolation, or combined with other structured variables as an input into another model.

LOS 5.b: Describe **objectives, steps, and examples of preparing and wrangling data.**

CFA® Program Curriculum, Volume 1, page 333

This critical step involves cleansing and organizing raw data for use in a model, and takes most of the project's time and resources. Once a problem is defined, appropriate data to be collected is identified with the help of domain experts. Data collection involves downloading data from internal and external sources. While accessing a database, appropriate caution must be exercised to ensure data validity. **README files** associated with a database usually contain information about how, what, and where data is stored. External data can also be obtained from third-party vendors using an **application programming interface (API)**. External data comes with a price, but saves time and money in the data wrangling step. One issue with using external data in financial forecasting is that other market participants can use the same data, diminishing the firm's proprietary advantage.

Data cleansing deals with reducing errors in the raw data. For structured data, errors in raw data include:

- Missing values.
- Invalid values (i.e., data is outside of a meaningful range).
- Inaccurate values.
- Non-uniform values due to use of wrong format or unit of measurement.
- Duplicate observations.

Data cleansing is accomplished via automated, rules-based algorithms as well as human intervention. **Metadata** (summary data) for the raw data set may serve as a starting point for error identification. Observations with erroneous values that cannot be cleansed would be dropped.

Data wrangling involves preprocessing data for model use. Preprocessing includes data transformation and scaling.

Data transformation types include:

- Extraction (e.g., extracting number of years employed based on dates provided).
- Aggregation, which involves consolidating two related variables into one, using appropriate weights.
- Filtration, which involves removing irrelevant observations.

Reading 5

■ Selection, which involves removing features (i.e., data columns) not needed for processing.

■ Conversion of data of diverse types (e.g., nominal, ordinal).

Outliers in the data set can be identified via statistical techniques (e.g., any value further than three standard deviations from the mean) and replaced with algorithm-determined values. Alternatively, the observation may be deleted. One approach to removing outliers is known as **trimming**, whereby the highest and lowest *x*% of observations are excluded. In **winsorization**, extreme values may be replaced by the maximum value allowable for that variable.

Conversion of data features to a common unit of measurement is known as **scaling**. Some ML algorithms (e.g., neural networks, SVM) require features to be homogenous (i.e., feature values in the same range). Two common methods of scaling are **normalization** and **standardization**.

Normalization scales variable values between 0 and 1.

$$\text{normalized } X_i = \frac{X_i - X_{min}}{X_{max} - X_{min}}$$

Standardization centers the variables at 0 and scales them as units of standard deviations from the mean.

$$\text{standardized } X_i = \frac{X_i - \mu}{\sigma}$$

A standardized variable has a normal distribution with a mean of 0 and a standard deviation of 1. A standardized variable value of +1.22 is interpreted as having a value of 1.22 standard deviations above its mean.

Unlike normalization, standardization is not sensitive to outliers, but assumes that the variable is normally distributed.

LOS 5.e: Describe preparing, wrangling, and exploring text-based data for financial forecasting.

CFA® Program Curriculum, Volume 1, page 369

Unstructured, text-based data is more suitable for human use rather than for processing by a computer. For analysis, unstructured data has to be converted into structured data. **Text processing** is the cleansing and preprocessing of text-based data.

Text Preparation or Cleansing

Text cleansing involves the following steps:

1. *Remove HTML tags.* Text collected from web pages has embedded HTML tags, which may need to be removed before processing. A **regular expression (regex)** is a text string used to identify characters in a particular order.

2. *Remove punctuations.* Text analysis usually does not need punctuations, so these need to be removed as well. Some punctuations (e.g., %, $, ?) may be needed for analysis, and if so, they are replaced with annotations (i.e., textual expressions) for model training.

3. *Remove numbers.* Digits are removed or replaced with annotations to let the ML program know that a number is present, but its value is not important in the analysis. If the value of a number is important for analysis, such values are first extracted via text applications.

4. *Remove white spaces.* Extra formatting-related white spaces (e.g., tabs, indents) do not serve any purpose in text processing and are removed.

Text Wrangling (Preprocessing)

Cleansed text is then normalized using the following steps:

1. *Lowercasing.* So as to not discriminate between *market* and *Market*.

2. *Removal of stop words.* In some ML applications, stop words such as *the*, *is*, and so on do not carry any semantic meaning; hence, they are removed to reduce the number of tokens in the training data.

3. *Stemming.* This is a rules-based algorithm that converts all variations of a word into a common value. For example, *integrate*, *integration*, and *integrating* are all assigned a common value of *integrat*. While stemming makes the text confusing for human processing, it is ideally suited for machines.

4. *Lemmatization.* This involves the conversion of inflected forms of a word into its *lemma* (i.e., morphological root). Lemmatization is similar to stemming, but is more computationally advanced and resource intensive.

In text wrangling, a **token** is a word, and **tokenization** is the process of splitting a sentence into tokens. For example, consider the sentence, "It is a beautiful day." This may be assigned five tokens: (1) it, (2) is, (3) a, (4) beautiful, and (5) day.

After the data is cleansed and normalized, a **bag-of-words (BOW)** procedure is applied, which simply collects all the words or tokens without regard to the sequence of occurrence. A **document term matrix** is then used to convert the unstructured data into structured data. In this matrix, each text document is a row, and the columns are represented by tokens. The cell value represents the number of occurrences of a token in a document (i.e., row).

If the sequence of text is important, **N-grams** can be used to represent word sequences. A two-word sequence is a bigram, a three-word sequence is trigram, and so forth. Consider the sentence, "The market is up today." Bigrams of this sentence include "the_market," "market_is," "is_up," and "up_today." BOW is then applied to the bigrams instead of the original words. N-gram implementation will affect the normalization of the BOW because stop words will not be removed.

Reading 5

MODULE QUIZ 5.1

To best evaluate your performance, enter your quiz answers online.

1. Which of the following is *least likely* to be a step in data analysis?
   A. Structured formative analysis.
   B. Data collection.
   C. Data preparation.

2. Which of the following shortcomings of a feature is *least likely* to be addressed by data cleansing?
   A. Missing values.
   B. Common values.
   C. Non-uniform values.

3. The process of adjusting variable values so that they fall between 0 and 1 is *most* commonly referred to as:
   A. scaling.
   B. standardization.
   C. normalization.

MODULE 5.2: DATA EXPLORATION

Video covering this content is available online.

LOS 5.c: Describe objectives, methods, and examples of data exploration.

CFA® Program Curriculum, Volume 1, page 347

Data exploration seeks to evaluate the data set and determine the most appropriate way to configure it for model training.

Steps in data exploration include the following:

1. **Exploratory data analysis (EDA)** involves looking at data descriptors such as summary statistics, heat maps, word clouds, and so on. The objectives of EDA include:

   – Understanding data properties, distributions, and other characteristics.

   – Finding patterns or relationships, and evaluating basic questions and hypotheses.

   – Planning modeling in future steps.

2. **Feature selection** is a process to select only the needed attributes of the data for ML model training. The higher the number of features selected, the higher the model complexity and training time.

3. **Feature engineering** is the process of creating new features by transforming (e.g., taking the natural logarithm), decomposing, or combining multiple features. A related term is **feature extraction**, whereby a feature is created from the data set (e.g., creating a value for age using date-of-birth data).

Model performance depends heavily on feature selection and engineering, and it is common for the analyst to recursively go back to this step and apply tweaks until model performance is acceptable.

Data Exploration for Structured Data

With **EDA**, structured data is organized in rows (observations) and columns (features). EDA can be performed for a single feature (one dimension) or multiple features (multidimension). When the number of features is large, dimension reduction models such as **principal component analysis (PCA)** can facilitate data exploration.

■ For a single feature, summary statistics include the mean, standard deviation, skewness, and kurtosis. EDA visualizations include box plots, histograms, density plots, and bar charts. Histograms capture the frequency of observations in a series of equal-width bins. Density plots are smoothed histograms for continuous data overlaid on top of histograms. Bar charts show frequency distributions of categorical variables (e.g., proportion of the population in each of the five geographical zones of the country). Box plots are used for continuous variables and highlight the median, quartiles, and outliers of a normally distributed feature.

■ For multiple features, the summary statistic can be a correlation matrix. Data can be visually graphed using a scatterplot, box plots, stacked bar or a line graph. Multiple box plots can be plotted on the same line with each plot representing a feature. Parametric statistical tests include ANOVA tables, correlation tables, and *t*-tests. Nonparametric statistical tests include the Spearman rank-order correlation and the chi-square test.

With **feature selection**, we try to select only the features that contribute to the out-of-sample predictive power of the model. A parsimonious model (i.e., a model with fewer features) reduces feature-induced noise and improves the model's prediction accuracy. Feature selection requires a good understanding of the business environment and the interrelationships among the features identified in the EDA. For structured data, feature selection is an iterative, methodical process. Features can be assigned an importance score using statistical methods and then ranked and selected based on that score. Dimension reduction algorithms may be employed to reduce the number of features needed so as to reduce processing time during model training.

Feature Engineering (FE) involves optimizing and improving the selected features. Model training results depend on how the features are presented to the algorithm. Feature engineering involves either decomposing a feature into multiple features or converting an existing feature into a new feature. **One-hot encoding (OHE)** is a process used to convert a categorical feature into a binary (dummy) variable suitable for machine processing. Feature engineering seeks to make model training faster and easier.

Reading 5

LOS 5.f: Describe methods for extracting, selecting and engineering features from textual data.

CFA® Program Curriculum, Volume 1, page 371

Data Exploration for Unstructured Data

Unstructured text can be tokenized, and summary statistics such as **term frequency** (number of times the word appears in the text) and **co-occurrence** (where two or more words appear together) can be analyzed. A **word cloud** is a visual representation of all the words in a BOW, such that words with higher frequency have a larger font size. This allows the analyst to determine which words are contextually more important. Figure 5.1 shows an example of a word cloud.

Figure 5.1:   Word Cloud, Apple (NASDAQ: AAPL) SEC Filing

Source: Apple SEC Filing: Form PX14A6G, February 5, 2019

Feature Selection

Feature selection involves selecting a subset of tokens in the BOW. Reduction in BOW size makes the model more parsimonious and reduces feature-induced noise. Noisy features do not contribute to prediction accuracy. High- and low-frequency words are often eliminated, resulting in a more concise BOW. High-frequency words tend to be stop words (if not removed during the data wrangling phase) or common vocabulary words. Low-frequency words may be irrelevant. Consider a model to predict bankruptcy: to effectively separate defaulters from nondefaulters, tokens that are associated with both categories should be removed. Feature selection methods include:

- *Frequency.* One of the tools used for feature selection in textual data is the **document frequency (DF)**. The DF of a token is calculated as the number of documents containing that token divided by the total number of documents.

- *Chi-square.* This test is used to rank tokens by their usefulness to a class in text classification problems. Tokens with the highest chi-square test statistic occur more frequently with a specific class; hence, they are useful in training ML algorithms for discriminant analysis.

- *Mutual information.* This is a numerical value indicating the contribution of a token to a class of texts. If the token appears in all classes, it is not considered a useful discriminant, and its **mutual information (MI)** equals 0. Tokens associated with only one or a few classes would have MI approaching 1.

Feature Engineering (FE)

Techniques of FE include:

- **Numbers.** Tokens with standard lengths are identified and converted into a token such as /numberX/. Four-digit numbers may be associated with years and are assigned a value of /number4/.

- **N-grams.** These are multiword patterns, and if they are useful, the order is preserved. For example, the words *expansionary monetary policy* may be best kept as a sequence rather than broken into three different tokens, and therefore would be replaced by a single token, expansionary_monetary_policy.

- **Name entity recognition (NER).** NER algorithms search for token values, in the context it was used, against their internal library and assign a NER tag to the token. For example, Microsoft would be assigned a NER tag of *ORG* and Europe would be assigned a NER tag of *Place*. NER object class assignment is meant to make the selected features more discriminatory.

- **Parts of speech (POS).** This uses language structure dictionaries to contextually assign tags (POS) to text. For example, Microsoft would be assigned a POS tag of *NNP* (indicating a proper noun), and the year 1969 would be assigned a POS tag of *CD* (indicating a cardinal number).

MODULE QUIZ 5.2

To best evaluate your performance, enter your quiz answers online.

1. The process used to convert a categorical feature into a binary (dummy) variable is *best* described as:
   A. one-hot encoding (OHE).
   B. parts of speech (POS).
   C. name entity recognition (NER).

2. To make a bag-of-words (BOW) concise, the *most appropriate* procedure would be to:
   A. eliminate high- and low-frequency words.
   B. use a word cloud.
   C. use N-grams.

Reading 5

3. Mutual information (MI) of tokens that appear in one or few classes is *most likely* to be:
   A. close to 0.
   B. close to 1.
   C. close to 100.

Video covering this content is available online.

MODULE 5.3: MODEL TRAINING AND EVALUATION

LOS 5.d: Describe objectives, steps, and techniques in model training.

CFA® Program Curriculum, Volume 1, page 359

Before model training, it is important to define the objective(s) of data analysis, identify useful data points, and conceptualize the model. Model conceptualization is the iterative planning phase that lays out the process to be followed. This process gets tweaked until the desired results are achieved. It is important that ML engineers work with domain experts so as to identify data characteristics and relationships (e.g., the relation between inflation and exchange rates).

Once the unstructured data has been processed and codified in a structured form such as a data matrix, model training is similar to that of structured data. ML seeks to identify patterns in the data set via a set of rules. Model fitting describes how well the model generalizes to new data (i.e., how the model performs out of sample).

Model fitting errors can be caused by:

■ *Size of the training sample*. Small data sets do not provide adequate training and can lead to an underfit model that does not recognize important patterns.

■ *Number of features*. Fewer features can also lead to an underfitting problem; the small number of features may not carry enough information to identify patterns in the training sample. On the other hand, data sets with a large number of features can lead to overfitting due to fewer degrees of freedom. Overfit models do not generalize well in the validation sample. The feature selection step discussed earlier is important in mitigating the overfitting and underfitting problems. FE, when properly done, tends to reduce the underfitting problem.

PROFESSOR'S NOTE

Model fitting is discussed in detail in the topic review on machine learning.

The three tasks of model training are as follows:

1. **Method selection** is the art and science of choosing the appropriate ML method (i.e., algorithm) given the objectives and data characteristics. Method selection is based on the following factors:

   – *Supervised or unsupervised learning*. Supervised learning is used when the training data contains the **ground truth** or the known outcome (i.e., the target variable). In such cases, available methods include regression, ensemble trees, **support vector machines (SVMs)**, and **neural networks (NN)**. Unsupervised learning occurs when there is no target variable. Unsupervised learning methods include clustering, dimension reduction, and anomaly detection.

– *Type of data.* For numerical data (e.g., predicting earnings) we may use classification and regression tree (CART) methods. For text data, we can use **generalized linear models (GLMs)** and SVMs. For image data, neural networks and deep learning methods can be employed.

– *Size of data.* Large data sets with many observations and features can be handled with SVMs. Neural networks work better with a large number of observations, but few features.

PROFESSOR'S NOTE

These methods and their applications are discussed in detail in the topic review on machine learning.

Once a method is selected, the researcher has to specify appropriate hyperparameters (e.g., the number of hidden layers in a neural network). For mixed data sets (containing numerical and textual data), multiple methods are often used. Sometimes, the output of one method (e.g., classification of financial news text for a company as positive or negative) may be used as an input to another model. Sometimes, multiple models are employed, and a weighted average of the forecasts from those models is used.

For supervised learning, before model training begins, the data set is divided into three parts. The larger part ($\approx$ 60%) is used for model training. A second part ($\approx$ 20%) is used for validation and model tuning. The last part ($\approx$ 20%) is the test set, and is used to check the out-of-sample performance of the model. Due to the absence of labeled training data, no splitting of the data set is needed for unsupervised learning.

For a model to be able to discriminate well, it should be provided with a wide variety of training data. **Class imbalance** occurs when one class has a large number of observations relative to other classes. For example, in a model for predicting bond default, if the data set has a large number of high-grade bonds (i.e., those that would be less likely to default), then the model would be more likely to predict nondefault for a new observation. The training data set should have a variety of high- and low-grade bonds so as to have enough diversity to make correct predictions. One way to overcome class imbalance is to undersample the overrepresented class and oversample the underrepresented class.

2. **Performance evaluation** is the process of assessing model efficacy; various tools are used to quantify and critique model performance.

3. **Tuning** is the process of implementing changes to improve model performance.

These steps are recursively applied until a desired level of model performance is attained. We will next explore the performance evaluation and tuning steps in detail.

Reading 5

LOS 5.g: Evaluate the fit of a machine learning algorithm.

CFA® Program Curriculum, Volume 1, page 385

Techniques to Measure Model Performance

In order to validate a model, we must measure its training performance or goodness of fit. We will next consider a few methods to measure this performance. (These techniques are particularly suited to evaluating binary classification models.)

1. **Error analysis.** Errors in classification problems can be false positives (type I error) or false negatives (type II error). A **confusion matrix** shows the results of a classification problem, as in Figure 5.2.

Figure 5.2: Classification of Defaulters

	Actual: Default	Actual: No Default
Prediction: Default	True positive (TP)	False positive (FP, type I)
Prediction: No Default	False negative (FN, type II)	True negative (TN)

Metrics such as **precision** (the ratio of true positives to all predicted positives) and **recall** (the ratio of TPs to all actual positives) can be used. High precision is valued when the cost of a type I error is large, while high recall is valued when the cost of a type II error is large.

$$\text{precision (P)} = TP / (TP + FP)$$

$$\text{recall (R)} = TP / (TP + FN)$$

While FP and FN are both errors, they may not be equally important. The tradeoff between precision and recall is a business decision, and depends on the model application. For example, a lender may want to avoid lending to potential defaulters, and so will want to maximize recall. Together, model precision and recall determine model **accuracy**, which is the proportion of correct forecasts out of a total number of forecasts. The **F1 score** is the harmonic mean of precision and recall.

$$\text{accuracy} = (TP + TN) / (TP + TN + FP + FN)$$

$$\text{F1 score} = (2 \times P \times R) / (P + R)$$

2. **Receiver operating characteristic (ROC).** Also used for classification problems, the ROC is a curve that plots the tradeoff between FPs and TPs. The true positive rate (TPR) is the same as recall, and is plotted along the Y-axis. The false positive rate (FPR) is the ratio of FPs to all actual negatives, and is plotted along the X-axis.

$$TPR = TP / (TP + FN)$$

$$FPR = FP / (FP + TN)$$

Figure 5.3 shows the performance of the three models used to predict defaults. The area under the curve (AUC) is a value from 0 to 1. The closer the value of AUC is to 1, the higher the predictive accuracy of the model. An AUC value of 0.50 (indicated by a straight line, for model 1) indicates that the model makes a random guess. The higher the convexity of the ROC curve, the higher its AUC.

Figure 5.3: ROC Curves and AUC

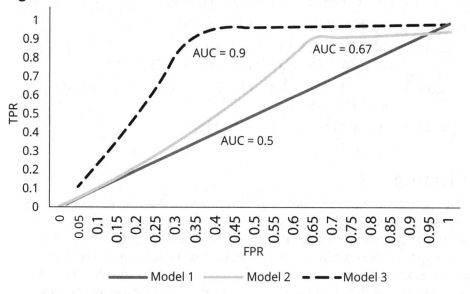

3. **Root mean square error (RMSE).** This is useful for data predictions that are continuous, such as regression models. The RMSE is a single metric summarizing the prediction error in a sample.

$$\text{RMSE} = \sqrt{\frac{\sum_{i=1}^{n}\left(\text{predicted}_i - \text{actual}_i\right)^2}{n}}$$

EXAMPLE: Model evaluation

Dave Kwah is evaluating a model that predicts whether a company is likely to have a dividend cut next year. The model uses a binary classification: cut versus not cut. In the test sample consisting of 78 observations, the model correctly classified 18 companies that had a dividend cut, as well as 46 companies that did not have a dividend cut. The model failed to identify three companies that actually had a dividend cut.

1. Calculate the model's precision and recall.

2. Calculate the model's accuracy and F1 score.

3. Calculate the model's FPR.

Reading 5

Answer:

	Actual: Cut	Actual: Not Cut
Prediction: Cut	TP = 18	FP = 11
Prediction: Not Cut	FN = 3	TN = 46

1. Precision = TP / (TP + FP) = 18 / (18 + 11) = 0.62

   Recall = TP / (TP + FN) = 18 / (18 + 3) = 0.86

2. Accuracy = (TP + TN) / (TP + TN + FP + FN)
   = (18 + 46) / (18 + 3 + 11 + 46) = 64 / 78 = 0.82

   F1 score = (2 × P × R) / (P + R) = (2 × 0.62 × 0.86) / (0.62 + 0.86)
   = 1.07 / 1.48 = 0.72

3. FPR = FP / (TN + FP) = 11 / (46 + 11) = 0.19

Model Tuning

After model evaluation, the model needs to be revised until it reaches an acceptable performance level. **Bias error** is the prediction error in the training data resulting from underfit models. Bias errors occur from oversimplified models, which don't learn adequately from the training sample. **Variance error** is the prediction error in the validation sample resulting from overfitting models that do not generalize well. Overfitting is an issue with supervised ML that results when too many features are included in the training sample (i.e., the model is too complicated). It is necessary to find an optimum tradeoff between bias and variance errors, such that the model is neither underfitting nor overfitting.

A **fitting curve** is a plot of training error and cross-validation prediction error with varying model complexity (more complex = more features). An example of a fitting curve is shown in Figure 5.4.

Figure 5.4: Fitting Curve

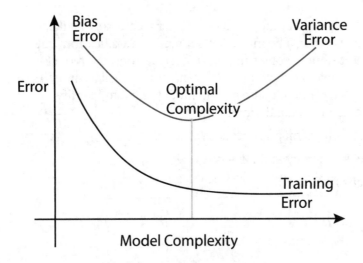

As a model's complexity increases, it starts overfitting the training sample, and training error (i.e., bias error) declines. However, this decrease in bias error comes at the cost of increasing variance error. Regularization seeks to reduce model complexity by imposing a penalty on features that don't meaningfully contribute to the predictive power of the model. Optimal model complexity balances the tradeoff between bias and variance error.

Parameters are estimated by the model (e.g., slope coefficients in a regression model) using an optimization technique on the training sample. **Hyperparameters** (e.g., the number of hidden layers in a neural network, or the p-threshold in logistic regression) are specified by ML engineers, and are independent of the training sample.

Tuning involves altering the hyperparameters until a desirable level of model performance is achieved. For each specification of hyperparameter(s), a confusion matrix is prepared based on the classification results, and accuracy and F1 scores are compiled. Rather than using a trial-and-error approach, especially if there are multiple hyperparameters in the model, one can use a **grid search**. A grid search is an automated process of selecting the best combination of hyperparameters.

Ceiling analysis is an evaluation and tuning of each of the components in the entire model-building pipeline. It identifies the weak link in the process, which can be tuned to improve the performance of the model.

MODULE QUIZ 5.3

To best evaluate your performance, enter your quiz answers online.

1. When the training data contains the ground truth, the *most appropriate* learning method is:
    A. supervised learning.
    B. unsupervised learning.
    C. machine learning.

Use the following information to answer Questions 2 through 6.

While analyzing health care stocks, Ben Stokes devises a model to classify the stocks as those that will report earnings above consensus forecasts versus those that won't. Stokes prepares the following confusion matrix using the results of his model.

Confusion Matrix for Earnings Outperformance

	Actual: Beat Forecast	Actual: Not Beat
Prediction: Beat Forecast	12	4
Prediction: Not Beat	2	7

2. The model's accuracy score is *closest* to:
    A. 0.44.
    B. 0.76.
    C. 0.89.

3. The model's recall is *closest* to:
   A. 0.67.
   B. 0.72.
   C. 0.86.

4. The model's precision is *closest* to:
   A. 0.64.
   B. 0.72.
   C. 0.75.

5. The model's F1 score is *closest* to:
   A. 0.80.
   B. 0.89.
   C. 0.94.

6. To reduce type I error, Stokes should *most* appropriately increase the model's:
   A. precision.
   B. recall.
   C. accuracy.

KEY CONCEPTS

LOS 5.a

The steps involved in a data analysis project include (1) conceptualization of the modeling task, (2) data collection, (3) data preparation and wrangling, (4) data exploration, and (5) model training.

LOS 5.b

Data cleansing deals with missing, invalid, inaccurate, and non-uniform values as well as with duplicate observations. Data wrangling or preprocessing includes data transformation and scaling. Data transformation types include extraction, aggregation, filtration, selection, and conversion of data. Scaling is the conversion of data to a common unit of measurement. Common scaling techniques include normalization and standardization. Normalization scales variables between the values of 0 and 1, while standardization centers the variables at a mean of 0 and a standard deviation of 1. Unlike normalization, standardization is not sensitive to outliers, but it assumes that the variable distribution is normal.

LOS 5.c

Data exploration involves exploratory data analysis (EDA), feature selection, and feature engineering (FE). EDA looks at summary statistics describing the data and any patterns or relationships that can be observed. Feature selection involves choosing only those features that meaningfully contribute to the model's predictive power. FE optimizes the selected features.

LOS 5.d

Before model training, the model is conceptualized where ML engineers work with domain experts to identify data characteristics and relationships. ML seeks to identify patterns in the training data, such that the model is able to generalize to out-of-sample data. Model fitting errors can be caused by using a small training sample or by using an inappropriate number of features. Too few features may underfit the data, while too many features can lead to the problem of overfitting.

Model training involves model selection, model evaluation, and tuning.

LOS 5.e

Text processing involves removing HTML tags, punctuations, numbers, and white spaces. Text is then normalized by lowercasing of words, removal of stop words, stemming, and lemmatization. Text wrangling involves tokenization of text. N-grams is a technique that defines a token as a sequence of words, and is applied when the sequence is important. A bag-of-words (BOW) procedure then collects all the tokens in a document. A document term matrix organizes text as structured data: documents are represented by words, and tokens by columns. Cell values reflect the number of times a token appears in a document.

Reading 5

LOS 5.f

Summary statistics for textual data includes term frequency and co-occurrence. A word cloud is a visual representation of all the words in a BOW, such that words with higher frequency have a larger font size. This allows the analyst to determine which words are contextually more important. Feature selection can use tools such as document frequency, the chi-square test, and mutual information (MI). FE for text data includes identification of numbers, usage of N-grams, name entity recognition (NER), or parts of speech (POS) tokenization.

LOS 5.g

Model performance can be evaluated by using error analysis. For a classification problem, a confusion matrix is prepared, and evaluation metrics such as precision, recall, accuracy score, and F1 score are calculated.

precision (P) = true positives / (false positives + true positives)

recall (R) = true positives / (true positives + false negatives)

accuracy = (true positives + true negatives) / (all positives and negatives)

F1 score = $(2 \times P \times R) / (P + R)$

The receiver operating characteristic (ROC) plots a curve showing the tradeoff between false positives and true positives.

Root mean square error (RMSE) is used when the target variable is continuous.

$$RMSE = \sqrt{\frac{\sum_{i=1}^{n} \left(predicted_i - actual_i \right)^2}{n}}$$

Model tuning involves balancing bias error versus variance error, and selecting the optimal combination of hyperparameters.

ANSWER KEY FOR MODULE QUIZZES

Module Quiz 5.1

1. **A** Structured formative analysis is not a term defined in the curriculum. The five steps of data analysis include conceptualization of modeling task; data collection; data preparation and wrangling; data exploration; and model training. (LOS 5.a)

2. **B** Common values are not *cleansed*. Missing, invalid, non-uniform, and inaccurate values are *cleaned*. (LOS 5.b)

3. **C** Normalization scales variable values between 0 and 1. (LOS 5.b)

Module Quiz 5.2

1. **A** OHE is a process used to convert a categorical feature into a binary (dummy) variable suitable for machine processing. POS and NER are mechanisms used to assign tags to tokens. (LOS 5.c)

2. **A** To make a BOW concise, usually high- and low-frequency words are eliminated. High-frequency words tend to be stop words or common vocabulary words. A word cloud is a text data visualization tool. N-grams are used when the sequence of words is important. (LOS 5.f)

3. **B** MI is a numerical value indicating the contribution of a token to a class of text. Tokens appearing in all classes will have an MI value close to 0, while tokens in one or a few classes should have an MI value close to 1. (LOS 5.f)

Module Quiz 5.3

1. **A** Supervised learning is used when the training data contains ground truth (i.e., the known outcome, or target variable). Unsupervised learning is used when there is no known target variable. Machine learning (ML) includes a broad array of algorithms, including supervised and unsupervised ML. (LOS 5.d)

Reading 5

The following matrix answers Questions 2 through 6:

Confusion Matrix for Earnings Outperformance

	Actual: Beat Forecast	Actual: Not Beat
Prediction: Beat Forecast	TP = 12	FP = 4
Prediction: Not Beat	FN = 2	TN = 7

2. **B** Accuracy = (TP + TN) / (TP + TN + FP + FN) = 19 / 25 = 0.76. (LOS 5.g)

3. **C** Recall (R) = TP / (TP + FN) = 12 / 14 = 0.86. (LOS 5.g)

4. **C** Precision (P) = TP/ (TP + FP) = 12 / 16 = 0.75. (LOS 5.g)

5. **A** F1 score = (2 × P × R) / (P + R) = (2 × 0.75 × 0.86) / (0.75 + 0.86) = 0.80. (LOS 5.g)

6. **A** High precision is valued when the cost of a type I error (i.e., FP) is large, while high recall is valued when the cost of a type II error (i.e., FN) is large. (LOS 5.g)

TOPIC QUIZ: QUANTITATIVE METHODS

You have now finished the Quantitative Methods topic section. On your Schweser online dashboard, you can find a Topic Quiz that will provide immediate feedback on how effective your study of this material has been. The test is best taken timed; allow three minutes per question. Topic Quizzes are more exam-like than typical QBank questions or module quiz questions. A score less than 70% suggests that additional review of the topic is needed.

The following is a review of the Economics principles designed to address the learning outcome statements set forth by CFA Institute. Cross-Reference to CFA Institute Assigned Reading #6.

READING 6

Currency Exchange Rates: Understanding Equilibrium Value

EXAM FOCUS

There's no fluff here; you need it all. Take it slow and get a good understanding of quotes, currency cross rates, triangular arbitrage, all parity conditions, and their interrelationships. Forecasting exchange rates has important applications for valuation (which is the focus of Level II). Accordingly, theories of exchange rate determination as well as factors influencing exchange rates are all important. Be prepared to identify warning signs of currency crises.

MODULE 6.1: FOREX QUOTES, SPREADS, AND TRIANGULAR ARBITRAGE

Video covering this content is available online.

LOS 6.a: Calculate and interpret the bid–offer spread on a spot or forward currency quotation and describe the factors that affect the bid–offer spread.

CFA® Program Curriculum, Volume 1, page 418

PROFESSOR'S NOTE

The "bid–offer" spread is also known as the "bid–ask" spread: the terms "ask" and "offer" mean the same thing. Accordingly, we will be using them interchangeably.

EXCHANGE RATES

An **exchange rate** is simply the price of one currency in terms of another. For example, a quote of 1.4126 USD/EUR means that each euro costs $1.4126. In this example, the euro is called the *base* currency and the USD the *price* currency. Hence, a quote is the price of one unit of the base currency in terms of the price currency.

A **spot exchange rate** is the currency exchange rate for immediate delivery, which for most currencies means the exchange of currencies takes place two days after the trade. A **forward exchange rate** is a currency exchange rate for an exchange to be done in the future. Forward rates are quoted for various future dates (e.g., 30 days, 60 days, 90 days, or one year). A forward contract is an agreement to exchange a specific amount of one currency for a specific amount of another currency on a future date specified in the forward agreement.

Dealer quotes often include both bid and offer (ask) rates. For example, the euro could be quoted as $1.4124 − 1.4128. The bid price ($1.4124) is the price at which the dealer will buy euros, and the offer price ($1.4128) is the price at which the dealer will sell euros.

FOREIGN EXCHANGE SPREAD

The difference between the offer and bid price is called the *spread*. Spreads are often stated as "pips." When the spot quote has four decimal places, one pip is 1/10,000. In the above example, the spread is $0.0004 (4 pips) reflecting the dealer's profit. Dealers manage their foreign currency inventories by transacting in the interbank market (think of this as a wholesale market for currency). Spreads are narrow in the interbank market.

The spread quoted by a dealer depends on:

- **The spread in an interbank market for the same currency pair.** Dealer spreads vary directly with spreads quoted in the interbank market.

- **The size of the transaction.** Larger, liquidity-demanding transactions generally get quoted a larger spread.

- **The relationship between the dealer and client.** Sometimes dealers will give favorable rates to preferred clients based on other ongoing business relationships.

The interbank spread on a currency pair depends on:

- **Currencies involved.** Similar to stocks, high-volume currency pairs (e.g., USD/EUR, USD/JPY, and USD/GBP) command lower spreads than do lower-volume currency pairs (e.g., AUD/CAD).

- **Time of day.** The time overlap during the trading day when both the New York and London currency markets are open is considered the most liquid time window; spreads are narrower during this period than at other times of the day.

- **Market volatility.** Spreads are directly related to the exchange rate volatility of the currencies involved. Higher volatility leads to higher spreads to compensate market makers for the increased risk of holding those currencies. Spreads change over time in response to volatility changes.

In addition to these factors, spreads in forward exchange rate quotes increase with maturity. The reasons for this are: longer maturity contracts tend to be less liquid, counterparty credit risk in forward contracts increases with maturity, and interest rate risk in forward contracts increases with maturity.

WARM-UP: WORKING WITH FOREIGN EXCHANGE QUOTES

Earlier, we stated that a dealer will sell a currency at the ask price and purchase it at the bid price. We need to be a bit more specific. For example, imagine that you are given a USD/AUD bid and ask quote of 1.0508-1.0510. Investors can buy AUD (i.e., the base currency) from the dealer at the ask price of USD 1.0510. Similarly, investors can sell AUD to the dealer at the bid price of USD 1.0508. Remember, investors always take a loss due to the spread. So the rule is *buy the base currency at ask, and sell the base currency at bid*.

For transactions in the price currency, we do the opposite. If we need to buy USD (i.e., the price currency) using AUD (i.e., selling the base currency), we now use the dealer *bid* quote. Similarly, to sell the price currency, we use the dealer *ask* quote. So the rule is *buy the price currency at bid, and sell the price currency at ask*.

Alternatively, it is useful to follow the *up-the-bid-and-multiply, down-the-ask-and-divide rule*. Again given a USD/AUD quote, if you want to convert USD into AUD (you are going down the quote—from USD on top to AUD on bottom), use the *ask* price for that quote. Conversely, if you want to convert AUD into USD, you are going up the quote (from bottom to top) and, hence, use the *bid* price.

> **EXAMPLE: Converting currencies using spot rates**
>
> A dealer is quoting the AUD/GBP spot rate as 1.5060 – 1.5067. How would we:
>
> 1. Compute the proceeds of converting 1 million GBP.
>
> 2. Compute the proceeds of converting 1 million AUD.
>
> **Answer:**
>
> 1. To convert 1 million GBP into AUD, we go "up the quote" (i.e., from GBP in the denominator to AUD in the numerator). Hence, we would use the *bid* price of 1.5060 and multiply.
>
>   1 million GBP × 1.5060 = 1,506,000 AUD
>
> 2. To convert 1 million AUD into GBP, we go "down the quote" (i.e., from AUD in the numerator to GBP in the denominator). Hence, we would use the *ask* price of 1.5067 and divide.
>
>   1 million AUD / 1.5067 = 663,702.13 GBP

LOS 6.b: Identify a triangular arbitrage opportunity and calculate its profit, given the bid–offer quotations for three currencies.

CFA® Program Curriculum, Volume 1, page 422

CROSS RATE

The **cross rate** is the exchange rate between two currencies implied by their exchange rates with a common third currency. It is necessary to use cross rates when there is no active foreign exchange (FX) market in the currency pair being considered. The cross rate must be computed from the exchange rates between each of these two currencies and a major third currency, usually the USD or EUR.

Suppose we have the following quotes:

USD/AUD = 0.60 and MXN/USD = 10.70. What is the cross rate between Australian dollars and pesos (MXN/AUD)?

$$\frac{MXN}{AUD} = \frac{\cancel{USD}}{AUD} \times \frac{MXN}{\cancel{USD}} = 0.60 \times 10.70 = 6.42$$

So our MXN/AUD cross rate is 6.42 pesos per Australian dollar. The key to calculating cross rates is to make sure the common currency cancels out.

CROSS RATES WITH BID-ASK SPREADS

Bid-ask spreads complicate the calculation of cross rates considerably. Suppose we are given three currencies A, B, and C; we can have three pairs of currencies (i.e., A/B, A/C, and B/C).

Rules:

$$\left(\frac{A}{C}\right)_{bid} = \left(\frac{A}{B}\right)_{bid} \times \left(\frac{B}{C}\right)_{bid}$$

$$\left(\frac{A}{C}\right)_{offer} = \left(\frac{A}{B}\right)_{offer} \times \left(\frac{B}{C}\right)_{offer}$$

To compute the cross rate for A/C, given A/B and B/C, we can follow the above rules to obtain the bid and offer prices. If we are instead given A/B and C/B rates, we will have to make adjustments to obtain the B/C bid and offer rates from the C/B bid and offer rates, because A/B × C/B ≠ A/C. The process is as follows:

$$\left(\frac{B}{C}\right)_{bid} = \frac{1}{\left(\frac{C}{B}\right)_{offer}}$$

$$\left(\frac{B}{C}\right)_{offer} = \frac{1}{\left(\frac{C}{B}\right)_{bid}}$$

TRIANGULAR ARBITRAGE

Real-world currency dealers will maintain bid/ask quotes that ensure a profit to the dealer, regardless of which currencies customers choose to trade. If this was not the case, customers could earn profits through the process of triangular arbitrage. In **triangular arbitrage**, we begin with three pairs of currencies, each with bid and ask quotes, and construct a triangle where each node in the triangle represents one currency. To check for arbitrage opportunities, we go around the triangle clockwise (and later, counterclockwise) until we reach our starting point. As before, we follow the up-the-bid-and-multiply, down-the-ask-and-divide rule.

The following example will illustrate triangular arbitrage.

Study Session 3
Cross-Reference to CFA Institute Assigned Reading #6 – Currency Exchange Rates: Understanding Equilibrium Value

Reading 6

EXAMPLE: Triangular arbitrage

The following quotes are available from the interbank market:

Quotes:

USD/AUD 0.6000 – 0.6015
USD/MXN 0.0933 – 0.0935

1. Compute the implied MXN/AUD cross rate.

2. If your dealer quotes MXN/AUD = 6.3000 – 6.3025, is an arbitrage profit possible? If so, compute the arbitrage profit in USD if you start with USD 1 million.

Answer:

1. To compute implied cross rates, we need:

$$\left(\frac{MXN}{AUD}\right)_{bid} = \left(\frac{USD}{AUD}\right)_{bid} \times \left(\frac{MXN}{USD}\right)_{bid}$$

Since we are given USD/MXN quotes instead of MXN/USD quotes, we first invert these quotes:

$$\left(\frac{MXN}{USD}\right)_{bid} = \frac{1}{\left(\frac{USD}{MXN}\right)_{offer}} = \left(\frac{1}{0.0935}\right) = 10.70 \text{ MXN/USD}$$

and

$$\left(\frac{MXN}{USD}\right)_{offer} = \frac{1}{\left(\frac{USD}{MXN}\right)_{bid}} = \left(\frac{1}{0.0933}\right) = 10.72 \text{ MXN/USD}$$

Now, the implied cross rates:

$$\left(\frac{MXN}{AUD}\right)_{bid} = \left(\frac{USD}{AUD}\right)_{bid} \times \left(\frac{MXN}{USD}\right)_{bid} = 0.60 \times 10.70 = 6.42$$

$$\left(\frac{MXN}{AUD}\right)_{offer} = \left(\frac{USD}{AUD}\right)_{offer} \times \left(\frac{MXN}{USD}\right)_{offer} = 0.6015 \times 10.72 = 6.4481$$

2. Since the dealer quote of MXN/AUD = 6.3000 – 6.3025 falls outside of these cross rates, arbitrage profit may be possible (we have to check this). Remember to use the dealer quotes in the triangle and not the cross rates we computed.

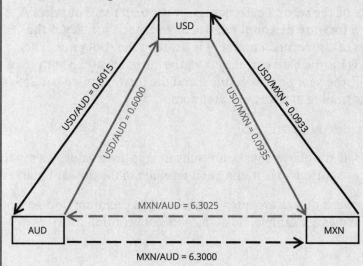

To label the arrows in this triangle, we follow the "up the bid, down the offer" rule. To convert from USD to MXN, ("down" with respect to the USD/MXN quote), we use the offer rate of 0.0935.

Going clockwise and starting with USD 1 million:

1. Convert USD 1 million into MXN @ 0.0935 USD/MXN. Note that the quote is USD/MXN and hence we are going down, and thus need to use the ask. Also remember: down, divide. We get 1 million/0.0935 = 10,695,187 MXN.

2. Next, we convert 10,695,187 MXN into AUD @ 6.3025 MXN/AUD to get 1,696,975 AUD.

3. Finally, we convert AUD 1,696,975 into USD @ 0.6000 USD/AUD. Here the quote is USD/AUD and we are converting from AUD to USD, so we are going "up the quote" and need to multiply by the bid. (Remember: up, multiply.) We get 1,696,975 × 0.60 = 1,018,185 USD – a profit of 18,185 USD.

We can also check for arbitrage in the counter-clockwise direction (even though we can never earn an arbitrage profit in both directions):

1. Convert USD 1 million into AUD using 0.6015. Again, the quote is USD/AUD and we are going down, so use the ask price and divide. We get 1 million/0.6015 = 1,662,510 AUD.

2. Next, we convert 1,662,510 AUD into MXN using 6.3000 to get 10,473,814 MXN.

3. Finally, we convert MXN 10,473,814 into USD at 0.0933 to get 977,207 USD – a loss of 22,793 USD.

LOS 6.c: Explain spot and forward rates and calculate the forward premium/discount for a given currency.

CFA® Program Curriculum, Volume 1, page 426

A currency is quoted at a **forward premium** relative to a second currency if the forward price (in units of the second currency) is *greater* than the spot price. A currency is quoted at a **forward discount** relative to a second currency if the forward price (in units of the second currency) is *less* than the spot price. The premium or discount is for the base currency (i.e., the currency at the bottom of the quote). For example, if the spot price is 1.20$/€ and the forward price is 1.25$/€, we say that the euro is trading at a forward premium.

$$\text{forward premium (discount)} = F - S_0$$

Given a quote of A/B, if the above equation results in a positive value, we say that currency B (i.e., the base currency) is trading at a *premium* in the forward market.

In the FX markets, forward quotes are often presented as a premium or discount over spot rates. The following example illustrates this convention.

Study Session 3
Cross-Reference to CFA Institute Assigned Reading #6 – Currency Exchange Rates: Understanding Equilibrium Value

Reading 6

EXAMPLE: Spot and forward quotes

Given the following quotes for AUD/CAD, compute the bid and offer rates for a 30-day forward contract.

Maturity	Rate
Spot	1.0511/1.0519
30-day	+3.9/+4.1
90-day	+15.6/+16.8
180-day	+46.9/+52.3

Answer:

Since the forward quotes presented are all positive, the CAD (i.e., the base currency) is trading at a forward *premium*.

30-day bid = 1.0511 + 3.9/10,000 = 1.05149

30-day offer = 1.0519 + 4.1/10,000 = 1.05231

The 30-day all-in forward quote for AUD/CAD is 1.05149/1.05231.

PROFESSOR'S NOTE

For an investor wishing to convert AUD into CAD in the forward market, the relevant quote would be the ask rate (remember the "down-the-ask" rule) of 1.05231. This is also known as the all-in (i.e., after adding (subtracting) the forward premium (discount) rate for the investor in question.

MODULE QUIZ 6.1

To best evaluate your performance, enter your quiz answers online.

1. All of the factors below would contribute to an increase in USD/EUR dealer spread except:
   A. increase in the volatility of EUR/USD spot rate.
   B. increase in the EUR/USD spread in the interbank market.
   C. smaller order size.

2. The bid-ask quotes for the USD, GBP, and EUR are:

   EUR/USD: 0.7000 − 0.7010

   USD/GBP: 1.7000 − 1.7010

   EUR/GBP: 1.2000 − 1.2010

   The potential arbitrage profit from a triangular arbitrage based on an initial position of 1 million USD is *closest* to:
   A. USD0.
   B. USD7,212.
   C. USD6,372.

Video covering this content is available online.

MODULE 6.2: MARK-TO-MARKET VALUE, AND PARITY CONDITIONS

LOS 6.d: Calculate the mark-to-market value of a forward contract.

CFA® Program Curriculum, Volume 1, page 430

If the forward contract price is consistent with covered interest rate parity (discussed later), the value of the contract at initiation is zero to both parties. After initiation, the value of the forward contract will change as forward quotes for the currency pair change in the market.

Mark-to-Market Value

The value of a forward currency contract prior to expiration is also known as the *mark-to-market value*. To compute the value of a forward contract prior to expiration, we take the difference between the forward price we locked-in and the current forward price, multiply that by the size of the contract, and then discount for the time period remaining until the contract settlement date.

$$V_t = \frac{(FP_t - FP)(\text{contract size})}{\left[1 + R\left(\frac{\text{days}}{360}\right)\right]}$$

where:

V_t = value of the forward contract at time t (to the party buying the base currency), ($t < T$) denominated in price currency

FP_t = forward price (to sell base currency) at time t in the market for a new contract maturing at time T

FP = forward price specified in the contract at inception (to buy the base currency)

days = number of days remaining to maturity of the forward contract ($T - t$)

R = interest rate of price currency

> **EXAMPLE: Valuing a forward contract prior to maturity**
>
> Yew Mun Yip has entered into a 90-day forward contract long CAD 1 million against AUD at a forward rate of 1.05358 AUD/CAD. Thirty days after initiation, the following AUD/CAD quotes are available:
>
> | Maturity | FX Rate |
> |----------|---------|
> | Spot | 1.0612/1.0614 |
> | 30-day | +4.9/+5.2 |
> | 60-day | +8.6/+9.0 |
> | 90-day | +14.6/+16.8 |
> | 180-day | +42.3/+48.3 |

Study Session 3
Cross-Reference to CFA Institute Assigned Reading #6 – Currency Exchange Rates: Understanding Equilibrium Value

Reading 6

The following information is available (at t = 30) for AUD interest rates:

30-day rate: 1.12%

60-day rate: 1.16%

90-day rate: 1.20%

What is the mark-to-market value in AUD of Yip's forward contract?

Answer:

Yip's contract calls for long CAD (i.e., converting AUD to CAD). To value the contract, we would look to unwind the position. To unwind the position, Yip can take an offsetting position in a new forward contract with the same maturity. Hence, Yip would be selling CAD in exchange for AUD and, hence, going up the bid (i.e., use the bid price). Note that after 30 days, 60 more days remain in the original contract.

The forward bid price for a new contract expiring in T − t = 60 days is 1.0612 + 8.6/10,000 = 1.06206.

The interest rate to use for discounting the value is also the 60-day AUD interest rate of 1.16%:

$$V_t = \frac{(FP_t - FP)(\text{contract size})}{\left[1 + R\left(\frac{\text{days}}{360}\right)\right]} = \frac{(1.06206 - 1.05358)(1,000,000)}{\left[1 + 0.0116\left(\frac{60}{360}\right)\right]}$$

$$= 8,463.64$$

Thirty days into the forward contract, Yip's position has gained (positive value) AUD 8,463.64. This is because Yip's position is long CAD, which has appreciated relative to AUD since inception of the contract. Yip can close out the contract on that day and receive AUD 8,463.64.

Note: Be sure to use the AUD (price currency) interest rate.

LOS 6.e: Explain international parity conditions (covered and uncovered interest rate parity, forward rate parity, purchasing power parity, and the international Fisher effect).

CFA® Program Curriculum, Volume 1, page 435

Covered Interest Rate Parity

The word 'covered' in the context of covered interest parity means bound by arbitrage. **Covered interest rate parity** holds when any forward premium or discount exactly offsets differences in interest rates, so that an investor would earn the same return investing in either currency. If euro interest rates are higher than dollar interest rates, the forward discount on the euro relative to the dollar will just offset the higher euro interest rate.

Formally, covered interest rate parity requires that (given A/B quote structure):

$$F = \frac{\left[1 + R_A\left(\frac{days}{360}\right)\right]}{\left[1 + R_B\left(\frac{days}{360}\right)\right]} S_0$$

where:
F   = forward rate (quoted as A/B)
S_0 = spot rate (quoted as A/B)
days = number of days in the underlying forward contract
R_A = interest rate for Currency A
R_B = interest rate for Currency B

PROFESSOR'S NOTE

For all parity relations, follow the numerator-denominator rule. If you are given a USD/EUR quote, the USD interest rate should be in the numerator and the EUR interest rate in the denominator of the parity equation.

Recall that:

$$\text{forward premium (discount)} = F - S_0 = \left[\frac{1 + R_A\left(\frac{days}{360}\right)}{1 + R_B\left(\frac{days}{360}\right)} - 1\right] S_0$$

or

$$\text{forward premium (discount)} = F - S_0 = S_0\left[\frac{\left(\frac{days}{360}\right)}{1 + R_B\left(\frac{days}{360}\right)}\right](R_A - R_B)$$

EXAMPLE: Covered interest arbitrage

The U.S. dollar interest rate is 8%, and the euro interest rate is 6%. The spot exchange rate is $1.30 per euro (USD/EUR), and the 1-year forward rate is $1.35 per euro. Determine whether a profitable arbitrage opportunity exists, and illustrate such an arbitrage if it does.

Answer:

First, we note that the forward value of the euro is too high. Interest rate parity would require a forward rate of:

$1.30(1.08 / 1.06) = $1.3245

Because the market forward rate of $1.35 is higher than that implied by interest rate parity, we should sell euros in the forward market and do the opposite (i.e., buy euros) in the spot market. The steps in the covered interest arbitrage are as follows.

Initially:

Step 1: Borrow $1,000 at 8%.

Step 2: Purchase 1,000 / 1.30 = 769.23 euros in the spot market.

Step 3: Invest the euros at 6%.

Step 4: Enter into a forward contract to sell the expected proceeds at the end of one year (i.e., 769.23 × 1.06 = 815.38 euros), at $1.35 each.

After one year:

Step 1: Sell the 815.38 euros under the terms of the forward contract at $1.35 to get $1,100.76.

Step 2: Repay the $1,000 8% loan, which requires $1,080.

Step 3: Keep the difference of $20.76 as an arbitrage profit.

Uncovered Interest Rate Parity

With covered interest rate parity, arbitrage will force the forward contract exchange rate to a level consistent with the difference between the two country's nominal interest rates. If forward currency contracts are not available, or if capital flows are restricted so as to prevent arbitrage, the relationship need not hold. **Uncovered interest rate parity** refers to such a situation; uncovered in this context means not bound by arbitrage.

Consider Country A where the interest rate is 4%, and Country B where the interest rate is 9%. Under uncovered interest rate parity, currency B is expected to depreciate by 5% annually relative to currency A, so that an investor should be indifferent between investing in Country A or B.

Given a quote structure of A/B, the base currency (i.e., currency B) is expected to appreciate by approximately $R_A - R_B$. (When $R_A - R_B$ is negative, currency B is expected to depreciate). Mathematically:

$$E(\%\Delta S)_{(A/B)} = R_A - R_B$$

The following example illustrates the use of uncovered interest rate parity to *forecast* future spot exchange rates using market interest rates.

> **EXAMPLE: Forecasting spot rates with uncovered interest rate parity**
>
> Suppose the spot exchange rate quote is ZAR/EUR = 8.385. The 1-year nominal rate in the eurozone is 10% and the 1-year nominal rate in South Africa is 8%. Calculate the expected percentage change in the exchange rate over the coming year using uncovered interest rate parity.

> **Answer:**
>
> The rand interest rate is less than the euro interest rate, so uncovered interest rate parity predicts that the value of the rand will rise (it will take fewer rand to buy one euro) because of higher interest rates in the eurozone. The euro (the base currency) is expected to "appreciate" by approximately $R_{ZAR} - R_{EUR} = 8\% - 10\% = -2\%$. (Note the *negative* 2% value.) Thus the euro is expected to *depreciate* by 2% relative to the rand, leading to a change in exchange rate from 8.385 ZAR/EUR to 8.217 ZAR/EUR over the coming year.

Comparing covered and uncovered interest parity, we see that covered interest rate parity derives the *no-arbitrage forward rate*, while uncovered interest rate parity derives the *expected future spot rate* (which is not market traded). Covered interest parity is assumed by arbitrage, but this is not the case for uncovered interest rate parity.

Under uncovered interest rate parity, if the foreign interest rate is higher by 2%, the foreign currency is expected to depreciate by 2%, so the investor should be indifferent between investing in the foreign currency or in their own domestic currency. An investor that chooses to invest in the foreign currency without any additional return (the interest rate differential is offset by currency value changes) is not demanding a risk premium for the foreign currency risk. Hence, uncovered interest rate parity assumes that the investor is *risk-neutral*.

If the forward rate is equal to the expected future spot rate, we say that the forward rate is an **unbiased predictor** of the future spot rate. In such an instance, $F = E(S_1)$; this is called **forward rate parity**. In this special case, if covered interest parity holds (and it will; by arbitrage) uncovered interest parity would also hold (and vice versa). Stated differently, if uncovered interest rate parity holds, forward rate parity also holds (i.e., the forward rate is an unbiased predictor of the future spot rate).

There is no reason that uncovered interest rate parity must hold in the short run, and indeed it typically does not. There is evidence that it does generally hold in the long run, so longer-term expected future spot rates based on uncovered interest rate parity are often used as forecasts of future exchange rates.

(Domestic) Fisher Relation

Professor Irving Fisher originated the idea that the nominal rate of return is (approximately) the sum of the real rate and the expected rate of inflation.

We can write this relation (known as the Fisher relation) as:

$$R_{nominal} = R_{real} + E(\text{inflation})$$

Study Session 3
Cross-Reference to CFA Institute Assigned Reading #6 – Currency Exchange Rates: Understanding Equilibrium Value

Reading 6

International Fisher Relation

Under **real interest rate parity**, real interest rates are assumed to converge across different markets. Taking the Fisher relation and real interest rate parity together gives us the **international Fisher effect**:

$$R_{nominal\ A} - R_{nominal\ B} = E(inflation_A) - E(inflation_B)$$

This tells us that the difference between two countries' nominal interest rates should be equal to the difference between their expected inflation rates.

The argument for the equality of real interest rates across countries is based on the idea that with free capital flows, funds will move to the country with a higher real rate until real rates are equalized.

> **EXAMPLE: Calculating the real interest rate**
>
> Suppose the nominal South African interest rate is 9.0% and the expected inflation rate is 3.5%. Calculate the real interest rate.
>
> **Answer:**
>
> $$0.090 = real\ r_{ZAR} + 0.035$$
> $$real\ r_{ZAR} = 0.090 - 0.035 = 0.055,\ or\ 5.5\%$$

If we move to a 2-country scenario, we will now have two nominal interest rates and two expected inflation rates. If the real rates for both countries are assumed to be equal, they drop out of the equation, and we are left with the international Fisher relation, as shown in the following example.

> **EXAMPLE: Using the international Fisher relation**
>
> Suppose that the eurozone expected annual inflation rate is 9.0%, and that the expected South African inflation rate is 13.0%. The nominal interest rate is 10.09% in the eurozone. Use the international Fisher relation to estimate the nominal interest rate in South Africa.
>
> **Answer:**
>
> real rate ZAR = real rate EUR $\approx$ (nominal interest rate in the eurozone) – (eurozone expected annual inflation rate) = 10.09% – 9% = 1.09%
>
> R_{ZAR} = (expected South African inflation rate) + (real ZAR interest rate)
> = 13% + 1.09% = 14.09%

Purchasing Power Parity

The law of one price states that identical goods should have the same price in all locations. For instance, a pair of designer jeans should cost the same in Paris as they do in New York, after adjusting for the exchange rate. The potential for arbitrage is the basis for the law of one price: if designer jeans cost less in New York than they do in Paris, an enterprising individual will buy designer jeans in New York and sell them in Paris, until this action causes the price differential to disappear. Note, however, that the law of one price does not hold in practice, due to the effects of frictions such as tariffs and transportation costs.

Instead of focusing on individual products, **absolute purchasing power parity** (absolute PPP) compares the average price of a representative basket of consumption goods between countries. Absolute PPP requires only that the law of one price be correct *on average*, that is, for like baskets of goods in each country.

$$S(A/B) = CPI(A) / CPI(B)$$

In practice, even if the law of one price held for every good in two economies, absolute PPP might not hold because the weights (consumption patterns) of the various goods in the two economies may not be the same (e.g., people eat more potatoes in Russia and more rice in Japan).

Relative Purchasing Power Parity

Relative purchasing power parity (relative PPP) states that changes in exchange rates should exactly offset the price effects of any inflation differential between two countries. Simply put, if (over a 1-year period) Country A has a 6% inflation rate and Country B has a 4% inflation rate, then Country A's currency should *depreciate* by approximately 2% relative to Country B's currency over the period.

The equation for relative PPP is as follows:

$$\%\Delta S_{(A/B)} = \text{Inflation}_{(A)} - \text{Inflation}_{(B)}$$
where:
$\%\Delta S_{(A/B)}$ = change in spot price (A/B)

Relative PPP is based on the idea that even if absolute PPP does not hold, there may still be a relationship between changes in the exchange rate and differences between the inflation rates of the two countries.

Ex-Ante Version of PPP

The ex-ante version of purchasing power parity is the same as relative purchasing power parity except that it uses *expected* inflation instead of actual inflation.

The following example illustrates the use of the ex-ante version of the PPP relation.

> **EXAMPLE: Calculating the exchange rate predicted by the ex-ante version of PPP**
>
> The current spot rate is USD/AUD = 1.00. You expect the annualized Australian inflation rate to be 5%, and the annualized U.S. inflation rate to be 2%. According to the ex-ante version of PPP, what is the expected change in the spot rate over the coming year?

> **Answer:**
>
> Since the AUD has the higher expected inflation rate, we expect that the AUD will depreciate relative to the USD. To keep the cost of goods and services the same across borders, countries with higher rates of inflation should see their currencies depreciate. The expected change in the spot rate over the coming year is inflation(USD) − inflation(AUD) = 2% − 5% = −3%. This predicts a new USD/AUD exchange rate of approximately 0.97 USD/AUD.

Because there is no true arbitrage available to force relative PPP to hold, violations of relative PPP in the short run are common. However, because the evidence suggests that the relative form of PPP holds approximately in the long run, it remains a useful method for estimating the relationship between exchange rates and inflation rates.

LOS 6.f: Describe relations among the international parity conditions.

CFA® Program Curriculum, Volume 1, page 436

It is useful to establish how all the parity relations described earlier fit together. Figure 6.1 shows the interrelationships among parity conditions. Though these relationships are not all exact, together they provide an extremely useful framework for thinking about exchange rates.

Figure 6.1:   The International Parity Relationships Combined

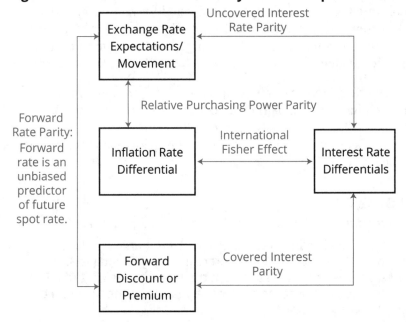

Several observations can be made from the relationships among the various parity conditions:

- Covered interest parity holds by arbitrage. If forward rate parity holds, uncovered interest rate parity also holds (and vice versa).

- Interest rate differentials should mirror inflation differentials. This holds true if the international Fisher relation holds. If that is true, we can also use inflation differentials to forecast future exchange rates—which is the premise of the ex-ante version of PPP.

- If the ex-ante version of relative PPP as well as the international Fisher relation both hold, uncovered interest rate parity will also hold.

LOS 6.g: Evaluate the use of the current spot rate, the forward rate, purchasing power parity, and uncovered interest parity to forecast future spot exchange rates.

LOS 6.h: Explain approaches to assessing the long-run fair value of an exchange rate.

CFA® Program Curriculum, Volume 1, pages 436 and 447

We can use ex-ante PPP, uncovered interest rate parity, or forward rates to forecast future spot rates. As stated earlier, uncovered interest rate parity and PPP are not bound by arbitrage and seldom work over the short and medium terms. Similarly, the forward rate is not an unbiased predictor of future spot rate. However, PPP holds over reasonably long time horizons. If relative PPP holds at any point in time, the real exchange rate (i.e., the exchange rate adjusted for relative historical inflation between the currency pair) would be constant. However, since relative PPP seldom holds over the short term, the real exchange rate fluctuates around its mean-reverting equilibrium value.

The international Fisher effect (and real rate parity) assumes that there are no differences between sovereign risk premia (i.e., all countries are perceived to be equally risky by investors). This is obviously untrue as investors do demand a higher real rate of return (i.e., a risk premium) for investing in emerging market currencies that are perceived to be riskier.

MODULE QUIZ 6.2

To best evaluate your performance, enter your quiz answers online.

1. Suppose the spot exchange rate quote is 1.0120 Canadian dollars (C$) per U.S. dollar. The 1-year nominal interest rate in Canada is 3.0% and the 1-year nominal interest rate in the United States is 1.0%. The expected exchange rate at the end of the year using the uncovered interest rate parity is *closest* to:
   A. C$1.0322.
   B. C$0.9923.
   C. C$0.9918.

2. The international parity relationships indicate that the expected return on risk-free securities should be the same in all countries and exchange rate risk is really just inflation risk. Which of the following is *least likely* to be considered a practical implication of this framework?
   A. Investors will earn the same real rate of return on investments once their own currency impact is accounted for.
   B. Interest rate differentials reflect currency expectations. As a result, covered interest arbitrage will provide a return in any foreign currency that is equal to the domestic return.
   C. There are significant rewards for bearing foreign exchange risk.

3. For uncovered interest rate parity to hold, which condition is necessary?
   A. Forward rate parity holds.
   B. Covered interest rate parity holds and ex-ante relative PPP holds.
   C. Real interest rate parity and ex-ante relative PPP holds.

Use the following information to answer Questions 4 through 9.

Sally Franklin, CFA, is a financial advisor to Jamie Curtess, a U.S. citizen interested in learning more about how her investments will be affected by exchange rates and differences in interest rates internationally. Franklin has gathered the following information based on Curtess's investment interests.

The current spot exchange rate: $1 = €0.74.

	Europe	United States
Nominal 1-year interest rate:	4%	?
Expected annual inflation:	2%	1%

Franklin also gathers the following information:

	Switzerland	South Africa
Nominal 1-year interest rate:	5%	7%
Expected annual inflation:	3%	5%

4. According to the international Fisher relation, the 1-year nominal interest rate in the United States should be *closest* to:
   A. 3.00%.
   B. 4.34%.
   C. 6.00%.

5. If the relative form of the PPP holds, the expected exchange rate in one year is *closest* to:
   A. $1.3378 per €.
   B. $0.7463 per €.
   C. $1.3647 per €.

6. For this question only, assume that the U.S. interest rate is 3.5%. The 1-year forward rate should be *closest* to:
   A. $1.3647 per €.
   B. $0.7463 per €.
   C. $1.3449 per €.

7. Curtess wonders how spot rates are expected to change in the future and asks the following question: "What are the implications for the South African rand relative to the Swiss franc under uncovered interest rate parity, and the implications for the euro relative to the U.S. dollar under the relative form of purchasing power parity?" Franklin responds by making two statements:

Statement 1: The South African rand is expected to depreciate relative to the Swiss franc.

Statement 2: The euro is expected to depreciate relative to the U.S. dollar.

Based upon the underlying parity relationships cited, are Franklin's statements accurate?
A. No, both statements are inaccurate.
B. Yes, both statements are accurate.
C. One statement is accurate and one is inaccurate.

8. For this question only, imagine that the nominal interest rate in the United States is 3%. Real interest rates, using the Fisher relation, are *most likely* to be:
A. greater in the United States than in Europe.
B. lower in Europe than in South Africa.
C. equal among Europe, South Africa, Switzerland, and the United States.

9. A forecasted $/€ exchange rate in one year equal to the current 1-year forward rate is *most likely* to be based on the assumption that:
A. absolute PPP holds.
B. investors are risk neutral.
C. real interest rate parity holds.

Video covering this content is available online.

MODULE 6.3: EXCHANGE RATE DETERMINANTS, CARRY TRADE, AND CENTRAL BANK INFLUENCE

LOS 6.i: Describe the carry trade and its relation to uncovered interest rate parity and calculate the profit from a carry trade.

CFA® Program Curriculum, Volume 1, page 451

FX Carry Trade

Uncovered interest rate parity states that a currency with a high interest rate should depreciate relative to a currency with a lower interest rate, so that an investor would earn the same return investing in either currency. For example, suppose that short-term interest rates are 3% in the U.K. and 1% in the United States. Uncovered interest rate parity implies that the GBP should depreciate by 2% relative to the USD over the coming year.

However, uncovered interest rate parity is not bound by arbitrage. If the GBP depreciates by less than 2% (or even appreciates), an investor who has invested in the higher yielding GBP using funds borrowed in USD will earn excess profits.

Study Session 3
Cross-Reference to CFA Institute Assigned Reading #6 – Currency Exchange Rates: Understanding Equilibrium Value

Reading 6

In a **FX carry trade**, an investor invests in a higher yielding currency using funds borrowed in a lower yielding currency. The lower yielding currency is called the *funding currency*.

Consider the following example.

EXAMPLE: Carry trade

Interest Rates	Currency Pair	Exchange Rates	
		Today	*One year later*
U.K 3%	USD/GBP	1.50	1.50
U.S. 1%			

Compute the profit to an investor borrowing in the United States and investing in the U.K.

Answer:

return = interest earned on investment − funding cost
　　　　 − currency depreciation

$= 3\% - 1\% - 0\%$

$= 2\%$

The FX carry trade attempts to capture an interest rate differential and is a bet *against* uncovered interest rate parity. Carry trades typically perform well during low-volatility periods. Sometimes, higher yields attract larger capital flows, which in turn lead to an economic boom and appreciation (instead of depreciation) of the higher yielding currency. This could make the carry trade even more profitable, because the investor earns a return from currency appreciation in addition to the return from the interest rate spread.

Risks of the Carry Trade

As discussed earlier, the carry trade is profitable only if uncovered interest rate parity does not hold over the investment horizon. The risk is that the funding currency may appreciate significantly against the currency of the investment, which would reduce a trader's profit—or even lead to a loss. Furthermore, the return distribution of the carry trade is not normal; it is characterized by negative skewness and excess kurtosis (i.e., fat tails), meaning that the probability of a large loss is higher than the probability implied under a normal distribution. We call this high probability of a large loss the *crash risk* of the carry trade.

Crash risk stems from the carry trade's leveraged nature: an investor borrows a low-yielding (funding) currency and then invests in a high-yielding currency. As more investors follow and adopt the same strategy, the demand for high-yielding currency actually pushes its value *up*. However, with this herding behavior comes the risk that all investors may attempt to exit the trade at the same time. (This is especially true if investors use stop-loss orders in their carry trades.) During turbulent times, as investors exit their positions (i.e., a flight to safety), the high-yielding currency can experience a steep decline in value, generating large losses for traders pursuing FX carry trades.

LOS 6.j: Explain how flows in the balance of payment accounts affect currency exchange rates.

CFA® Program Curriculum, Volume 1, page 454

BALANCE OF PAYMENTS

Balance-of-payments (BOP) accounting is a method used to keep track of transactions between a country and its international trading partners. It includes government transactions, consumer transactions, and business transactions. The BOP accounts reflect all payments and liabilities *to* foreigners as well as all payments and obligations received *from* foreigners.

The **current account** measures the exchange of goods, the exchange of services, the exchange of investment income, and unilateral transfers (gifts to and from other nations). The current account balance summarizes whether we are selling more goods and services to the rest of the world than we are buying from them (a current account surplus) or buying more from the rest of the world than we are selling to them (a current account deficit).

The **financial account** (also known as the **capital account**) measures the flow of funds for debt and equity investment into and out of the country.

When a country experiences a current account deficit, it must generate a surplus in its capital account (or see its currency depreciate). Capital flows tend to be the dominant factor influencing exchange rates in the short term, as capital flows tend to be larger and more rapidly changing than goods flows.

INFLUENCE OF BOP ON EXCHANGE RATES

Current Account Influences

Current account deficits lead to a depreciation of domestic currency via a variety of mechanisms:

- **Flow supply/demand mechanism.** Current account deficits in a country increase the supply of that currency in the markets (as exporters to that country convert their revenues into their own local currency). This puts downward pressure on the exchange value of that currency. The decrease in the value of the currency *may* restore the current account deficit to a balance—depending on the following factors:

    - *The initial deficit.* The larger the initial deficit, the larger the depreciation of domestic currency needed to restore current account balance.

    - *The influence of exchange rates on domestic import and export prices.* As a country's currency depreciates, the cost of imported goods increases. However, some of the increase in cost may not be passed on to consumers.

    - *Price elasticity of demand of the traded goods.* If the most important imports are relatively price inelastic, the quantity imported will not change.

©2021 Kaplan, Inc.

Study Session 3
Cross-Reference to CFA Institute Assigned Reading #6 – Currency Exchange Rates: Understanding Equilibrium Value

Reading 6

- **Portfolio balance mechanism.** Countries with current account surpluses usually have capital account deficits, which typically take the form of investments in countries with current account deficits. As a result of these flows of capital, investor countries may find their portfolios' composition being dominated by few investee currencies. When investor countries decide to rebalance their investment portfolios, it can have a significant negative impact on the value of those investee country currencies.

- **Debt sustainability mechanism.** A country running a current account deficit may be running a capital account surplus by borrowing from abroad. When the level of debt gets too high relative to GDP, investors may question the sustainability of this level of debt, leading to a rapid depreciation of the borrower's currency.

Capital Account Influences

Capital account flows are one of the major determinants of exchange rates. As capital flows into a country, demand for that country's currency increases, resulting in appreciation. Differences in real rates of return tend to be a major determinant of the flow of capital: higher relative real rates of return attract foreign capital. Capital flows into a country may be needed to overcome a shortage of internal savings to fund investments needed for economic growth. However, capital flows in excess of needed investment capital pose several problems. This is especially problematic for emerging markets.

Excessive capital inflows into emerging markets create problems for those countries such as:

- Excessive real appreciation of the domestic currency.

- Financial asset and/or real estate bubbles.

- Increases in external debt by businesses or government.

- Excessive consumption in the domestic market fueled by credit.

Emerging market governments often counteract excessive capital inflows by imposing capital controls or by direct intervention in the foreign exchange markets. We will discuss this further in a subsequent LOS.

LOS 6.k: Explain the potential effects of monetary and fiscal policy on exchange rates.

CFA® Program Curriculum, Volume 1, page 464

MUNDELL-FLEMING MODEL

Developed in early 1960s, the **Mundell-Fleming model** evaluates the short-term impact of monetary and fiscal policies on interest rates—and consequently on exchange rates. The model assumes that there is sufficient slack in the economy to handle changes in aggregate demand, and that inflation is not a concern. Accordingly, changes in inflation rates due to changes in monetary or fiscal policy are not explicitly modeled by the Mundell-Fleming model.

We will look at the implications of this model for flexible exchange rate regimes as well as for fixed exchange rate regimes.

Flexible Exchange Rate Regimes

In a flexible ("floating") exchange rate system, rates are determined by supply and demand in the foreign exchange markets. We will examine the influence of monetary and fiscal policies when international capital flows are relatively unrestricted (high mobility of capital) versus when capital flows are relatively restricted (low mobility of capital), both under a flexible exchange rate system.

High Capital Mobility

Expansionary **monetary policy** and expansionary **fiscal policy** are likely to have opposite effects on exchange rates. Expansionary monetary policy will reduce the interest rate and, consequently, reduce the inflow of capital investment in physical and financial assets. This decrease in financial inflows (deterioration of the financial account) reduces the demand for the domestic currency, resulting in depreciation of the domestic currency. Restrictive monetary policy should have the opposite effect, increasing interest rates and leading to an appreciation in the value of the domestic currency.

Expansionary fiscal policy (an increased deficit from lower taxes or higher government spending) will increase government borrowing and, consequently, interest rates. An increase in interest rates will attract foreign investment, improve the financial account, and consequently, *increase* the demand for the domestic currency.

Low Capital Mobility

Our discussion so far has assumed free flow of capital, which is a valid assumption with respect to developed markets. In emerging markets, however, capital flows may be restricted. In that case, the impact of trade imbalance on exchange rates (goods flow effect) is greater than the impact of interest rates (financial flows effect). In such a case, expansionary fiscal or monetary policy leads to increases in net imports, leading to depreciation of the domestic currency. Similarly, restrictive monetary or fiscal policy leads to an appreciation of domestic currency. Figure 6.2 summarizes the influence of fiscal and monetary policy on exchange rates.

Figure 6.2: Monetary and Fiscal Policy and Exchange Rates

Monetary Policy/Fiscal Policy	Capital Mobility	
	High	Low
Expansionary/Expansionary	Uncertain	Depreciation
Expansionary/Restrictive	Depreciation	Uncertain
Restrictive/Expansionary	Appreciation	Uncertain
Restrictive/Restrictive	Uncertain	Appreciation

Study Session 3
Cross-Reference to CFA Institute Assigned Reading #6 – Currency Exchange Rates: Understanding Equilibrium Value

Reading 6

 PROFESSOR'S NOTE
Candidates are often confused by the implication under the Mundell-Fleming model that a higher-interest-rate currency will appreciate relative to a lower-interest-rate currency, because this is exactly the opposite of what we learned under uncovered interest rate parity. Note though that uncovered interest rate parity assumed that real interest rates are equal globally, and thus that nominal interest rates merely mirror expected inflation. That condition no longer holds under the Mundell Fleming model, which does not consider inflation.

Fixed Exchange Rate Regimes

Under a fixed exchange rate regime, the government fixes the rate of exchange of its currency relative to one of the major currencies.

An expansionary (restrictive) monetary policy would lead to depreciation (appreciation) of the domestic currency as stated previously. Under a fixed rate regime, the government would then have to purchase (sell) its own currency in the foreign exchange market. This action essentially reverses the expansionary (restrictive) stance.

This explains why in a world with mobility of capital, governments cannot both manage exchange rates as well as pursue independent monetary policy. If the government wants to manage monetary policy, it must either let exchange rates float freely or restrict capital movements to keep them stable.

MONETARY APPROACH TO EXCHANGE RATE DETERMINATION

Monetary models only take into account the effect of monetary policy on exchange rates (fiscal policy effects are not considered). With the Mundell-Fleming model, we assume that inflation (price levels) plays no role in exchange rate determination. Under monetary models, we assume that output is fixed, so that monetary policy primarily affects inflation, which in turn affects exchange rates. There are two main approaches to monetary models:

1. **Pure monetary model**. Under a pure monetary model, the PPP holds at any point in time and output is held constant. An expansionary (restrictive) monetary policy leads to an increase (decrease) in prices and a decrease (increase) in the value of the domestic currency. Therefore an x% increase in the money supply leads to an x% increase in price levels and then to an x% depreciation of domestic currency. The pure monetary approach does not take into account expectations about future monetary expansion or contraction.

2. **Dornbusch overshooting model**. This model assumes that prices are sticky (inflexible) in the short term and, hence, do not immediately reflect changes in monetary policy (in other words, PPP does not hold in the short term). The model concludes that exchange rates will overshoot the long-run PPP value in the short term. In the case of an expansionary monetary policy, prices increase, but over time. Expansionary monetary policy leads to a *decrease* in interest

rates—and a larger-than-PPP-implied depreciation of the domestic currency due to capital outflows. In the long term, exchange rates gradually increase toward their PPP implied values.

Similarly, a restrictive monetary policy leads to excessive appreciation of the domestic currency in the short term, and then a slow depreciation toward the long-term PPP value.

PORTFOLIO BALANCE APPROACH TO EXCHANGE RATE DETERMINATION

The portfolio balance approach focuses only on the effects of *fiscal* policy (and not monetary policy). While the Mundell-Fleming model focuses on the short-term implications of fiscal policy, the **portfolio balance approach** takes a long-term view and evaluates the effects of a sustained fiscal deficit or surplus on currency values.

When the government runs a fiscal deficit, it borrows money from investors. Under the portfolio balance approach, investors evaluate the debt based on expected risk and return. A sovereign debt investor would earn a return based on both the debt's yield and its currency return. (When we invest in a foreign-currency-denominated security, our realized return will be comprised of the return earned on that security in its local currency, as well as a return from the performance of that foreign currency versus our domestic currency.) When a government pursues a long-term stance of expansionary fiscal policy, an investor should evaluate the implications of such a policy on expected risk and return (typically the yield should increase due to a higher risk premium). If investors perceive that the yield and/or currency return is sufficient, they will continue to purchase the bonds. However, continued increases in fiscal deficits are unsustainable and investors may refuse to fund the deficits— leading to currency depreciation.

Combining the Mundell-Fleming and portfolio balance approaches, we find that in the short term, with free capital flows, an expansionary fiscal policy leads to domestic currency appreciation (via high interest rates). In the long term, the government has to reverse course (through tighter fiscal policy) leading to depreciation of the domestic currency. If the government does not reverse course, it will have to monetize its debt (i.e., print money—monetary expansion), which would also lead to depreciation of the domestic currency.

LOS 6.1: Describe objectives of central bank or government intervention and capital controls and describe the effectiveness of intervention and capital controls.

CFA® Program Curriculum, Volume 1, page 472

A combination of "push" and "pull" factors determine the flow of capital into a country. Pull factors are favorable developments that make a country an attractive destination for foreign capital. These include relative price stability, a flexible exchange rate regime, improved fiscal position, privatization of state-owned enterprises etc. Push factors are largely driven by mobile international capital seeking high returns from a diversified portfolio.

Study Session 3
Cross-Reference to CFA Institute Assigned Reading #6 – Currency Exchange Rates: Understanding Equilibrium Value

Reading 6

As stated earlier, capital flows can lead to excessive appreciation of a currency. This can lead to several problems including loss of competitiveness of exports in the global markets, asset price bubbles, and excessive consumption fueled by credit creation. Excessive capital inflows to a country can also lead to a currency crisis when such capital is eventually withdrawn from the country. To reduce these problems, policymakers may intervene by imposing capital controls or by direct intervention in the foreign exchange market by the central bank.

Objectives

The objectives of capital controls or central bank intervention in FX markets are to:

- Ensure that the domestic currency does not appreciate excessively.

- Allow the pursuit of independent monetary policies without being hindered by their impact on currency values. For example, an emerging market central bank seeking to reduce inflation may pursue a restrictive monetary policy, increasing interest rates. However, these higher rates may attract large inflows of foreign capital, pushing up the value of the domestic currency.

- Reduce the aggregate volume of inflow of foreign capital.

Effectiveness

For developed market countries, the volume of trading in a country's currency is usually very large relative to the foreign exchange reserves of its central bank. Evidence has shown that for developed markets, central banks are relatively ineffective at intervening in the foreign exchange markets due to lack of sufficient resources. Evidence in the case of emerging markets is less clear: central banks of emerging market countries may be able to accumulate sufficient foreign exchange reserves (relative to trading volume) to affect the supply and demand of their currencies in the foreign exchange markets.

LOS 6.m: Describe warning signs of a currency crisis.

CFA® Program Curriculum, Volume 1, page 474

History has shown that market participants have failed to predict crises and typically are surprised by them. When market sentiment changes significantly, crises may occur *even for countries with sound economic fundamentals.*

The following conditions have been identified as warning signs in the period leading up to a currency crisis:

- Terms of trade (i.e., ratio of exports to imports) deteriorate.

- Fixed or partially-fixed exchange rates (versus floating exchange rates).

- Official foreign exchange reserves dramatically decline.

- Currency value that has risen above its historical mean.

- Inflation increases.

- Liberalized capital markets, that allow for the free flow of capital.

- Money supply relative to bank reserves increases.
- Banking crises (may also be coincident).

MODULE QUIZ 6.3

To best evaluate your performance, enter your quiz answers online.

1. Vilasram Deshmukh is forecasting JPY/USD exchange rates based on balance of payments analysis. He notes that the United States is running large current account deficits relative to Japan. Based on this information, he concludes that the JPY/USD rate should decrease. His conclusion is *most likely* supported by the:
   A. flow mechanism of the current account influences.
   B. portfolio composition mechanism of the current account influences.
   C. capital account influences.

2. Stephen Hall is forecasting USD/GBP exchange rates. He consults forecasts of the money supply for the United States and U.K. made by his firm's chief economist, and he notes the following statement from a report published by the chief economist: "The U.S. money supply is expected to grow at a much faster pace than the U.K. or European money supplies."

   Hall makes the following statement: "Under the pure monetary approach model, an increase in the future growth rate of the money supply would lead to an immediate depreciation in the currency's value." Hall's statement is *most likely*:
   A. correct.
   B. incorrect, as the future growth rate in the money supply would not immediately affect currency values under the pure monetary approach model.
   C. incorrect, as the future growth rate in money supply would actually increase the currency value under the pure monetary approach.

3. Chintan Rajyaguru works for a currency dealer in London. He is evaluating the implications of changes in fiscal and monetary policies occurring in Zambola, an emerging market country with low capital mobility. He concludes that Zambola's central bank is pursuing a restrictive monetary policy to curb inflation. Additionally, the Zambolan government has been reducing budget deficits to comply with new IMF lending terms. According to the Mundell-Fleming model, the change in monetary and fiscal policy is *most likely* to cause the Zambolan currency to:
   A. appreciate.
   B. depreciate.
   C. remain unchanged.

Use the following information to answer Questions 4 through 9.

Agnetha Poulsen works as an analyst in the foreign exchange overlay strategies department for CFN, a large asset management firm serving institutional clients. She is concerned about the excessive unhedged currency exposure taken on by the overlay strategies department. She makes an appointment with Alvilda Kristensen, director of risk management, to discuss this matter. Prior to the meeting, Poulsen collects information on foreign currency quotes and on interest rates as shown in Figure 1 and Figure 2.

Figure 1: Current Spot and Forward Exchange Rate Quotes

Quotes	USD/CHF	USD/EUR
Spot	0.9817/0.9821	1.2235/1.2238
30-day forward	–7.6/–6.9	–7.21/–6.80
60-day forward	–15.3/–13.3	–14.56/–13.76
90-day forward	–24.3/–23.05	–23.84/–22.77

Figure 2: Selected Interest Rates

Interest Rates	USD	EUR	CHF
30-day rate	0.20%	0.91%	1.13%
60-day rate	0.21%	0.93%	1.15%
90-day rate	0.26%	1.04%	1.25%

Poulsen also reviews the current open forward contracts. As an example, she reviews two contracts. Contract FX2001 is a 90-day forward contract initiated 60 days ago. The contract calls for purchase of CHF 200 million at an all-in rate of USD 0.9832. Contract FX2051 is a 90-day contract initiated 30 days ago to purchase 100 million EUR at an all-in rate of 1.2242.

During her meeting with Kristensen, Poulsen expresses concern about traders establishing FX carry trades in several emerging market currencies. Kristensen assures Poulsen that CFN has adequate monitoring mechanisms. She continues that these carry trades have been generating significant positive returns for the clients and Poulsen should not worry about it. Poulsen counters by stating that carry trade returns distributions are characterized by negative kurtosis and excess skewness.

Poulsen reviews her notes and decides to prepare a report on currency crises. She compiles a list of indicators of an impending currency crisis based on empirical analysis.

Poulsen then turns her attention to the firm's investments in Zambola, an emerging market. She realizes that currently the currency overlay strategy department has no trades involving the free-floating Zambolan currency, the Zu. Poulsen is concerned about significant long exposure of the portfolio in Zu. Zambola is enjoying large capital inflows drawn by Zambola's attractive yields. Her analysis indicates that Zambola has been running large current account deficits. A trend analysis on Zu indicates a steep upward trend continuing above its PPP value.

4. The 30-day forward spread on USD/CHF is *closest* to:
   A. 0.0005.
   B. 0.0007.
   C. 0.7000.

5. The current mark-to-market value of the forward contract FX2001 in USD is *closest* to:
   A. –USD460,000.
   B. –USD451,924.
   C. –USD357,940.

6. The current mark-to-market value of the forward contract FX2051 in USD is *closest* to:
   A. –USD215,900.
   B. –USD107,900.
   C. –USD216,000.

7. Poulsen's description of the carry trade return distribution is *best* described as:
   A. correct.
   B. incorrect about skewness only.
   C. incorrect about both skewness and kurtosis.

8. Which of the following indicators of impending currency crises should Poulsen exclude from her report?
   A. Terms of trade improve.
   B. Increase in money supply relative to bank reserves.
   C. Increase in inflation.

9. If Zambolan government wanted to reduce the inflow of foreign capital, it should:
   A. pursue expansionary monetary policies.
   B. pursue policies consistent with currency appreciation.
   C. reduce inflation by increasing interest rates.

Study Session 3
Cross-Reference to CFA Institute Assigned Reading #6 – Currency Exchange Rates: Understanding Equilibrium Value

Page 176 ©2021 Kaplan, Inc.

Study Session 3
Cross-Reference to CFA Institute Assigned Reading #6 – Currency Exchange Rates: Understanding Equilibrium Value

Reading 6

KEY CONCEPTS

LOS 6.a

bid-ask spread (for base currency) = ask quote − bid quote

Dealer spreads depend on spreads in the interbank market, the transaction size, and the dealer-client relationship. Interbank spreads depend on the currencies involved, time of day, and volatility in the currency pair. Forward spreads increase with maturities.

LOS 6.b

To calculate the profits from triangular arbitrage, start in the home currency and go around the triangle by exchanging the home currency for the first foreign currency, then exchanging the first foreign currency for the second foreign currency, and then exchanging the second foreign currency back into the home currency. If we end up with more money than what we had when we started, we've earned an arbitrage profit. The bid-ask spread forces us to buy a currency at a higher rate going one way than we can sell it for going the other way.

LOS 6.c

A spot exchange rate is for immediate delivery, while a forward exchange rate is for future delivery.

premium (discount) for base currency = forward price − spot price

LOS 6.d

The mark-to-market value of a forward contract reflects the profit that would be realized by closing out the position at current market prices, which is equivalent to offsetting the contract with an equal and opposite forward position:

$$V_t = \frac{(FP_t - FP)(\text{contract size})}{\left[1 + R\left(\frac{\text{days}}{360}\right)\right]}$$

where:
V_t = value of the forward contract at time t (to the party buying the base currency), ($t < T$) denominated in price currency
FP_t = forward price (to sell base currency) at time t in the market for a new contract maturing at time T
FP = forward price specified in the contract at inception (to buy the base currency)
days = number of days remaining to maturity of the forward contract ($T − t$)
R = interest rate of price currency

LOS 6.e

Covered interest arbitrage:

$$F = \frac{\left[1 + R_A\left(\dfrac{days}{360}\right)\right]}{\left[1 + R_B\left(\dfrac{days}{360}\right)\right]} S_0$$

Uncovered interest rate parity:

$$E(\%\Delta S)_{(A/B)} = R_A - R_B$$

International Fisher relation:

$$R_{nominal\ A} - R_{nominal\ B} = E(inflation_A) - E(inflation_B)$$

Relative PPP:

$$\%\Delta S_{(A/B)} = inflation_A - inflation_B$$

Forward rate parity:

$$F = E(S_T)$$

LOS 6.f

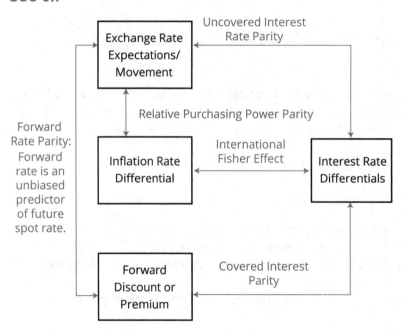

LOS 6.g, 6.h

Future spot rates can be forecasted using PPP or by uncovered interest rate parity. However, neither relationship is bound by arbitrage, nor do these relationships necessarily work in the short term. Forward exchange rates, on the other hand, can be estimated using covered interest parity, and this relationship is bound by arbitrage. If uncovered interest parity holds, then we say that the forward rate parity holds, i.e., the forward rate is an unbiased estimate of the future spot rate.

LOS 6.i

The FX carry trade seeks to profit from the failure of uncovered interest rate parity to work in the short run. In an FX carry trade, the investor invests in a high-yielding currency while borrowing in a low-yielding currency. If the higher yielding currency does not depreciate by the interest rate differential, the investor makes a profit. Carry trade has exposure to crash risk.

> profit on carry trade
> = interest differential − change in the spot rate of the investment currency

LOS 6.j

BOP influence on exchange rate can be analyzed based on current account influence and capital account influence. Current account influences include flow mechanism, portfolio composition mechanism, and debt sustainability mechanism. Capital account inflows (outflows) are one of the major causes of increases (decreases) in exchange rates.

LOS 6.k

The Mundell-Fleming model of exchange rate determination evaluates the impact of monetary and fiscal policies on interest rates and consequently on exchange rates.

Under monetary models, we assume that output is fixed and, hence, monetary policies primarily affect inflation, which in turn affects exchange rates.

The portfolio balance (asset market) model evaluates the long-term implications of sustained fiscal policy (deficit or surplus) on currency values.

Monetary and Fiscal Policy and Exchange Rates

Monetary Policy/Fiscal Policy	Capital Mobility	
	High	Low
Expansionary/Expansionary	Uncertain	Depreciation
Expansionary/Restrictive	Depreciation	Uncertain
Restrictive/Expansionary	Appreciation	Uncertain
Restrictive/Restrictive	Uncertain	Appreciation

Under the pure monetary approach, PPP holds at any point in time.

Under the Dornbusch overshooting model, a restrictive (expansionary) monetary leads to an appreciation (depreciation) of domestic currency in the short term, and then slow depreciation (appreciation) towards the long-term PPP value.

Combining the Mundell-Fleming and portfolio balance approaches, we find that in the short term, an expansionary (restrictive) fiscal policy leads to domestic currency appreciation (depreciation). In the long term, the impact on currency values is opposite.

LOS 6.l

Capital controls and central bank intervention aim to reduce excessive capital inflows, which could lead to speculative bubbles. The success of central bank intervention depends on the size of official FX reserves at the disposal of the central bank relative to the average trading volume in the country's currency. For developed markets, the central bank resources on a relative basis are too insignificant to be effective at managing exchange rates. However, some emerging market countries with large FX reserves relative to trading volume have been somewhat effective.

LOS 6.m

Warning signs of currency crises include: deterioration in terms of trade, a dramatic decline in official foreign exchange reserves, an exchange rate substantially higher than its mean-reverting level, increases in the inflation rate, a fixed- or partially-fixed exchange rate, an increase in money supply relative to bank reserves, and banking crises.

ANSWER KEY FOR MODULE QUIZZES

Module Quiz 6.1

1. **C** Dealer spreads are lower for smaller orders as compared to larger orders. Dealer spreads are larger when spreads in the interbank market are higher. An increase in spot rate volatility will increase spreads in the interbank market. (LOS 6.a)

2. **C** Here is what the triangle looks like with the bid-ask quotes filled in:

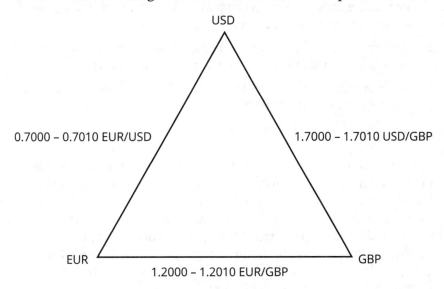

If we start with 1 million USD and move clockwise around the triangle (USD to GBP to EUR to USD), we first convert 1 million USD into GBP at the ask:

$$\frac{1 \text{ million USD}}{1.7010 \text{ USD/GBP}} = 587{,}889 \text{ GBP}$$

Then we sell the GBP for EUR at the bid:

$$587{,}889 \text{ GBP} \times \left(\frac{1.2000 \text{ EUR}}{\text{GBP}}\right) = 705{,}467 \text{ EUR}$$

Finally, we purchase USD at the ask in euros:

$$\frac{705{,}467 \text{ EUR}}{0.7010} = 1{,}006{,}372 \text{ USD}$$

Arbitrage profits are 1,006,372 USD – 1,000,000 USD = 6,372 USD. (LOS 6.b)

Module Quiz 6.2

1. **A** Because of a lower interest rate, the USD (base currency) will appreciate by 2% to $1.012 × 1.02 = C$1.0322. (LOS 6.e)

2. **C** Combining all parity relationships indicates that the expected return on risk-free securities should be the same in all countries and exchange rate risk is really just inflation risk. There are four practical implications from this framework:
   1. The real, risk-free return will be the same in all countries.
   2. Investing in countries with high nominal interest rates will not generate excess returns because the high nominal interest rates will be accompanied by local currency depreciation.
   3. All investors will earn the same expected return in their own currency on any investment denominated in a foreign currency.
   4. Exchange rate risk is simply inflation risk, so investors interested in real returns will not face exchange rate risk.

   (LOS 6.f)

3. **A** Covered interest parity is forced by arbitrage, which is not the case for uncovered interest rate parity. If the forward rate is equal to the expected future spot rate, we say that the forward rate is an unbiased predictor of the future spot rate: $F = E(S_1)$. In this special case, given that covered interest parity holds, uncovered interest parity would also hold (and vice versa). In other words, if uncovered interest rate parity (and covered interest parity) holds, the forward rate is unbiased predictor of future spot rate (i.e., forward rate parity holds). (LOS 6.e)

4. **A** According to the international Fisher relation:

   r = real r + E(I)

   From European data:

   4% = real r + 2%

   real r = 2%

   For United States:

   r = 2% + 1%

   r = 3%

   (LOS 6.e)

5. **A** Since inflation in Europe is higher than the inflation in the U.S. by 1%, the Euro is expected to depreciate by 1% annually against the dollar.

   The current spot rate is $(1/0.74) per Euro or $1.3513/€.

   expected exchange rate in 1 year = 1.3513(0.99) = $1.3378/€

   (LOS 6.e)

Study Session 3
Cross-Reference to CFA Institute Assigned Reading #6 – Currency Exchange Rates: Understanding Equilibrium Value

Reading 6

6. **C** Using covered interest parity, the forward rate in one year (in $ per €) can be calculated as follows:

$$\text{Spot rate} = €0.74 \text{ per } \$ = \$\left(\frac{1}{0.74}\right) \text{ per } €$$

$$F = S_0 \times \left(\frac{1 + r_\$}{1 + r_€}\right) = \left(\frac{1}{0.74}\right) \times \left(\frac{1.035}{1.04}\right) = \$1.3449 \text{ per } €$$

(LOS 6.e)

7. **B** Franklin is correct with respect to both of his statements: the rand should depreciate relative to the franc and the euro should depreciate relative to the dollar.

    The relative form of purchasing power parity predicts that countries with higher expected inflation will experience a depreciation of their currencies. South Africa's expected inflation rate (5%) is higher than the expected inflation rate in Switzerland (3%). The expected inflation rate in Europe (2%) is higher than the expected inflation rate in the United States (1%). According to purchasing power parity, the rand should depreciate relative to the franc, and the euro should depreciate relative to the U.S. dollar.

    Uncovered interest parity makes the same predictions with regard to relative interest rates: countries with higher nominal interest rates can be expected to experience currency depreciation. The South African interest rate (7%) is higher than the Swiss rate (5%), so uncovered interest rate parity predicts that the rand will depreciate with respect to the franc. The interest rate in Europe (4%) is higher than the interest rate in the United States (3%), so the euro should depreciate relative to the U.S. dollar. (LOS 6.e)

8. **C** According to the international Fisher relation, the real interest rate is equal to the nominal interest rate minus the expected inflation rate. The real interest rate in each of the four countries is 2%. (LOS 6.e)

9. **B** The 1-year expected spot rate should be equal to the current 1-year forward rate if uncovered interest rate parity holds. One of the assumptions of uncovered interest rate parity is that investors are risk neutral. Real interest rate parity states that real interest rates are equal across countries. Uncovered interest rate parity also would hold if both (1) relative (not absolute) PPP holds and (2) the international Fisher relationship holds. (LOS 6.e)

Module Quiz 6.3

1. **A** The flow mechanism of current account influences supports the view that current account deficits lead to depreciation of currency. In this example, the reduction in the JPY/USD rate implies depreciation of the USD. Under capital account influences, current account deficits imply capital account inflows and, hence, would lead to an appreciation of USD. The portfolio composition mechanism of current account influences supports the flow mechanism if investors rebalance a portion of their portfolio out of USD assets due to gradual buildup of USD assets over time in their portfolios. The question does not provide information to support this reallocation. (Module 6.3, LOS 6.j)

2. **B** Under the pure monetary approach, growth in the money supply leads to depreciation in currency. However, the future growth rate in money supply affects the trajectory of FX rates but not the current exchange rate. (Module 6.3, LOS 6.k)

3. **A** Under the Mundell-Fleming framework, low capital mobility and restrictive monetary and fiscal policy leads to better trade balance and appreciation of the country's currency. (Module 6.3, LOS 6.k)

4. **A** $(0.9821 - 0.00069) - (0.9817 - 0.00076) = 0.00047$

   (Module 6.1, LOS 6.c)

5. **B** The contract calls for purchase of 200 million CHF in 30 days. To compute the mark-to-market value, we would have to use the quote on 30-day forward contract to sell CHF. Given USD/CHF quote structure, we should use the bid price (going up the quote).

   all-in bid price for 30-day USD/CHF forward contract =
   $0.9817 - 7.6 / 10,000 = 0.98094$

   $$V_t = \frac{(FP_t - FP)(\text{contract size})}{\left[1 + R\left(\frac{\text{days}}{360}\right)\right]}$$

   $FP_t = 0.98094$ (computed above)

   $FP = 0.9832$ (given)

   R = 30-day USD interest rate (USD is the price currency)
   = 0.20%

   $$V_t = \frac{(0.98094 - 0.9832)(200,000,000)}{\left[1 + 0.002\left(\frac{30}{360}\right)\right]} = \frac{-452,000}{1.000166} = -451,924 \text{ USD}$$

   (Module 6.2, LOS 6.d)

6. **A** The contract calls for purchase of 100 million EUR in 60 days. To compute the mark-to-market value, we would have to use the quote on 60-day forward contract to sell EUR. Given USD/EUR quote structure, we should use the bid price (going up the quote).

    all-in bid price for 60-day USD/EUR forward contract
    = 1.2235 – 14.56 / 10,000 = 1.22204

$$V_t = \frac{(FP_t - FP)(\text{contract size})}{\left[1 + R\left(\frac{\text{days}}{360}\right)\right]}$$

    FP_t = 1.22204 (computed above)

    FP = 1.2242 (given)

    R = 60-day USD interest rate (USD is the price currency)

       = 0.21%

$$V_t = \frac{(1.22204 - 1.2242)(100,000,000)}{\left[1 + 0.0021\left(\frac{60}{360}\right)\right]} = \frac{-216,000}{1.00035} = -215,924 \text{ USD}$$

    (Module 6.2, LOS 6.d)

7. **C** Poulsen incorrectly described both the skewness as well as the kurtosis of carry trade returns. Carry trade return distributions generally have *negative skewness* and *excess kurtosis*. (Module 6.3, LOS 6.i)

8. **A** Deterioration (and not improvement) in terms of trade is an indicator of currency crisis. (Module 6.3, LOS 6.m)

9. **A** The Zu is overvalued per PPP, and Zambola is running a current account deficit. A depreciation of Zu would bring it closer to its long-run fair value. An increase in interest rates would lead to appreciation of Zu. Expansionary monetary policy would reduce interest rates and make Zambolan yields less attractive to foreign investors. (Module 6.3, LOS 6.j)

READING
7

Economic Growth and the Investment Decision

EXAM FOCUS

Forecasts of economic growth rates have important implications for investment decisions. Understand the preconditions of growth, how the growth rate can be increased, and what drives economic growth. Be able to compare and contrast competing theories of growth. Finally, be able to use growth accounting equations to forecast the potential growth rate of an economy.

MODULE 7.1: GROWTH FACTORS AND PRODUCTION FUNCTION

Video covering this content is available online.

LOS 7.a: Compare factors favoring and limiting economic growth in developed and developing economies.

CFA® Program Curriculum, Volume 1, page 501

Economists measure the economic output of a country by gross domestic product (GDP). A country's standard of living, however, is best measured by GDP per capita. Of particular concern to investors is not just the level of economic output but the growth rate of output.

Historically, there have been large variations in both GDP growth rates and per capita GDP across countries. Research has identified several factors that influence both the growth of GDP and the level of GDP.

PRECONDITIONS FOR GROWTH

1. **Savings and investment** are positively correlated with economic development. For countries to grow, private and public sector investment must provide a sufficient level of capital per worker. If a country has insufficient domestic savings, it must attract foreign investment in order to grow.

2. **Financial markets and intermediaries** augment economic growth by efficiently allocating resources in several ways. First, financial markets determine which potential users of capital offer the best returns on a risk-adjusted basis. Second, financial instruments are created by intermediaries that provide investors with liquidity and opportunities for risk reduction. Finally, by pooling small amounts of savings from investors, intermediaries can finance projects on larger scales than would otherwise be possible.

   Some caution is in order, however. Financial sector intermediation may lead to declining credit standards and/or increases in leverage, increasing risk but not economic growth.

3. The **political stability, rule of law, and property rights** environment of a country also influence economic growth. Countries that have not developed a system of property rights for both physical and intellectual property will have difficulty attracting capital. Similarly, economic uncertainty caused by wars, corruption, and other disruptions poses unacceptable risk to many investors, reducing potential economic growth.

4. **Investment in human capital**, the investment in skills and well-being of workers, is thought to be complementary to growth in physical capital. Consequently, countries that invest in education and health care systems tend to have higher growth rates. Developed countries benefit the most from post-secondary education spending, which has been shown to foster innovation. Less-developed countries benefit the most from spending on primary and secondary education, which enables the workforce to *apply* the technology developed elsewhere.

5. **Tax and regulatory systems** need to be favorable for economies to develop. All else equal, the lower the tax and regulatory burdens, the higher the rate of economic growth. Lower levels of regulation foster entrepreneurial activity (startups), which have been shown to be positively related to the overall level of productivity.

6. **Free trade and unrestricted capital flows** are also positively related to economic growth. Free trade promotes growth by providing competition for domestic firms, thus increasing overall efficiency and reducing costs. Additionally, free trade opens up new markets for domestic producers. Unrestricted capital flows mitigate the problem of insufficient domestic savings as foreign capital can increase a country's capital, allowing for greater growth. Foreign capital can be invested directly in assets such as property, physical plant, and equipment (foreign direct investment), or invested indirectly in financial assets such as stocks and bonds.

LOS 7.b: Describe the relation between the long-run rate of stock market appreciation and the sustainable growth rate of the economy.

CFA® Program Curriculum, Volume 1, page 507

Equity prices are positively related to earnings growth. Economy-wide, aggregate corporate earnings can grow if GDP grows or if the share of corporate earnings in GDP grows. Therefore, the **potential GDP** of a country—the upper limit of *real* growth for an economy—is an important factor in predicting returns on aggregate equity markets.

To understand this, consider that the growth in aggregate stock market valuation is a function of GDP growth, growth in earnings relative to GDP, and growth in the price to earnings ratio:

$$\Delta P = \Delta GDP + \Delta(E/GDP) + \Delta(P/E)$$

Over the long-term, we have to recognize that *growth* in earnings relative to GDP is zero; labor will be unwilling to accept an ever-decreasing share of GDP. Similarly, *growth* in the P/E ratio will also be zero over the long term; investors will not continue to pay an ever-increasing price for the same level of earnings forever (i.e., the P/E ratio cannot grow indefinitely). Hence over a sufficiently long time horizon, the potential GDP growth rate equals the growth rate of aggregate equity valuation.

LOS 7.c: Explain why potential GDP and its growth rate matter for equity and fixed income investors.

CFA® Program Curriculum, Volume 1, page 507

As indicated previously, growth in potential GDP represents the main driver of aggregate equity valuation. More generally, potential GDP also has implications for real interest rates. Positive growth in potential GDP indicates that future income will rise relative to current income. When consumers expect their incomes to rise, they increase current consumption and save less for future consumption (i.e., they are less likely to worry about funding their future consumption). To encourage consumers to delay consumption (i.e., to encourage savings), investments would have to offer a higher real rate of return. Therefore, higher potential GDP growth implies higher real interest rates and higher real asset returns in general.

In the short term, the relationship between actual GDP and potential GDP may provide insight to both equity and fixed-income investors as to the state of the economy. For example, since actual GDP in excess of potential GDP results in rising prices, the gap between the two can be used as a forecast of inflationary pressures—useful to all investors but of particular concern to fixed-income investors. Furthermore, central banks are likely to adopt monetary policies consistent with the gap between potential output and actual output. When actual GDP growth rate is higher (lower) than potential GDP growth rate, concerns about inflation increase (decrease) and the central bank is more likely to follow a restrictive (expansionary) monetary policy.

In addition to predicting monetary policy, the relationship between actual and potential GDP can also be useful in analyzing fiscal policies. It is more likely for a government to run a fiscal deficit when actual GDP growth rate is lower than its potential growth rate.

Finally, because of the credit risk assumed by fixed-income investors, growth in GDP may be used to gauge credit risk of both corporate and government debt. A higher potential GDP growth rate reduces expected credit risk and generally increases the credit quality of all debt issues.

LOS 7.d: Contrast capital deepening investment and technological progress and explain how each affects economic growth and labor productivity.

CFA® Program Curriculum, Volume 1, page 511

FACTOR INPUTS AND ECONOMIC GROWTH

Economies are complex systems of many economic inputs. To simplify analysis, we examine a 2-factor (labor and capital) aggregate production function in which output (Y) is a function of labor (L) and capital (K), given a level of technology (T).

To examine the effect of capital investment on **economic growth** and **labor productivity**, consider a **Cobb-Douglas production function**, which takes the form:

$$Y = TK^{\alpha}L^{(1-\alpha)}$$

where:

α and $(1 - \alpha)$ = the share of output allocated to capital (K) and labor (L), respectively [α and $(1 - \alpha)$ are also referred to as capital's and labor's share of **total factor cost**, where $\alpha < 1$]

T = a scale factor that represents the **technological progress** of the economy, often referred to as *total factor productivity* (TFP)

The Cobb-Douglas function essentially states that output (GDP) is a function of labor and capital inputs and their productivity. It exhibits **constant returns to scale**; increasing both inputs by a fixed percentage leads to the same percentage increase in output.

Dividing both sides by L in the Cobb-Douglas production function, we can obtain the output per worker (labor productivity).

output per worker = $Y/L = T(K/L)^{\alpha}$

Labor productivity is similar to GDP per capita, a standard of living measure. The previous equation has important implications about the effect of capital investment on the standard of living. Assuming the number of workers and α remain constant, increases in output can be gained by increasing capital per worker (**capital deepening**) or by improving technology (increasing TFP).

However, since α is less than one, additional capital has a diminishing effect on productivity: the lower the value of α, the lower the benefit of capital deepening.

Developed markets typically have a high capital to labor ratio and a lower α compared to developing markets, and therefore developed markets stand to gain less in increased productivity from capital deepening.

> **PROFESSOR'S NOTE**
>
> We need to distinguish between marginal product of capital and marginal productivity of capital. Marginal product of capital is the additional output for one additional unit of capital. Marginal productivity of capital is the increase in output per worker for one additional unit of capital per labor (i.e., increasing capital while keeping labor constant).

In steady state (i.e., equilibrium), the marginal product of capital (MPK = $\alpha Y/K$) and marginal cost of capital (i.e., the *rental price of capital*, r) are equal; hence:

$$\alpha Y/K = r$$

or

$$\alpha = rK/Y$$

> **PROFESSOR'S NOTE**
>
> In the previous equation, r is rate of return and K is amount of capital. rK measures the amount of return to providers of capital. The ratio of rK to output (Y) measures the amount of output that is allocated to providers of capital. This is precisely our definition of α.

The productivity curves in Figure 7.1 show the effect of increasing capital per worker on output per worker. Capital deepening is a movement *along* the productivity curve. The curvature of the relationship derives from the diminishing marginal productivity of capital. Economies will increase investment in capital as long as MPK > r. At the level of K/L for which MPK = r, capital deepening stops and labor productivity becomes stagnant.

However, as technological progress occurs, both capital and labor can produce a higher level of output. An investment in capital leading to technological progress enhances the productivity of existing labor and capital. Technological progress, therefore, can lead to continued increases in output despite diminishing marginal productivity of capital. Technological progress *shifts* the productivity curve upward and will lead to increased productivity at all levels of capital per worker.

labor productivity growth rate

= growth due to technological change + growth due to capital deepening

Figure 7.1: Productivity Curves

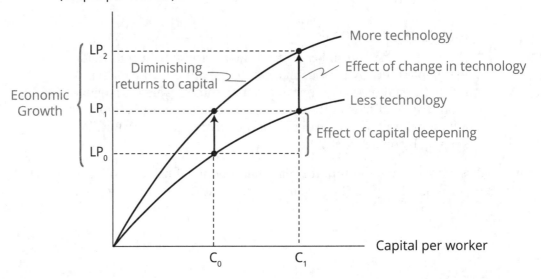

As stated earlier, for developed countries, the capital per worker ratio is relatively high (e.g., level C_1 in Figure 7.1), so those countries gain little from capital deepening and must rely on technological progress for growth in productivity. In contrast, developing nations often have low capital per worker ratios (e.g., C_0 in Figure 7.1), so capital deepening can lead to at least a short-term increase in productivity.

MODULE 7.2: GROWTH ACCOUNTING AND INFLUENCING FACTORS

LOS 7.e: Demonstrate forecasting potential GDP based on growth accounting relations.

CFA® Program Curriculum, Volume 1, page 511

GROWTH ACCOUNTING RELATIONS

Using the Cobb-Douglas production function, the growth in potential GDP can be expressed using the **growth accounting relation** as:

$$\Delta Y/Y = \Delta A/A + \alpha \times (\Delta K/K) + (1-\alpha) \times (\Delta L/L)$$

where:
Y   = output
A   = technology
K   = capital
L   = labor
α = elasticity of output with respect to capital = share of income paid to capital
$(1 - \alpha)$ = elasticity of output with respect to labor = share of income paid to labor

or:

growth rate in potential GDP = long-term growth rate of technology

$$+ \alpha \text{ (long-term growth rate of capital)}$$

$$+ (1 - \alpha) \text{ (long-term growth rate of labor)}$$

In practice, levels of capital and labor are forecasted from their long-term trends, and the shares of capital and labor determined from national income accounts. The change in total factor productivity (technology) is not directly observable. Therefore, it must be estimated as a residual: the ex-post (realized) change in output minus the output implied by ex-post changes in labor and capital.

The growth accounting equation is also useful in determining the comparative effects of increasing different inputs. If labor growth accounts for the majority of economic growth, for example, analysts should be concerned with a country's ability to continue to increase its labor force. The relation can also be used to estimate potential output, as illustrated in the following example.

> **EXAMPLE: Estimating potential GDP growth rate**
>
> Azikland is an emerging market economy where labor cost accounts for 60% of total factor cost. The long-term trend of labor growth of 1.5% is expected to continue. Capital investment has been growing at 3%. The country has benefited greatly from borrowing the technology of more developed countries; total factor productivity is expected to increase by 2% annually. Compute the potential GDP growth rate for Azikland.
>
> **Answer:**
>
> Using the growth accounting equation:
>
> growth rate in potential GDP = 2% + (0.4)(3%) + (0.6)(1.5%) = 4.1%

Another approach to forecasting potential GDP growth is the *labor productivity growth accounting equation*, which focuses on changes in labor as follows:

growth rate in potential GDP = long-term growth rate of labor force

$$+ \text{ long-term growth rate in labor productivity}$$

The long-term growth rate in labor productivity reflects both capital deepening and technological progress.

LOS 7.f: Explain how natural resources affect economic growth and evaluate the argument that limited availability of natural resources constrains economic growth.

CFA® Program Curriculum, Volume 1, page 518

Natural resources include both renewable resources, such as timber, and non-renewable resources, such as oil and gas. The role of natural resources in economic growth is complex. In some instances, countries with abundant natural resources (e.g., Brazil) have grown rapidly. Yet other countries (e.g., some of the resource-rich countries of Africa) have not. Conversely, some resource-poor countries have managed impressive growth.

One reason that limited natural resources do not necessarily constrain economic growth is that *access* to natural resources does not require *ownership* of resources. Resource-poor countries may be able to access resources via trade. Japan, for example, has managed impressive growth and high per capita GDP despite having limited ownership of natural resources.

Other theories contend that ownership of natural resources may actually inhibit growth, because the economic energy of a country rich in natural resources may be focused on recovering those resources rather than developing other industries. Furthermore, countries that own valuable resources can find their currency appreciating as the demand for those resources increases. The so-called "Dutch disease" refers to a situation where global demand for a country's natural resources drives up the country's currency values, making all exports more expensive and rendering other domestic industries uncompetitive in the global markets.

LOS 7.g: Explain how demographics, immigration, and labor force participation affect the rate and sustainability of economic growth.

CFA® Program Curriculum, Volume 1, page 520

As stated previously, an increase in the quantity of labor will increase output, but not per capita output. Quantity of labor is defined as the size of the labor force multiplied by average hours worked. **Labor force** is defined as the number of working age (ages 16–64) people available to work, both employed and unemployed.

LABOR SUPPLY FACTORS

1. **Demographics.** A country's demographics strongly influence its potential economic growth. As a country's population ages and individuals live beyond working age, the labor force declines. Conversely, countries with younger populations have higher *potential* growth. Furthermore, fertility rates drive population growth and thereby affect potential future economic output. Countries with low or declining fertility rates will likely face growth challenges from labor force declines.

2. **Labor force participation.** Labor force participation is defined as the proportion of working age population in the labor force.

   $$\text{labor force participation} = \frac{\text{labor force}}{\text{working age population}}$$

   Labor force participation can increase as more women enter the workforce.

3. **Immigration.** Immigration poses a potential solution to a declining labor force. Countries with low population growth or adverse demographic shifts (older population) may find their growth constrained. Since developed countries tend to have lower fertility rates than less developed countries, immigration represents a potential source of continued economic growth in developed countries.

4. **Average hours worked.** For most countries, the general trend in average hours worked is downward. Possible explanations include legislation limiting the number of hours worked, the "wealth effect" which induces individuals to take

more leisure time, high tax rates on labor income, and an increase in part-time and temporary workers.

EXAMPLE: Impact of demographics on economic growth

Data for Cangoria, a country in Asia, is shown below. Based upon this data, comment on the likely impact of Cangoria's demographic changes on its economic growth. Assume average world population growth rate is 1.2% per year.

	Population	Labor Force Participation	Median Age of Population
2000	23,400,400	60.4%	39.2
2010	28,040,300	70.3%	38.1

Answer:

Cangoria's population grew at an average annual compound growth rate of approximately 1.8% per year over the last ten years. Combined with the increase in labor force participation, labor supply growth should be above average in the future for Cangoria if those trends continue. The young median age of the population also indicates an expected increase in the labor pool in the future.

Changes in per capita GDP are difficult to predict. Output is expected to be higher due an increasing labor pool, but the larger population may mean there is no impact on per capita GDP.

LOS 7.h: Explain how investment in physical capital, human capital, and technological development affects economic growth.

CFA® Program Curriculum, Volume 1, page 526

Human capital. Human capital is knowledge and skills individuals possess. Unlike quantitative labor metrics, such as hours worked, human capital is a qualitative measure of the labor force. Increasing human capital through education or work experience increases productivity and economic growth. Furthermore, human capital may have external spillover effects as knowledgeable workers innovate. Innovations are then used by society in general creating greater efficiencies economy wide.

Physical capital. Physical capital is generally separated into infrastructure, computers, and telecommunications capital (ICT) and non-ICT capital (i.e., machinery, transportation, and non-residential construction). Empirical research has found a strong positive correlation between investment in physical capital and GDP growth rates.

This result may seem inconsistent given our previous discussion about capital deepening and diminishing marginal returns to capital. Several explanations exist to explain why capital increases may still result in economic growth. First, many countries (e.g., developing economies) have relatively low capital to labor ratios, so increases in capital may still have significant impact on economic growth. Second, capital investment can take different forms. Some capital investment actually influences technological progress, thereby increasing TFP and economic growth. For example, acceleration of spending in the IT sector has created what are termed *network externalities*. Investment in IT networks may have multiplicative effects on productivity since IT network investment actually becomes more valuable as more people are connected to the network.

Technological development. Investment in technology includes investment in both physical and human capital. Technological innovation can manifest itself in processes, knowledge, information, machinery, and software, among other things. Researchers have examined proxies for investment in technology such as research and development (R&D) spending or number of patents issued. Developed countries tend to spend the most on R&D since they rely on technological progress for growth given their high existing capital stock and slower population growth. In contrast, less developed countries often copy the technological innovations of developed countries and thus invest less in R&D as a percentage of GDP.

Ultimately, technological development should lead to increases in productivity as measured by GDP per worker. Developed countries tend to have very high levels of productivity by this measure while less developed countries tend to have greater potential for growth in productivity.

Public infrastructure. Investments in public infrastructure such as the construction of public roads, bridges, and municipal facilities, provide additional benefits to *private* investment. For example, an investment in distribution facilities by a private company would do little good without an interstate highway grid. The highway system, therefore, enhances total productivity for the economy by complementing the private investment and increasing total factor productivity.

MODULE QUIZ 7.1, 7.2

To best evaluate your performance, enter your quiz answers online.

Use the following information to answer questions 1 through 6.

Jay Smith, an analyst for Mako Capital, is evaluating investment prospects in Minikaz, an emerging market economy. Minikaz has experienced moderate growth in the past four years, after decades of stagnation. Smith is evaluating changes in government policies that would foster a higher level of growth. Figure 1 shows the summary of his findings.

Figure 1:   Proposed Changes in Minikaz Government Policies

1. Consumer protection will be at the forefront of government's agenda.

2. The government will lower the entry barriers for foreign financial institutions to operate as intermediaries in Minikaz capital markets.

3. The government will expand public domain legislation to acquire private property for public works projects.

Smith reviews a report published by the Minikaz commerce department. The report indicates that the long-term real growth rate of Minikaz GDP is 2.5%, corporate profits as a percentage of GDP increased by 2% last year, and the P/E ratio increased from 17 to 19 over the last two years. Separately, Smith also reviews World Bank reports indicating that Minikaz's potential GDP growth is 4% and that it has been experiencing actual GDP growth of approximately 2.5%. Finally, Smith reviews Minikaz's national income accounts and finds that Minikaz is experiencing both technological progress and making increased capital expenditures.

Separately, Smith evaluates the performance of Kinimaz, a neighboring republic. Kinimaz has had labor growth of 2% over the last several years and capital growth of 3%. Labor's share of total output is estimated to be 60%. Over the same period, Kinimaz's real GDP has grown by 3.7%. Comparing the two countries, Smith notes that Kinimaz has substantially higher amounts of natural resource endowments. He concludes that Minikaz's relatively lower GDP growth is due to lack of natural resources.

1. Which of the following actions by Minikaz's government is *most likely* to increase Minikaz's economic growth rate?
   A. Increasing protection for consumers through regulations.
   B. Allowing foreign financial institutions to enter the market.
   C. Expanding public domain legislation.

2. Based on the commerce department report, what would be the *most likely* forecast for the long-term aggregate stock market appreciation?
   A. 2.5%.
   B. 4.5%.
   C. 11.5%.

3. Based on World Bank report, which of the following conclusions is *most likely* regarding Minikaz?
   A. Inflation is 1.5%.
   B. Minikaz's government is likely to follow a restrictive fiscal policy.
   C. Minikaz's central bank is not likely to be worried about inflation.

4. Using the Cobb-Douglas production function and the concepts of capital deepening and total factor productivity, which of the following outcomes is *most likely*?
   A. Minikaz will experience an increase in sustainable growth of per capita output due to the increased capital expenditures.
   B. There will be no short-term increase in per capita output.
   C. There will be both short-term and long-term increases in Minikaz's GDP growth rate.

5. Using the Cobb-Douglas relation, total factor productivity growth for Kinimaz is *closest* to:
   A. 0.5%.
   B. 1.3%.
   C. 1.7%.

6. Smith's conclusion about Minikaz's relatively lower GDP growth is *most likely*:
   A. correct.
   B. correct because in some cases, natural resources may inhibit economic growth.
   C. incorrect because access to natural resources is more important than ownership.

7. Data for the labor market of countries X and Y over the past year appears below:

Country	Unemployment Rate	% Population < Age 15	Avg. Hours Worked/Week	Immigration Growth
X	16%	16%	37	3.5%
Y	3%	10%	36.5	3.0%

Both countries are expected to have moderate economic expansions over the next several years. Which of the following statements is *most accurate* regarding labor input of the countries in the next several years?
   A. Country X will have greater opportunities to increase labor input.
   B. Country Y will have greater opportunities to increase labor input.
   C. Neither Country X nor Country Y will be able to increase labor input.

8. Which of the following would *least likely* have externality effects on output growth for an economy?
   A. Human capital investment.
   B. ICT investment.
   C. Non-ICT investment.

Video covering this content is available online.

MODULE 7.3: GROWTH AND CONVERGENCE THEORIES

LOS 7.i: Compare classical growth theory, neoclassical growth theory, and endogenous growth theory.

CFA® Program Curriculum, Volume 1, page 538

Theories of economic growth are largely separated into three models with differing views on the steady state growth potential of an economy.

CLASSICAL GROWTH THEORY

Based on Malthusian economics, classical growth theory posits that, in the long-term, population growth increases whenever there are increases in per capita income above subsistence level due to an increase in capital or technological progress. Subsistence level is the minimum income needed to maintain life. Classical growth theory contends that growth in real GDP per capita is not permanent, because when real GDP per capita rises above the subsistence level, a population explosion occurs. Population growth leads to diminishing marginal returns to labor, which reduces productivity and drives GDP per capita back to the subsistence level. This mechanism would prevent long-term growth in per capita income. Classical growth theory is not supported by empirical evidence.

NEOCLASSICAL GROWTH THEORY

Neoclassical growth theory's primary focus is on estimating the economy's long-term **steady state growth rate** (sustainable growth rate or equilibrium growth rate). The economy is at equilibrium when the output-to-capital ratio is constant. When the output-to-capital ratio is constant, the labor-to-capital ratio and output per capita also grow at the equilibrium growth rate, g*. Under neoclassical theory, population growth is independent of economic growth.

PROFESSOR'S NOTE

Steady state growth rate for the purpose of neoclassical growth theory does not assume a constant level of technology and hence differs from the definition of steady state discussed earlier.

Based on the Cobb-Douglas function discussed earlier, neoclassical growth theory states that:

- Sustainable growth of output per capita (or output per worker)(g*) is equal to the growth rate in technology (θ) divided by labor's share of GDP (1 − α).

$$g^* = \frac{\theta}{(1 - \alpha)}$$

- Sustainable growth rate of output (G*) is equal to the sustainable growth rate of output per capita, plus the growth of labor (ΔL).

$$G^* = \frac{\theta}{(1 - \alpha)} + \Delta L$$

PROFESSOR'S NOTE

In the equations for sustainable growth (per capita or total), growth rate is not affected by capital (K). Hence, we say that capital deepening is occurring but it does not affect growth <u>rate</u> once steady state is achieved.

EXAMPLE: Estimating steady state growth rate

An analyst is forecasting steady state growth rates for Country X and Country Y and has collected the following estimates:

Country	TFP Growth Rate	Labor Force Growth Rate	Labor Cost as a Proportion of Total Factor Cost
X	2.0%	1.2%	0.60
Y	1.0%	2.6%	0.52

Calculate and comment on sustainable growth rates for the two countries.

Answer:

Sustainable growth rates:

Country X = (2.0% / 0.60) + 1.2% = 4.53%

Country Y = (1.0% / 0.52) + 2.6% = 4.52%

> Sustainable growth rates for the two countries are comparable. Country X's sustainable growth rate is primarily driven by higher growth rate in TFP. Country Y's sustainable growth rate is mostly driven by a higher population growth rate.

Under neoclassical theory:

- Capital deepening affects the *level* of output but not the *growth rate* in the long run. Capital deepening may temporarily increase the growth rate, but the growth rate will revert back to the sustainable level if there is no technological progress.

- An economy's growth rate will move towards its steady state regardless of the *initial* capital to labor ratio or level of technology.

- In the steady state, the growth rate in productivity (i.e., output per worker) is a function only of the growth rate of technology (θ) and labor's share of total output $(1 - \alpha)$.

- In the steady state, marginal product of capital (MPK) = $\alpha Y/K$ is constant, but marginal productivity is diminishing.

- An increase in savings will only temporarily raise economic growth. However, countries with higher savings rates will enjoy higher capital to labor ratio and higher productivity.

- Developing countries (with a lower level of capital per worker) will be impacted less by diminishing marginal productivity of capital, and hence have higher growth rates as compared to developed countries; there will be eventual convergence of growth rates.

ENDOGENOUS GROWTH THEORY

In contrast to the neoclassical model, **endogenous growth theory** contends that technological growth emerges as a *result* of investment in both physical and human capital (hence the name *endogenous* which means coming from within). Technological progress enhances productivity of both labor and capital. Unlike the neoclassical model, there is no steady state growth rate, so that increased investment can permanently increase the rate of growth.

The driving force behind the endogenous growth theory result is the assumption that certain investments increase TFP (i.e., lead to technological progress) from a societal standpoint. Increasing R&D investments, for example, results in benefits that are also external to the firm making the R&D investments. Those benefits raise the level of growth for the entire economy.

The endogenous growth model theorizes that returns to *capital* are constant. The key implication of constant returns to capital is the effect of an increase in savings: unlike the neoclassical model, the endogenous growth model implies that an increase in savings will permanently increase the growth rate.

The difference between neoclassical and endogenous growth theory relates to total factor productivity. Neoclassical theory assumes that capital investment will expand as technology improves (i.e., growth comes from increases in TFP not related to the investment in capital within the model). Endogenous growth theory, on the other

©2021 Kaplan, Inc.

hand, assumes that capital investment (R&D expenditures) may actually improve total factor productivity.

LOS 7.j: Explain and evaluate convergence hypotheses.

CFA® Program Curriculum, Volume 1, page 553

Empirical evidence indicates that there are large differences between productivity (output per capita) of different countries, with less developed countries experiencing much lower output per capita than their developed counterparts. The economic question is whether productivity, and hence, living standards tend to converge over time. Will less developed countries experience productivity growth to match the productivity of developed nations?

The **absolute convergence** hypothesis states that less-developed countries will converge to the *growth rate* (but not the level of per capita output) of more-developed countries. The neoclassical model assumes that every country has access to the same technology. This leads to countries having the same *growth rates* but not the same per capita income. The **conditional convergence** hypothesis states that convergence in living standards will only occur for countries with the same savings rates, population growth rates, and production functions. Under the conditional convergence hypothesis, the growth rate will be higher for less developed countries until they catch up and achieve a similar standard of living. Under the neoclassical model, once a developing country's standard of living converges with that of developed countries, the growth rate will then stabilize to the same steady state growth rate as that of developed countries.

An additional hypothesis is **club convergence**. Under this hypothesis, countries may be part of a 'club' (i.e., countries with similar institutional features such as savings rates, financial markets, property rights, health and educational services, etc.). Under club convergence, poorer countries that are part of the club will grow rapidly to catch up with their richer peers. Countries can 'join' the club by making appropriate institutional changes. Those countries that are not part of the club may never achieve the higher standard of living.

Empirical evidence shows that developing economies often (but not always) reach the standard of living of more developed ones. Over the past half century, about two-thirds of economies with a lower standard of living than the United States grew at a faster pace than the United States. Though they have not converged to standard of living of the United States, their more rapid growth provides at least some support for the convergence hypothesis. The club convergence theory may explain why some countries that have not implemented appropriate economic or political reforms still lag behind.

LOS 7.k: Describe the economic rationale for governments to provide incentives to private investment in technology and knowledge.

CFA® Program Curriculum, Volume 1, page 557

Firms accept projects when they provide an expected return greater than their risk-adjusted cost of capital. Under endogenous growth theory, private sector investments in R&D and knowledge capital benefit the society overall. For example, a new technology may initially benefit the firm that developed it but may also boost the country's overall productivity. The effects of 'social returns' or externalities are captured in the endogenous growth theory model, which concludes that economies may not reach a steady state growth but may permanently increase growth by expenditures that provide both benefits to the company (private benefits) and benefits to society (externalities).

When the external benefits to the economy (the social returns) of investing in R&D are not considered, many possible R&D projects do not have expected returns (private benefits) high enough to compensate firms for the inherent riskiness of R&D investments. From an aggregate, economy-wide viewpoint, the resultant level of R&D investment will be sub-optimal or too low. Government incentives that effectively subsidize R&D investments can theoretically increase private spending on R&D investments to its optimal level.

LOS 7.l: Describe the expected impact of removing trade barriers on capital investment and profits, employment and wages, and growth in the economies involved.

CFA® Program Curriculum, Volume 1, page 557

None of the growth theories that we have discussed account for potential trade and capital flows between countries. Removing trade barriers and allowing for free flow of capital is likely to have the following benefits for countries:

- Increased investment from foreign savings.
- Allows focus on industries where the country has a comparative advantage.
- Increased markets for domestic products, resulting in economies of scale.
- Increased sharing of technology and higher total factor productivity growth.
- Increased competition leading to failure of inefficient firms and reallocation of their assets to more efficient uses.

The neoclassical model's predictions in an open economy (i.e., an economy without any barriers to trade or capital flow) focus on the convergence. Since developing economies have not reached the point of significant diminishing returns on capital, they can attract capital through foreign investment and experience productivity growth as a result. Eventually, these economies will develop; their growth will slow and will converge to the steady state growth rate of developed economies.

The endogenous growth model also predicts greater growth with free trade and high mobility of capital since open markets foster increased innovation. As foreign competition increases, more efficient and innovative firms will survive. Those firms permanently increase the growth rate of the international economy by providing benefits beyond those simply captured by the firm. Economies of scale also increase output as firms serve larger markets and become more efficient.

In terms of convergence, removing barriers on capital and trade flows may speed the convergence of standard of living of less developed countries to that of developed countries. Research has shown that as long as countries follow outward-oriented policies of integrating their industries with the world economy and increasing exports, their standard of living tends to converge to that of more developed countries. Countries following inward-oriented policies and protecting domestic industries, can expect slower GDP growth and convergence may not occur.

MODULE QUIZ 7.3

To best evaluate your performance, enter your quiz answers online.

1. Country X has output elasticity of capital of 0.6 and population growth of 2%. If total factor productivity growth is 1%, what is the sustainable growth rate in output according to neoclassical theory?
   A. 2.0%.
   B. 2.7%.
   C. 4.5%.

2. Which of the following is the *most accurate* description of club convergence?
   A. Less developed countries will converge to living standards of other less developed countries.
   B. More developed countries may see their standard of living drop due to competition from less developed countries.
   C. Some less developed countries may converge to developed country living standards while others may not.

3. A chief economist argues that government policy should include an additional tax break for research and development expenses. The economist *most likely* agrees with:
   A. endogenous growth theory.
   B. neoclassical theory.
   C. classical theory.

Use the following information to answer questions 4 through 5.

Jignesh Sangani, an economist with a large asset management firm, makes the following statements about removal of barriers to trade and capital flows:

Statement 1: Removal of barriers is likely to lead to permanently higher global economic growth under the neoclassical theory.

Statement 2: Removal of barriers is likely to lead to permanently higher economic growth for developing countries only under the endogenous growth theory.

4. Sangani's statement 1 is *most likely*:
   A. correct.
   B. incorrect due to economic growth being permanent.
   C. incorrect due to economic growth being global.

5. Sangani's statement 2 is *most likely*:
    A. correct.
    B. incorrect due to economic growth being permanent.
    C. incorrect due to economic growth being limited to developing countries only.

6. Which of the following is *least likely* to be associated with the law of diminishing returns?
    A. Investment in labor.
    B. Investment in knowledge capital.
    C. Investment in physical capital.

KEY CONCEPTS

LOS 7.a

Significant differences in growth rates exist between economies. The following factors are positively related to growth rate:

- Sufficient level of savings and investment.
- Development of financial markets and financial intermediaries.
- Political stability, sound laws, and property rights.
- Investment in education and health care systems.
- Lower taxes and regulatory burdens.
- Free trade and unrestricted capital flows.

LOS 7.b

In the long-run, the rate of aggregate stock market appreciation is limited to the sustainable growth rate of the economy.

LOS 7.c

Potential GDP represents the maximum output of an economy without putting upward pressure on prices. Higher potential GDP growth increases the potential for stock returns but also increases the credit quality of all fixed-income investments, all else equal.

In the short term, the difference between potential GDP and actual GDP may be useful for predicting fiscal and monetary policy. If actual GDP is less than potential GDP, inflation is unlikely and the government may follow an expansionary monetary/fiscal policy.

LOS 7.d

Capital deepening is an increase in the capital stock and the capital to labor ratio. Due to diminishing marginal productivity of capital, capital deepening will lead to only limited increases in output and labor productivity if the capital to labor ratio is already high.

Technological progress enhances the productivity of both labor and capital but not the relative productivity of either. The long-term growth rate can be increased by technological progress (also called total factor productivity) since output and labor efficiency are increased at all levels of capital to labor ratios.

LOS 7.e

growth rate in potential GDP = long-term growth rate of technology

$+ \alpha$ (long-term growth rate in capital)

$+ (1 - \alpha)$ (long-term growth rate in labor)

or

growth rate in potential GDP = long-term growth rate of labor force

$+$ long-term growth rate in labor productivity

LOS 7.f

Natural resources are essential to economic growth. Empirical evidence has shown, however, that *ownership* of natural resources is not necessary for growth. As long as nations can acquire natural resources through trade, they can experience substantial growth. In some cases, ownership of natural resources may even inhibit growth since countries with abundant natural resources may not develop other industries.

LOS 7.g

Quantity of labor is a function of population growth, workforce participation, immigration, and average hours worked. All else equal, countries with higher population growth, higher workforce participation, younger working-age populations, higher average hours worked, and higher net immigration can grow faster due to higher labor input.

LOS 7.h

The economic growth rate of a country is positively correlated with investments in both physical and human capital. Furthermore, technological development (as evidenced by spending on R&D) is critical for economic growth. This is especially true for developed countries that already have large capital stock and a slower population growth rate.

LOS 7.i

Classical growth theory states that growth in real GDP per capita is temporary—when the GDP per capita rises above the subsistence level, a population explosion occurs, and GDP per capita is driven back to the subsistence level.

Neoclassical growth theory states that the sustainable growth rate of GDP is a function of population growth, labor's share of income, and the rate of technological advancement. Growth gains from other means such as increased savings are only temporary.

Endogenous growth theory includes the impact of technological progress within the model. Under endogenous growth theory, investment in capital can have constant returns, unlike neoclassical theory that assumes diminishing returns to capital. This assumption allows for a permanent increase in growth rate attributable to an increase in savings rate. Research and development expenditures are often cited as examples of capital investment that increase technological progress.

LOS 7.j

Absolute convergence states that the per capita growth *rates* (not growth *level)* will converge (i.e., be the same across all countries). The conditional convergence hypothesis assumes that convergence in living standards (i.e., *level* of per capita output) will only occur for countries with the same savings rate, population growth, and production functions.

The club convergence hypothesis contends that living standards in some less developed countries may converge to living standards of developed standards if they are in the same "club." A club comprises countries with similar institutional structures (such as property rights and political stability). Countries outside of the club (without the appropriate institutional structures) will not see their living standards converge.

LOS 7.k

Under the endogenous growth theory, investments in R&D, though risky, often enhance the productivity of the entire economy. Since the private investor only reaps part of the benefit of those investments, it is likely that private sector investments in R&D will be less than what would be optimal for the economy. Government subsidies can make these investments more attractive to private businesses.

LOS 7.l

Economies grow faster in an environment of no trade barriers and free capital flows. Higher growth rates are possible because foreign investment can provide capital to less developed countries (neoclassical theory). The larger markets and greater opportunity to take advantage of innovation will also increase the growth rate in open economies (endogenous growth theory).

Finally, convergence of living standards is likely to be quicker in an open economy.

ANSWER KEY FOR MODULE QUIZZES

Module Quiz 7.1, 7.2

1. **B** Financial intermediary development helps foster economic growth by allowing more efficient allocation of capital and risk. (Module 7.1, LOS 7.a)

2. **A** Long-term growth in the stock market is a function of GDP growth. The other factors—profits as a percentage of GDP and P/E ratios—will have a long-term growth rate of approximately zero and will not impact a forecast of long-term growth in the stock market. (Module 7.1, LOS 7.a)

3. **C** Potential GDP can be interpreted as the highest growth that can be obtained without pressure on prices. Since actual GDP is lower than potential, there is little risk of inflation. (Module 7.1, LOS 7.b)

4. **C** Since Minikaz is a developing country, it is likely to have a low capital base. With a low capital base, increased capital expenditures will still have an impact on output per worker. Technological progress always has a positive impact on output per worker. (Module 7.1, LOS 7.d)

5. **B** Use the growth accounting relations and solving for growth in TFP.

   $$3.7\% = \Delta TFP + 0.4(3\%) + 0.6(2\%)$$

   $$\Delta TFP = 1.3\%$$

   (Module 7.2, LOS 7.e)

6. **C** Empirical evidence has shown that for economic growth, access to natural resources is more important than ownership. Natural resources may inhibit growth if countries that own them do not develop other industries. However, that is not the conclusion Smith reaches. (Module 7.2, LOS 7.f)

7. **A** Country X will have the greater opportunity due to the younger workforce, potential labor input from unemployed workers, and immigration. (Module 7.2, LOS 7.g)

8. **C** Both human capital and ICT investment tend to have societal benefits. This spillover effect enhances overall growth rate. (Module 7.2, LOS 7.h)

Module Quiz 7.3

1. **C** Using the equation from neoclassical theory, $1\% / (1 - 0.6) + 2\% = 4.5\%$.
(LOS 7.i)

2. **C** The notion of the club is that some nations are not in the club and will not converge. (LOS 7.j)

3. **A** Endogenous growth theory includes the concept that R&D may have external benefits, and, therefore, should be subsidized by the government. (LOS 7.i)

4. **B** Under the neoclassical growth theory, the benefit of open markets is temporary. (LOS 7.i)

5. **C** Under the endogenous growth theory, open markets lead to higher rate of growth permanently for all markets. (LOS 7.i)

6. **B** Knowledge capital is a special type of public good that is not subject to the law of diminishing returns. Investment in labor and physical capital do exhibit diminishing returns, which are reflected in the shape of the productivity curve. (LOS 7.k)

READING
8

Economics of Regulation

EXAM FOCUS

Regulations have important implications for economic growth and for valuation of companies. Understand the implications of regulations on financial markets, the cost benefit analysis of regulation, regulatory interdependence, and implications for valuation. There is a lot of new terminology introduced in this topic review that needs to be memorized.

MODULE 8.1: ECONOMICS OF REGULATION

LOS 8.a: Describe the economic rationale for regulatory intervention.

Video covering this content is available online.

CFA® Program Curriculum, Volume 1, page 582

Economic Rationale for Regulation

Regulations are often required when markets cannot provide efficient solutions (also known as Pareto optimal, which means that one cannot make any participant better off without making some other participant worse off) for all problems. Regulations are needed in the presence of informational frictions, externalities, weak competition, and social objectives.

Informational frictions occur when information is not equally available or distributed. A situation where some market participants have access to information unavailable to others is called *information asymmetry*. Regulations are put in place in an attempt to ensure that no participant is treated unfairly or is at a disadvantage.

Externalities are costs or benefits that affect a party that did not choose to incur that cost or benefit. For example, a polluter may not bear the full cost of their actions.

Weak competition can lead to fewer choices, higher prices, and lack of innovation. Antitrust regulations (discussed later) seek to mitigate this problem.

Social objectives are achieved via provision of public goods (e.g., roads and police protection). A public good is a resource that can be enjoyed by a person without making it unavailable to others. Since people share in the consumption of public goods but don't necessarily bear a cost that is proportionate to consumption, regulations are necessary to ensure an optimal level of production of such public goods. Regulatory obligations imposed on firms (e.g., telecommunications firms should serve rural markets) can also serve social objectives.

LOS 8.b: Explain the purposes of regulating commerce and financial markets.

CFA® Program Curriculum, Volume 1, page 586

1. **Regulating commerce.** Government regulations provide an essential framework to facilitate business decision-making. Examples of regulations covering commerce include company laws, tax laws, contract laws, competition laws, labor laws, banking laws, bankruptcy laws, and dispute resolution systems.

   Regulations may facilitate or hinder commerce. For example, protections of intellectual property facilitate long-term investments in research. Similarly, trade agreements promote commerce internationally. Lack of enforcement or generally poor protection of intellectual property rights globally remains a concern. With increasing use of big data by businesses, privacy and data protection rules are concerns that are best addressed by regulation.

2. **Regulating financial markets.** Financial market regulations include regulation of securities markets and regulation of financial institutions. Regulation of financial markets is critical to prevent failures of the financial system and to maintain the integrity of markets. The objectives of securities regulations include three interrelated goals: protect investors, create confidence in the markets, and enhance capital formation.

Regulation of Security Markets

Ensuring the fairness and integrity of capital markets and thereby protecting investors is a key role of financial market regulators. Several observations can be made about securities markets regulations:

- Disclosure requirements are a key element of security markets regulations. Disclosures provide transparency (i.e., reduce information asymmetry) in financial markets and hence promote investor confidence.

- Many securities regulations are directed toward mitigating agency problems. In the financial markets, investors often work through intermediaries (agents) whose interests often diverge from the interests of investors. Regulations imposing fiduciary duties seek to mitigate such agency problems.

- Regulations have historically focused on protecting small (retail) investors (hence the relatively lax regulatory coverage of hedge funds and private equity funds that are marketed only to qualified investors).

Regulation of Financial Institutions

Prudential Supervision

Prudential supervision refers to the monitoring and regulation of financial institutions to reduce system-wide risks and to protect investors. Prudential supervision is important because the failure of one financial institution can have a far-reaching impact and may result in a loss of confidence. Due to high mobility of capital across the developed world, shocks in one part of the system can affect the whole system, leading to a global contagion. Prudential supervision focuses on diversification of assets, an adequate capital base, and risk management activities of financial institutions.

The cost benefit analysis of financial market regulations should also include hidden costs. For example, FDIC insurance for banks may incentivize them with excessive risk-taking (a moral hazard problem).

LOS 8.c: Describe anticompetitive behaviors targeted by antitrust laws globally and evaluate the antitrust risk associated with a given business strategy.

CFA® Program Curriculum, Volume 1, page 587

Antitrust Regulation

While regulations often hinder foreign competition (to protect domestic businesses), they seek to promote competition among domestic businesses. Antitrust laws work to promote domestic competition by monitoring and restricting activities that reduce or distort competition.

Regulators often block a merger that leads to an excessive concentration of market share. Anticompetitive behavior such as price collusion, discriminatory pricing, bundling, and exclusive dealing is often also prohibited. Internationally, companies need to evaluate their product and marketing strategies in the context of multiple (and varying) regulatory regimes. For example, a multinational company may be subject to U.S. antitrust laws as well as EU antitrust laws.

When evaluating an announced merger or acquisition, an analyst should consider the anticipated response by regulators as part of the analysis.

LOS 8.d: Describe classifications of regulations and regulators.

CFA® Program Curriculum, Volume 1, page 588

Regulations have important implications on businesses and the overall economy. Regulations can be classified as **statutes** (laws made by legislative bodies), **administrative regulations** (rules issued by government agencies or other bodies authorized by the government), or **judicial law** (findings of the court).

Regulators

Regulators can be government agencies or **independent regulators**. Independent regulators are given recognition by government agencies and have power to make rules and enforce them. However, independent regulators are usually not funded by the government and hence are politically independent. The Public Company Accounting Oversight Board (PCAOB), an independent regulator, is a nonprofit corporation established by the U.S. Congress to oversee audits of public companies and is primarily funded by annual fees paid by public companies, brokers, and dealers.

Industry **self-regulatory bodies (SRBs)** are private organizations that represent as well as regulate their members. Members of SRBs have to adhere to its rules. SRBs may have inherent conflicts of interest. These conflicts of interest may reduce the effectiveness of SRBs, especially in the presence of a more formal and effective regulatory structure. SRBs nonetheless are attractive in that they increase the overall level of regulatory resources, utilize the industry professionals with the requisite expertise, and allow regulators to devote resources to other priorities.

SRBs that are recognized by the government and given enforcement powers are self-regulating organizations (SROs). SROs are also independently funded and, as such, are politically independent. SROs regulate the behavior of their members and often provide public goods in the form of standards. Because of their recognition by the government, SROs fall within the category of independent regulators.

Outside bodies are not regulators themselves, but their product is referenced by regulators. Examples of outside bodies include FASB and IASB.

LOS 8.e: Describe uses of self-regulation in financial markets.

CFA® Program Curriculum, Volume 1, page 588

FINRA is an SRO recognized by the SEC in the United States. FINRA's primary objective is to protect investors by maintaining the fairness of the U.S. capital markets. FINRA has the authority to enforce security laws and regulations. Similar SRBs can be found globally.

However, the use of SROs in civil-law countries is not common; in such countries, formal government agencies fulfill the role of SROs. In these civil-law countries, nonindependent SRBs may support the regulatory framework via guidelines, codes of conduct, and continuing education.

In common-law countries such as the United Kingdom and the United States, SROs have historically enjoyed recognition.

LOS 8.f: Describe regulatory interdependencies and their effects.

CFA® Program Curriculum, Volume 1, page 592

Regulatory Interdependencies

Regulation does not always conflict with the interests of the regulated. The **regulatory capture** is based upon the assumption that, regardless of the original purpose behind its establishment, a regulatory body will, at some point in time, be influenced or even possibly controlled by the industry that is being regulated. The rationale behind the theory is that regulators often have experience in the industry, and this affects the regulators' ability to render impartial decisions. Regulatory capture is more likely to be a concern with SROs than with government agencies. For example, regulatory capture is often cited as a concern with the commercialization of financial exchanges.

Regulatory differences between jurisdictions can lead to **regulatory competition**, in which regulators compete to provide the most business-friendly regulatory environment. **Regulatory arbitrage** occurs when businesses shop for a country that allows a specific behavior rather than changing the behavior. Regulatory arbitrage also entails exploiting the difference between the economic substance and interpretation of a regulation.

To avoid regulatory arbitrage, cooperation at a global level to achieve a cohesive regulatory framework is necessary. For example, regulations limiting greenhouse gas emissions should be consistent globally; otherwise, polluters will simply relocate to less restrictive jurisdictions and the objectives of the regulations will not be achieved. Similarly, efforts to reduce the risk of a global financial crisis have been hampered by the lack of a cohesive global regulatory framework.

Even within a country, there may be a conflict between the objectives of different regulatory bodies, leading to an inconsistent overall regulatory framework. For example, regulations seeking higher fuel efficiency standards for automobiles may conflict with regulations from another agency seeking to make the automobiles safer.

LOS 8.g: Describe tools of regulatory intervention in markets.

CFA® Program Curriculum, Volume 1, page 596

Tools of Regulatory Intervention

Three **regulatory tools** are available to regulators:

1. **Price mechanisms.** Price mechanisms such as taxes and subsidies can be used to further specific regulatory objectives; for example, sin taxes are often used to deter consumption of alcohol. Conversely, subsidies such as those on green energy can encourage specific economic behaviors. Per the Coase theorem, if an externality can be traded (and absent transaction costs), then the allocation of property rights will be efficient, and the resource allocation will not depend

on the initial assignment of property rights. SROs and outside bodies are least likely to use price mechanisms.

2. **Restricting or requiring certain activities.** Regulators may ban certain activities (e.g., use of specific chemicals) or require that certain activities be performed (e.g., filing of 10-K reports by publicly listed companies) to further their objectives.

3. **Provision of public goods or financing of private projects.** Regulators may provide public goods (e.g., national defense) or fund private projects (e.g., small-business loans, student loans) depending on their political priorities and objectives.

Newer regulatory tools continue to be developed as governments face new challenges. For example, following the financial crisis of 2008, to reduce systemic risk of financial contagion, the Financial Stability Board and the G20 introduced a new bail-in tool to deal with the failure of a financial institution. Under this framework, a clear set of rules was designed to ensure that the cost of failure is borne by the shareholders and creditors, not the taxpayers. Regulatory tools developed in response to past events may not necessarily work well under a different set of circumstances in the future; the jury is still out on the bail-in process.

Sometimes, a combination of regulatory tools may work better in conjunction. For example, in deterring consumption of junk foods, regulators may both tax the product category as well as require appropriate nutritional labeling for food.

The effectiveness of regulatory tools depends on the enforcement abilities (e.g., sanctioning violators) of the regulators. Furthermore, the enforcement should have the desired effect of compliance with the regulations. For example, regulations seeking to protect investors in a public company may specify sanctions for violations. If the sanctions are borne by the company (and ultimately the shareholders) and not the individuals perpetrating the violations (i.e., management), then the sanctions end up hurting those that the regulations were intended to protect in the first place.

LOS 8.h: Describe benefits and costs of regulation.

CFA® Program Curriculum, Volume 1, page 599

Cost Benefit Analysis of Regulation

A regulatory framework needs to be assessed in terms of the cost of the framework relative to the benefit it provides. U.S. federal regulatory agencies are required to conduct a cost benefit analysis prior to issuing a regulation.

The costs and benefits of regulations may be easy to view but difficult to quantify. The cost of a regulation is not limited to the implementation cost (i.e., the cost of operating a government agency to provide the monitoring and supervision); an analyst should also consider the cost of the regulation to the private sector.

Regulatory burden (also known as government burden) refers to the cost of compliance for the regulated entity. Regulatory burden minus the private benefits of regulation is known as the **net regulatory burden**.

Regulators should be aware of unintended consequences of regulations. For example, regulations mandating an increase in automobile fuel efficiency standards may encourage consumers to drive more, reducing the effectiveness of the regulation. Regulatory burden is generally difficult to measure as it includes the indirect costs related to changes in economic behavior.

Regulatory costs are difficult to assess before a regulation is put in place. For this reason, many regulatory provisions include a sunset clause that requires regulators to revisit the cost benefit analysis based on actual outcomes before renewing the regulation.

LOS 8.i: Describe the considerations when evaluating the effects of regulation on an industry.

CFA® Program Curriculum, Volume 1, page 602

Regulations can help or hinder a company or industry. Regulations may shrink the size of one industry (e.g., if it is heavily taxed) while increasing the size of another (e.g., an industry receiving subsidies). Analysts should review the impact of current and proposed regulations on an industry or company because regulations can have a large impact on valuation.

Regulations are not always costly for those that end up being regulated. If the regulator is captive, regulations may end up benefiting the regulated entities.

Regulations may introduce inefficiencies in the market. For example, past government bailouts of financial institutions have conveyed a message of future implicit guarantees. For this reason, the credit spreads on bonds issued by the financial sector may not fully reflect their risk.

Some regulations may be specifically applicable to certain sectors, while others may have broad implications affecting a number of sectors. Certain industries have more exposure to certain types of regulations. For example, environmental laws have greater implications for the mining, oil, and gas sectors than they do for the retail or health care sectors. Similarly, labor laws are most relevant to labor-intensive industries.

MODULE QUIZ 8.1

To best evaluate your performance, enter your quiz answers online.

Use the following information to answer Questions 1 through 7.

Gyaneshwar Dharampal, CFA, is one of the newer analysts at Paramus Funds and has been assigned to cover the global financial services industry. Dharampal is currently reviewing the Zambolan financial services industry. Zambola is a rapidly growing emerging market country. The Zambolan currency is known as the Zu.

The governance of commercial banks in Zambola is covered by the Zambola Financial Institutions Act as amended (2018) (the act). The act provides the regulatory framework for security markets, commercial banks, and other financial intermediaries.

The Zambolan Finance Commission (ZFC) has enforcement and supervisory powers over commercial banks. In its regulatory role, ZFC specifies minimum capital requirements and underwriting standards for loans and investments for commercial banks in Zambola. Currently, the minimum credit rating for bonds eligible for investment by commercial banks is stipulated to be *B* as rated by JBL Services, an independent rating agency.

The act also provides that the operation of the Zambolan stock exchange be supervised by the Exchange Association (a self-regulating organization). To promote independence of the Exchange Association, the act exempts it from supervisory review by ZFC.

To curb predatory lending, the act imposes a ceiling on interest rates that banks can charge on consumer loans. However, a recent decision by a Zambolan high court overturned that provision of the act. In response, in the new revenue bill, the Zambolan government included punitive taxes on earnings of commercial banks that are attributable to interest rates higher than the previously specified ceiling.

Dharampal notes that a new regulation would impose additional taxes on Zambolan manufacturers and require them to make certain workplace safety-related modifications. He estimates that the tax revenue from the new regulation would be 100 million Zu. The tax revenue would be used to cover the salaries of newly hired personnel at the government agency in charge of enforcing the regulation. The aggregate cost to the manufacturing sector for compliance with the new regulation is estimated to be 300 million Zu. It is also estimated that the aggregate benefit to private sector builders as a result of the new regulation would be 30 million Zu.

Finally, Dharampal notes that Zambola is in the process of introducing a national health care system wherein taxes on tobacco and alcohol will fund government-subsidized health care.

1. The removal of the interest rate ceiling on consumer loans is *most likely* an example of:
    A. a judicial law.
    B. a statute.
    C. an administrative regulation.

2. JBL Services is *best* described as:
    A. a self-regulating organization.
    B. a government agency.
    C. an outside body.

3. Which of the following is *not* a good reason to delegate supervisory authority to the Exchange Association?
    A. Increase in overall regulatory resources.
    B. Exemption from supervisory review by ZFC.
    C. Additional knowledge and expertise of industry professionals.

4. Which of the following is *most likely* to be a concern related to the regulatory authority of the Exchange Association?
    A. Regulatory arbitrage.
    B. Regulatory capture.
    C. Regulatory competition.

5. The Zambolan government's action of charging punitive taxes on interest earnings of commercial banks is *best* described as:
    A. a price mechanism.
    B. a restriction on certain activities.
    C. a provision of a public good.

6. The net regulatory burden of the new workplace safety regulation is *closest* to:
    A. 170 million Zu.
    B. 270 million Zu.
    C. 430 million Zu.

7. Based on the information provided, which sector of the Zambolan economy is *most likely* to grow?
    A. Commercial banks.
    B. Health care.
    C. Alcoholic beverage producers.

8. Which of the following would *least accurately* be described as regulations of commerce?
    A. Antitrust regulations.
    B. Dispute resolution regulations.
    C. Prudential supervision regulations.

KEY CONCEPTS

LOS 8.a

Regulations are needed in the presence of informational frictions and externalities. Informational frictions arise in the presence of information asymmetry. Externalities deal with the provision of public goods.

LOS 8.b

Examples of regulations covering commerce include company law, tax law, contract law, competition law, banking law, bankruptcy law, and dispute resolution systems. Governments may facilitate or hinder commerce.

Financial market regulations seek to protect investors and to ensure stability of financial systems. Securities market regulations include disclosure requirements, regulations to mitigate agency conflicts, and regulations to protect small investors.

Prudential supervision is the regulation and monitoring of financial institutions to reduce system-wide risks and protect investors.

LOS 8.c

Regulators often block a merger that would lead to an excessive concentration of market share. Additionally, anticompetitive behavior such as discriminatory pricing, bundling, and exclusive dealing is often prohibited.

LOS 8.d

Regulations can be classified as statutes, administrative regulations, or judicial law.

Regulators can be government agencies or independent regulators. Self-regulating organizations (SROs) are given government recognition and authority. Self-regulatory bodies do not have government recognition, and they represent as well as regulate their members. Outside bodies are not regulators themselves, but their product may be referenced by regulators.

LOS 8.e

Self-regulating organizations, when properly supervised by regulatory agencies, have been effective in carrying out the objectives of regulations. Use of SROs is more prevalent in common-law countries than in civil-law countries.

LOS 8.f

The regulatory capture theory is based upon the assumption that a regulatory body will be influenced or even controlled by the industry that is being regulated. Regulatory differences between jurisdictions can lead to regulatory competition wherein regulators compete to provide the most business-friendly regulatory environment. Firms may use regulatory arbitrage to exploit the difference between the substance and interpretation of a regulation.

LOS 8.g

Regulatory tools include price mechanisms, restrictions on or requirement of certain activities, and provision of public goods or financing of private projects.

LOS 8.h

Regulatory burden refers to the cost of compliance for the regulated entity. Regulatory burden minus the private benefits of regulation is known as the net regulatory burden. Indirect costs of regulations need to be included in the cost benefit analysis of regulations but are difficult to measure ex ante. Sunset clauses require a cost benefit analysis to be revisited before the regulation is renewed.

LOS 8.i

Regulations can have material impacts on industries and companies. Certain industries have more exposure to certain types of regulations. Analysts should review the impact of current and proposed regulations as regulations can have a large impact on valuations for a particular company or industry.

Reading 8

ANSWER KEY FOR MODULE QUIZZES

Module Quiz 8.1

1. **A** Judicial law is the finding of the court and is applicable in this case. Statutes are laws made by legislative bodies, while administrative regulations are rules issued by government agencies or other bodies authorized by the government. (LOS 8.d)

2. **C** JBL Services is neither a government agency nor an SRO and is best described as an outside body. The work of such outside bodies is sometimes referenced by regulatory authorities in their regulations. (LOS 8.d)

3. **B** The Exchange Association is an SRO and hence increases overall regulatory resources. Its members also bring knowledge and expertise of industry professionals. However, due to the inherent conflict of interest in an association regulating its own members, adequate regulatory oversight would be necessary. (LOS 8.e)

4. **B** The Exchange Association is exposed to conflict of interest in regulating its members. Hence, regulatory capture (where a regulatory body is influenced or controlled by the industry that is being regulated) is a concern. Regulatory differences between jurisdictions can lead to regulatory competition; regulators compete to provide a business-friendly regulatory environment. Firms may also resort to regulatory arbitrage to exploit the difference between the substance and interpretation of a regulation. Neither regulatory competition nor regulatory arbitrage is applicable in this case. (LOS 8.f)

5. **A** Taxes and subsidies as regulatory tools are examples of price mechanisms. (LOS 8.g)

6. **B** Net regulatory burden is the cost of compliance for the regulated entity minus the private benefits of regulation. (LOS 8.h)

7. **B** Everything else held constant, sectors being taxed (i.e., commercial banks, alcohol, and tobacco) would be expected to shrink, while sectors that are subsidized (i.e., health care) would be expected to grow. (LOS 8.i)

8. **C** Prudential supervision deals with regulating financial markets rather than regulating commerce. Antitrust regulations and dispute resolution regulations are elements of the regulation of commerce. (LOS 8.b)

TOPIC QUIZ: ECONOMICS

You have now finished the Economics topic section. On your Schweser online dashboard, you can find a Topic Quiz that will provide immediate feedback on how effective your study of this material has been. The test is best taken timed; allow three minutes per question. Topic Quizzes are more exam-like than typical QBank questions or module quiz questions. A score less than 70% suggests that additional review of the topic is needed.

FORMULAS

Study Sessions 1 & 2: Quantitative Methods

Simple Linear Regression

slope coefficient: $\hat{b}_1 = \dfrac{\text{cov}_{XY}}{\sigma_X^2}$

intercept term: $\hat{b}_0 = \overline{Y} - \hat{b}_1\overline{X}$

coefficient t-test: $t_{b_1} = \dfrac{\hat{b}_1 - b_1}{s_{\hat{b}_1}}$ with $n - 2$ df

predicted value of the dependent variable: $\hat{Y} = \hat{b}_0 + \hat{b}_1 X_p$

confidence interval for a predicted value (simple linear regression only):

$$\hat{Y} \pm \left(t_c \times s_f\right) \Rightarrow \left[\hat{Y} - \left(t_c \times s_f\right) < Y < \hat{Y} + \left(t_c \times s_f\right)\right]$$

ANOVA Table Information (Simple Linear Regression)

total sum of squares (SST): $\text{SST} = \sum\limits_{i=1}^{n} \left(Y_i - \overline{Y}\right)^2$

regression sum of squares (RSS): $\text{RSS} = \sum\limits_{i=1}^{n} \left(\hat{Y}_i - \overline{Y}\right)^2$

sum of squared errors (SSE): $\text{SSE} = \sum\limits_{i=1}^{n} \left(Y_i - \hat{Y}\right)^2$

coefficient of determination: $R^2 = \dfrac{\text{total variation} - \text{unexplained variation}}{\text{total variation}}$

$$= \dfrac{\text{SST} - \text{SSE}}{\text{SST}}$$

standard error of estimate (SEE): $\sqrt{\dfrac{\text{SSE}}{n-2}} = \sqrt{\text{MSE}}$

F-statistic $= \dfrac{\text{MSR}}{\text{MSE}} = \dfrac{\text{RSS}/k}{\text{SSE}/{n-k-1}}$ with $n - 2$ df

Multiple Regression

predicted y-value: $\hat{Y}_i = \hat{b}_0 + \hat{b}_1 X_{1i} + \hat{b}_2 X_{2i} + \ldots + \hat{b}_k X_{ki}$

t-test for regression coefficient: $t = \dfrac{\hat{b}_j - b_j}{s_{\hat{b}_j}}$ with $n - k - 1$ df

©2021 Kaplan, Inc.

ANOVA: total variation (SST) = explained variation (RSS) + unexplained variation (SSE)

mean squared error: $MSE = \dfrac{SSE}{n - k - 1}$

mean regression sum of squares: $MSR = \dfrac{RSS}{k}$

F-test for multiple regression: $F = \dfrac{MSR}{MSE} = \dfrac{RSS/k}{SSE/n - k - 1}$, with k and n − k − 1 df

adjusted R^2: $R_a^2 = 1 - \left[\left(\dfrac{n-1}{n-k-1}\right) \times \left(1 - R^2\right)\right]$

Breusch-Pagan Chi-square test for heteroskedasticity:

$\quad BP = n \times R_{resid}^2$ with k degrees of freedom

Time-Series Analysis

AR model of order p, AR(p): $x_t = b_0 + b_1 x_{t-1} + b_2 x_{t-2} + \ldots + b_p x_{t-p} + \varepsilon_t$

Mean reverting level of AR(1): $x_t = \dfrac{b_0}{\left(1 - b_1\right)}$

ARCH(1) model: $\hat{\varepsilon}_t^2 = a_0 + a_1 \hat{\varepsilon}_{t-1}^2 + \mu_t$

Big Data Projects

normalized $X_i = \dfrac{X_i - X_{min}}{X_{max} - X_{min}}$

standardized $X_i = \dfrac{X_i - \mu}{\sigma}$

accuracy = (TP + TN) / (TP + TN + FP + FN)

F1 score = (2 × P × R) / (P + R)

true positive rate (TPR) = TP / (TP + FN)

false positive rate (FPR) = FP / (FP + TN)

$RMSE = \sqrt{\dfrac{\sum\limits_{i=1}^{n}\left(\text{predicted}_i - \text{actual}_i\right)^2}{n}}$

Study Session 3: Economics

Where applicable, ALL notation assumes A/B currency quote convention.

bid-ask spread (for base currency) = ask quote − bid quote

cross rates with bid-ask spreads:

$$\left(\frac{A}{C}\right)_{bid} = \left(\frac{A}{B}\right)_{bid} \times \left(\frac{B}{C}\right)_{bid} \qquad \left(\frac{A}{C}\right)_{offer} = \left(\frac{A}{B}\right)_{offer} \times \left(\frac{B}{C}\right)_{offer}$$

forward premium = (forward price) − (spot price) = $F - S_0$

value of a forward currency contract prior to expiration:

$$V_t = \frac{(FP_t - FP)(\text{contract size})}{\left[1 + R\left(\frac{\text{days}}{360}\right)\right]}$$

covered interest rate parity:

$$F = \frac{\left[1 + R_A\left(\frac{\text{days}}{360}\right)\right]}{\left[1 + R_B\left(\frac{\text{days}}{360}\right)\right]} S_0$$

uncovered interest rate parity:

$$E(\%\Delta S)_{(A/B)} = R_A - R_B$$

Fisher relation:

$$R_{nominal} = R_{real} + E(\text{inflation})$$

international Fisher relation:

$$R_{nominal\,A} - R_{nominal\,B} = E(\text{inflation}_A) - E(\text{inflation}_B)$$

relative purchasing power parity:

$$\%\Delta S_{(A/B)} = \text{inflation}_{(A)} - \text{inflation}_{(B)}$$

where:

$$\%\Delta S_{(A/B)} = \text{change in spot price } (A/B)$$

labor productivity:

output per worker $Y/L = T(K/L)^{\alpha}$

©2021 Kaplan, Inc.

growth accounting relation:

growth rate in potential GDP = long-term growth rate of technology
+ α(long-term growth rate of capital)
+ $(1 - \alpha)$(long-term growth rate of labor)

or

growth rate in potential GDP = long-term growth rate of labor force
+ long-term growth rate in labor productivity

neoclassical growth theory:

sustainable growth of output per capita (g*) equals growth rate in technology (θ) divided by labor's share of GDP $(1 - \alpha)$

$$g* = \frac{\theta}{(1 - \alpha)}$$

sustainable growth rate of output (G*) equals sustainable growth rate of output per capita plus growth of labor (ΔL)

$$G* = \frac{\theta}{(1 - \alpha)} + \Delta L$$

APPENDIX A: STUDENT'S T-DISTRIBUTION

STUDENT'S T-DISTRIBUTION

	Level of Significance for One-Tailed Test					
df	0.100	0.050	0.025	0.01	0.005	0.0005

	Level of Significance for Two-Tailed Test					
df	0.20	0.10	0.05	0.02	0.01	0.001
1	3.078	6.314	12.706	31.821	63.657	636.619
2	1.886	2.920	4.303	6.965	9.925	31.599
3	1.638	2.353	3.182	4.541	5.841	12.294
4	1.533	2.132	2.776	3.747	4.604	8.610
5	1.476	2.015	2.571	3.365	4.032	6.869
6	1.440	1.943	2.447	3.143	3.707	5.959
7	1.415	1.895	2.365	2.998	3.499	5.408
8	1.397	1.860	2.306	2.896	3.355	5.041
9	1.383	1.833	2.262	2.821	3.250	4.781
10	1.372	1.812	2.228	2.764	3.169	4.587
11	1.363	1.796	2.201	2.718	3.106	4.437
12	1.356	1.782	2.179	2.681	3.055	4.318
13	1.350	1.771	2.160	2.650	3.012	4.221
14	1.345	1.761	2.145	2.624	2.977	4.140
15	1.341	1.753	2.131	2.602	2.947	4.073
16	1.337	1.746	2.120	2.583	2.921	4.015
17	1.333	1.740	2.110	2.567	2.898	3.965
18	1.330	1.734	2.101	2.552	2.878	3.922
19	1.328	1.729	2.093	2.539	2.861	3.883
20	1.325	1.725	2.086	2.528	2.845	3.850
21	1.323	1.721	2.080	2.518	2.831	3.819
22	1.321	1.717	2.074	2.508	2.819	3.792
23	1.319	1.714	2.069	2.500	2.807	3.768
24	1.318	1.711	2.064	2.492	2.797	3.745
25	1.316	1.708	2.060	2.485	2.787	3.725
26	1.315	1.706	2.056	2.479	2.779	3.707
27	1.314	1.703	2.052	2.473	2.771	3.690
28	1.313	1.701	2.048	2.467	2.763	3.674
29	1.311	1.699	2.045	2.462	2.756	3.659
30	1.310	1.697	2.042	2.457	2.750	3.646
40	1.303	1.684	2.021	2.423	2.704	3.551
60	1.296	1.671	2.000	2.390	2.660	3.460
120	1.289	1.658	1.980	2.358	2.617	3.373
∞	1.282	1.645	1.960	2.326	2.576	3.291

APPENDIX B: F-TABLE AT 5 PERCENT (UPPER TAIL)

F-TABLE, CRITICAL VALUES, 5 PERCENT IN UPPER TAIL

Degrees of freedom for the numerator along top row

Degrees of freedom for the denominator along side row

	1	2	3	4	5	6	7	8	9	10	12	15	20	24	30	40
1	161	200	216	225	230	234	237	239	241	242	244	246	248	249	250	251
2	18.5	19.0	19.2	19.2	19.3	19.3	19.4	19.4	19.4	19.4	19.4	19.4	19.4	19.5	19.5	19.5
3	10.1	9.55	9.28	9.12	9.01	8.94	8.89	8.85	8.81	8.79	8.74	8.70	8.66	8.64	8.62	8.59
4	7.71	6.94	6.59	6.39	6.26	6.16	6.09	6.04	6.00	5.96	5.91	5.86	5.80	5.77	5.75	5.72
5	6.61	5.79	5.41	5.19	5.05	4.95	4.88	4.82	4.77	4.74	4.68	4.62	4.56	4.53	4.50	4.46
6	5.99	5.14	4.76	4.53	4.39	4.28	4.21	4.15	4.10	4.06	4.00	3.94	3.87	3.84	3.81	3.77
7	5.59	4.74	4.35	4.12	3.97	3.87	3.79	3.73	3.68	3.64	3.57	3.51	3.44	3.41	3.38	3.34
8	5.32	4.46	4.07	3.84	3.69	3.58	3.50	3.44	3.39	3.35	3.28	3.22	3.15	3.12	3.08	3.04
9	5.12	4.26	3.86	3.63	3.48	3.37	3.29	3.23	3.18	3.14	3.07	6.01	2.94	2.90	2.86	2.83
10	4.96	4.10	3.71	3.48	3.33	3.22	3.14	3.07	3.02	2.98	2.91	2.85	2.77	2.74	2.70	2.66
11	4.84	3.98	3.59	3.36	3.20	3.09	3.01	2.95	2.90	2.85	2.79	2.72	2.65	2.61	2.57	2.53
12	4.75	3.89	3.49	3.26	3.11	3.00	2.91	2.85	2.80	2.75	2.69	2.62	2.54	2.51	2.47	2.43
13	4.67	3.81	3.41	3.18	3.03	2.92	2.83	2.77	2.71	2.67	2.60	2.53	2.46	2.42	2.38	2.34
14	4.60	3.74	3.34	3.11	2.96	2.85	2.76	2.70	2.65	2.60	2.53	2.46	2.39	2.35	2.31	2.27
15	4.54	3.68	3.29	3.06	2.90	2.79	2.71	2.64	2.59	2.54	2.48	2.40	2.33	2.29	2.25	2.20
16	4.49	3.63	3.24	3.01	2.85	2.74	2.66	2.59	2.54	2.49	2.42	2.35	2.28	2.24	2.19	2.15
17	4.45	3.59	3.20	2.96	2.81	2.70	2.61	2.55	2.49	2.45	2.38	2.31	2.23	2.19	2.15	2.10
18	4.41	3.55	3.16	2.93	2.77	2.66	2.58	2.51	2.46	2.41	2.34	2.27	2.19	2.15	2.11	2.06
19	4.38	3.52	3.13	2.90	2.74	2.63	2.54	2.48	2.42	2.38	2.31	2.23	2.16	2.11	2.07	2.03
20	4.35	3.49	3.10	2.87	2.71	2.60	2.51	2.45	2.39	2.35	2.28	2.20	2.12	2.08	2.04	1.99
21	4.32	3.47	3.07	2.84	2.68	2.57	2.49	2.42	2.37	2.32	2.25	2.18	2.10	2.05	2.01	1.96
22	4.30	3.44	3.05	2.82	2.66	2.55	2.46	2.40	2.34	2.30	2.23	2.15	2.07	2.03	1.98	1.94
23	4.28	3.42	3.03	2.80	2.64	2.53	2.44	2.37	2.32	2.27	2.20	2.13	2.05	2.01	1.96	1.91
24	4.26	3.40	3.01	2.78	2.62	2.51	2.42	2.36	2.30	2.25	2.18	2.11	2.03	1.98	1.94	1.89
25	4.24	3.39	2.99	2.76	2.60	2.49	2.40	2.34	2.28	2.24	2.16	2.09	2.01	1.96	1.92	1.87
30	4.17	3.32	2.92	2.69	2.53	2.42	2.33	2.27	2.21	2.16	2.09	2.01	1.93	1.89	1.84	1.79
40	4.08	3.23	2.84	2.61	2.45	2.34	2.25	2.18	2.12	2.08	2.00	1.92	1.84	1.79	1.74	1.69
60	4.00	3.15	2.76	2.53	2.37	2.25	2.17	2.10	2.04	1.99	1.92	1.84	1.75	1.70	1.65	1.59
120	3.92	3.07	2.68	2.45	2.29	2.18	2.09	2.02	1.96	1.91	1.83	1.75	1.66	1.61	1.55	1.50
∞	3.84	3.00	2.60	2.37	2.21	2.10	2.01	1.94	1.88	1.83	1.75	1.67	1.57	1.52	1.46	1.39

APPENDIX C: CHI-SQUARED TABLE

Values of χ^2 (Degrees of Freedom, Level of Significance)

Probability in Right Tail

Degrees of Freedom	0.99	0.975	0.95	0.9	0.1	0.05	0.025	0.01	0.005
1	0.000157	0.000982	0.003932	0.0158	2.706	3.841	5.024	6.635	7.879
2	0.020100	0.050636	0.102586	0.2107	4.605	5.991	7.378	9.210	10.597
3	0.1148	0.2158	0.3518	0.5844	6.251	7.815	9.348	11.345	12.838
4	0.297	0.484	0.711	1.064	7.779	9.488	11.143	13.277	14.860
5	0.554	0.831	1.145	1.610	9.236	11.070	12.832	15.086	16.750
6	0.872	1.237	1.635	2.204	10.645	12.592	14.449	16.812	18.548
7	1.239	1.690	2.167	2.833	12.017	14.067	16.013	18.475	20.278
8	1.647	2.180	2.733	3.490	13.362	15.507	17.535	20.090	21.955
9	2.088	2.700	3.325	4.168	14.684	16.919	19.023	21.666	23.589
10	2.558	3.247	3.940	4.865	15.987	18.307	20.483	23.209	25.188
11	3.053	3.816	4.575	5.578	17.275	19.675	21.920	24.725	26.757
12	3.571	4.404	5.226	6.304	18.549	21.026	23.337	26.217	28.300
13	4.107	5.009	5.892	7.041	19.812	22.362	24.736	27.688	29.819
14	4.660	5.629	6.571	7.790	21.064	23.685	26.119	29.141	31.319
15	5.229	6.262	7.261	8.547	22.307	24.996	27.488	30.578	32.801
16	5.812	6.908	7.962	9.312	23.542	26.296	28.845	32.000	34.267
17	6.408	7.564	8.672	10.085	24.769	27.587	30.191	33.409	35.718
18	7.015	8.231	9.390	10.865	25.989	28.869	31.526	34.805	37.156
19	7.633	8.907	10.117	11.651	27.204	30.144	32.852	36.191	38.582
20	8.260	9.591	10.851	12.443	28.412	31.410	34.170	37.566	39.997
21	8.897	10.283	11.591	13.240	29.615	32.671	35.479	38.932	41.401
22	9.542	10.982	12.338	14.041	30.813	33.924	36.781	40.289	42.796
23	10.196	11.689	13.091	14.848	32.007	35.172	38.076	41.638	44.181
24	10.856	12.401	13.848	15.659	33.196	36.415	39.364	42.980	45.558
25	11.524	13.120	14.611	16.473	34.382	37.652	40.646	44.314	46.928
26	12.198	13.844	15.379	17.292	35.563	38.885	41.923	45.642	48.290
27	12.878	14.573	16.151	18.114	36.741	40.113	43.195	46.963	49.645
28	13.565	15.308	16.928	18.939	37.916	41.337	44.461	48.278	50.994
29	14.256	16.047	17.708	19.768	39.087	42.557	45.722	49.588	52.335
30	14.953	16.791	18.493	20.599	40.256	43.773	46.979	50.892	53.672
50	29.707	32.357	34.764	37.689	63.167	67.505	71.420	76.154	79.490
60	37.485	40.482	43.188	46.459	74.397	79.082	83.298	88.379	91.952
80	53.540	57.153	60.391	64.278	96.578	101.879	106.629	112.329	116.321
100	70.065	74.222	77.929	82.358	118.498	124.342	129.561	135.807	140.170

APPENDIX D: CRITICAL VALUES FOR THE DURBIN-WATSON STATISTIC

CRITICAL VALUES FOR THE DURBIN-WATSON STATISTIC ($\alpha = 0.05$)

n	K = 1 D_l	K = 1 D_u	K = 2 D_l	K = 2 D_u	K = 3 D_l	K = 3 D_u	K = 4 D_l	K = 4 D_u	K = 5 D_l	K = 5 D_u
15	1.08	1.36	0.95	1.54	0.82	1.75	0.69	1.97	0.56	2.21
16	1.10	1.37	0.98	1.54	0.86	1.73	0.74	1.93	0.62	2.15
17	1.13	1.38	1.02	1.54	0.90	1.71	0.78	1.90	0.67	2.10
18	1.16	1.39	1.05	1.53	0.93	1.69	0.82	1.87	0.71	2.06
19	1.18	1.40	1.08	1.53	0.97	1.68	0.86	1.85	0.75	2.02
20	1.20	1.41	1.10	1.54	1.00	1.68	0.90	1.83	0.79	1.99
21	1.22	1.42	1.13	1.54	1.03	1.67	0.93	1.81	0.83	1.96
22	1.24	1.43	1.15	1.54	1.05	1.66	0.96	1.80	0.86	1.94
23	1.26	1.44	1.17	1.54	1.08	1.66	0.99	1.79	0.90	1.92
24	1.27	1.45	1.19	1.55	1.10	1.66	1.01	1.78	0.93	1.90
25	1.29	1.45	1.21	1.55	1.12	1.66	1.04	1.77	0.95	1.89
26	1.30	1.46	1.22	1.55	1.14	1.65	1.06	1.76	0.98	1.88
27	1.32	1.47	1.24	1.56	1.16	1.65	1.08	1.76	1.01	1.86
28	1.33	1.48	1.26	1.56	1.18	1.65	1.10	1.75	1.03	1.85
29	1.34	1.48	1.27	1.56	1.20	1.65	1.12	1.74	1.05	1.84
30	1.35	1.49	1.28	1.57	1.21	1.65	1.14	1.74	1.07	1.83
31	1.36	1.50	1.30	1.57	1.23	1.65	1.16	1.74	1.09	1.83
32	1.37	1.50	1.31	1.57	1.24	1.65	1.18	1.73	1.11	1.82
33	1.38	1.51	1.32	1.58	1.26	1.65	1.19	1.73	1.13	1.81
34	1.39	1.51	1.33	1.58	1.27	1.65	1.21	1.73	1.15	1.81
35	1.40	1.52	1.34	1.58	1.28	1.65	1.22	1.73	1.16	1.80
36	1.41	1.52	1.35	1.59	1.29	1.65	1.24	1.73	1.18	1.80
37	1.42	1.53	1.36	1.59	1.31	1.66	1.25	1.72	1.19	1.80
38	1.43	1.54	1.37	1.59	1.32	1.66	1.26	1.72	1.21	1.79
39	1.43	1.54	1.38	1.60	1.33	1.66	1.27	1.72	1.22	1.79
40	1.44	1.54	1.39	1.60	1.34	1.66	1.29	1.72	1.23	1.79
45	1.48	1.57	1.43	1.62	1.38	1.67	1.34	1.72	1.29	1.78
50	1.50	1.59	1.46	1.63	1.42	1.67	1.38	1.72	1.34	1.77
55	1.53	1.60	1.49	1.64	1.45	1.68	1.41	1.72	1.38	1.77
60	1.55	1.62	1.51	1.65	1.48	1.69	1.44	1.73	1.41	1.77
65	1.57	1.63	1.54	1.66	1.50	1.70	1.47	1.73	1.44	1.77
70	1.58	1.64	1.55	1.67	1.52	1.70	1.49	1.74	1.46	1.77
75	1.60	1.65	1.57	1.68	1.54	1.71	1.51	1.74	1.49	1.77
80	1.61	1.66	1.59	1.69	1.56	1.72	1.53	1.74	1.51	1.77
85	1.62	1.67	1.60	1.70	1.57	1.72	1.55	1.75	1.52	1.77
90	1.63	1.68	1.61	1.70	1.59	1.73	1.57	1.75	1.54	1.78
95	1.64	1.69	1.62	1.71	1.60	1.73	1.58	1.75	1.56	1.78
100	1.65	1.69	1.63	1.72	1.61	1.74	1.59	1.76	1.57	1.78

INDEX